# EVANSTON

## WYOMING

## Also available by Dennis J Ottley

*Remembering (Korea: 1950-1953)*

IZZARD PUBLISHING COMPANY
PO Box 522251
Salt Lake City, Utah 84152
www.izzardink.com

LIBRARY OF CONGRESS CONTROL NUMBER: 2018960342

*Designed by Alissa Rose Theodor*
*Cover Design by Andrea Ho*
*Cover Photograph by Shelly & Deann Horne of Creative Ink Images*
Cover Images: Robert Castillo/Shutterstock.com ivangal/Shutterstock.com
monofaction/Shutterstock.com

First Edition January 28, 2019

Contact the author at djottleybooks@gmail.com

Hardback ISBN: 978-1-64228-012-8
Softback ISBN: 978-1-64228-017-3
eBook ISBN: 978-1-64228-018-0

## 1967 TO 1995

# EVANSTON

# WYOMING

## VOLUME TWO

CITY OF
OPPORTUNITY
EQUALITY · FRIENDSHIP
EVANSTON WYO.

## BOOM-BUST-POLITICS

### "IN THE EYES OF A MAYOR"

# DENNIS J OTTLEY

IZZARD INK
—PUBLISHING—

# PART TWO

## "FIRST TERM MAYOR"

*"A community is like a ship, everyone ought to be prepared to take the helm."*

—QUOTE BY HENRIK IBSEN

# CHAPTER 13

**1**979....It was now 1979, and I was about to be sworn in as Mayor of the City of Evanston. I suppose being Mayor of any community is a tough job with a lot of responsibility, but Evanston was different at this time with the big boom going on. While the rest of the country was in a recession, a few areas of Wyoming were doing very well, and Evanston was facing one of the biggest booms in the history of Wyoming. I was sure that this would be a tough time to be Mayor.

I wasn't sure how I felt now that I had been elected, but in one way I was happy. It was a position that I had wanted for quite some time, but I have to admit that I was a bit worried. I was just glad that city politics were nonpartisan, and at least I didn't have to worry about political parties even though I am a registered Republican. I am no politician.

While campaigning, I promised that I would always have an "Open Office" for anyone who wished to visit me. I also promised that my interest would only be to better the community and keep everyone informed when possible. I read a quote by Albert Camus that said, *"Integrity has no need for rules."* And I believe that is very true.

But through my 12 years as a member of the city council there was one thing that I did learn. I learned that no matter how good the economy is, whether you are in a boom and things are going great, or whether you are in a bust and everything is going to hell, the number one priority for any elected official has got to be the economy. You never know what will happen from one year to the next. Whether you're a mayor, a county commissioner, governor or the president of the United States, your first and foremost concern must be the economy.

When your economy is good, everything else seems to take care of itself. A mayor needs to retain the employees he already has, and he needs to continue making an effort to bring in other industry with decent paying jobs. I have always believed that, with Interstate 80, the main line of the Union Pacific Railroad, and our location close to the Wasatch Front in Utah, Evanston is in a great location for any industry or business that may be looking for an additional location.

However, I promised to be very fair and honest with the public. As I said, *I am not a politician. I don't play games, I am a person of vision, but I get things done. And I am not afraid of stepping on toes.* I realize there is no way of getting around that, if you are trying to do what you feel is best for the community. Any decisions I made as mayor would be with good intent, right or wrong, and I would always uphold the Oath of Office.

On January 3, 1979, our first regular meeting of the year, Mayor Dan South opened the meeting with me as mayor-elect, and Councilmen David E. Bills, Jimmie L. Rice, and Russell "Bub" Albrecht, as well as councilmen-elect Ronald O. Davis, Roy Fruits and Russell "Rusty" Megeath, all in attendance.

Also present were City Attorney Dennis W. Lancaster, City Engineer John A. Proffit, General Superintendent J. Allen Kennedy, Building Inspector William "Bill" George, Chief of Police Dennis Harvey, Assistant Chief of Police Frank Chisholm, City Clerk and Treasurer Don U. Welling and his assistant, Phyllis J. Martin, and a large group of interested citizens.

Mayor South opened the meeting with his welcome and the Pledge of Allegiance, followed by the reading of the minutes of the last meeting of 1978, plus approval for payment of all outstanding bills. Both were approved by motion and seconded, with all voting in favor.

After the business of the previous administration had been taken care of, Mayor South called for City Clerk Welling to proceed with the swearing in of the newly elected officials. Welling read the Oath of Office to me as mayor-elect and to the three councilmen-elect which we all attested to by stating so and signing the Oath of Office.

Mayor South then gave a short speech concerning his accomplishments during his term as mayor, and reminded the new administration what to expect in the future. He also said that he was looking forward to working with the city as a member of the Uinta County Commission. Then, after thanking everyone for all their support during his term as mayor, he turned the gavel over to me. I then presented him with an attaché case from the city as a token of appreciation for his duties as mayor for the past four years.

Mayor South then left the chambers and I immediately took over the meeting, acting on my first duty, making my appointments of the city officials. Don Welling was appointed as City Clerk and Treasurer, and Phyllis Martin as Assistant Clerk and Treasurer; Dennis Harvey as Chief of Police and Frank Chisholm as Assistant Chief of Police; Dennis Lancaster as City Attorney; John Proffit as City Engineer; William George as City Building and Zoning Inspector; Allen Kennedy as General Superintendent of Public Works; Steven Aaron as Police Justice (City Judge); Gerald Cazin as Fire Chief and Calvin "Benny" Goodwin as Assistant Fire Chief.

Each appointment was accepted separately by a motion and seconded by a member of the council, with all voting in favor for everyone appointed.

My next order of business was to call for nominations for Council President. Councilman Albrecht nominated Ron Davis, who had seniority, to serve as the president of the council. Councilman Bills moved to cease nominations and elect Davis to the position, which was seconded by Rice, with all voting in favor.

At that time all appointed officials were sworn in and each signed the Oath of Office.

I made appointments of citizens to the various boards and commissions, such as the Airport Board, the Planning and Zoning Commission and the Parks and Recreation Board. Dennis Poppinga would continue his position as Director of Parks and Recreation. This is not an appointed position.

After making all the appointments to the various boards, motions were made and seconded with all voting in favor.

After the appointments to the boards I made the following Council assignments:

Streets and Alleys -- Bills and Davis

Parks and Recreation -- Fruits and Megeath

Cemetery -- Rice and Albrecht

Fire Department -- Megeath and me

Water and Sewer -- Albrecht, Rice and me

Planning and Zoning/Building -- Bills and Megeath

Police Department (Commission) -- Fruits, Albrecht and me, with me serving as Police Commissioner

Airport -- Rice and Megeath

Garbage (solid waste) and Landfill -- Davis and Fruits

Public Health and Safety -- Davis, Albrecht and Rice

Finance and Budget -- Fruits, Megeath and me

LUAG (Lincoln Uinta Association of Governments) -- Bills and me

W.A.M. (Wyoming Association of Municipalities) -- Albrecht and me

City Hall, Shop, Engineer, Attorney, Police Justice -- Myself and Council.

Following the assignments I read a letter from Brad "Jonesy" Fearn stating that he wished to resign from the Evanston City Police Department to serve as undersheriff to the Uinta County Sheriff's office. The motion was made and seconded to accept his letter of resignation and to wish him well in his new assignment. All voted in favor.

I also read a letter from Fire Chief Cazin concerning potential fire danger in various parts of town. City Attorney Lancaster and City Inspector George were directed to look into this matter.

Finally I read a letter of appreciation from David Lewis addressed to the mayor and council thanking the city for removing snow from around his mother's house at the time of her funeral. Also, the Masonic Cemetery Association sent a donation of $150 to the Cemetery Perpetual Care Fund. The council and I expressed our thanks for the generous donation.

Resolution 79-1, the first resolution of the year, was introduced by Councilman Bills. This was a resolution to petition for annexation of properties owned by the City of Evanston and Painter and Company, Inc. The petition was a request to include these properties within the city limits. A motion to adopt the resolution was made by the council and seconded, with all voting in favor.

A public hearing was then held at 7:30 p.m. concerning senior citizens housing. Questions were raised about how we could assist in the senior housing problem. The biggest concern was that elderly folks who were renting could not afford the high rents caused by the oil and gas boom. It was brought up that the first thing we had to do was form a Housing Authority so that we could receive assistance and subsidies from the U.S. Department of Housing and Urban Development (HUD). It was announced that the city is in the progress of doing just that.

Councilmen Albrecht and Fruits together with Steve Snyder, representing LUAG, along with Darlene Bennett, Art Ortega, and Marie Hicks were asked to head up a committee to find sites for building senior and low-income housing. It was suggested that this committee meet in the conference room at City Hall on Friday, January 5th at 5 p.m.

Mr. Jim Hanson, representing Ecotek Corp., the new owners of the Ramada Inn, made a presentation about their proposed expansion of the Ramada Inn complex. They explained that for mortgaging and financing, Ecotek needed an endorsement from the City of Evanston to sell tax-exempt bonds to finance their proposed construction. I directed the city attorney to work with the Ekotek people to see if an agreeable resolution could be drafted and brought to the council to act on. The council took no action at this time.

Questions about the business occupation and license ordinance came up with some suggestions and recommendations for some modifications and changes. As mayor, I appointed myself along with Councilmen Davis and Bills to check into this.

After becoming mayor of Evanston, the first proclamation that I signed was declaring January 27th as the official day for Chinese New Year, celebrating the Year of the Ram, and urging all Evanston area citizens to support and enjoy the occasion by wearing Chinese costumes and participating in the special events.

This year of 1979 would be the Centennial Year of the Chinese New Year celebration held in Evanston. The first Chinese New Year was held in 1879 by Chinese workers on the Union Pacific Railroad and in the Almy coal mines. The three-day celebration was the pride of the Chinese people because it gave then a once-a-year respite from their back-breaking labor and isolation from non-Chinese pioneers. It was the one time of the year when the two groups set aside their prejudices and joined together to celebrate the most colorful holiday in the Chinese culture. The Chinese were a very important part of the Evanston area's history.

*Uinta County Herald*, January 25, 1979.

This year Denice Wheeler, a very civic-minded person and historian, formed a committee and became chairman of the special event. The Chinese New Year was very successful and brought many Chinese dignitaries and others to town, some taking part, to enjoy the event. Many learned the ways of the Chinese and the part they played in the history of Evanston.

During the regular city council meeting of February 7th there was a bill in the amount of $43.20 from the Ottley Sport Center among the outstanding bills to be paid.

Councilman Bills made a motion to approve payment of all the bills, which was seconded by Davis, with all voting in favor.

At that time City Attorney Lancaster stated that there may be a conflict of interest in purchasing items from Ottley Sport Center by the recreation department or any department of the city. He said, *according to state law, a conflict of interest must be declared, and this will suffice for all subsequent bills from this firm while Mr. Ottley is Mayor.*

During this meeting Robert Koff, Harry Tate, Hal McVey, and Attorney Larry Lehman, representing Cities Service Company, met with the council regarding a drilling site within the city limits on the south side of Interstate 80. The council recommended they first meet with the Planning and Zoning Commission for proper zoning and a conditional use permit.

Also during the meeting Mr. Ted Taylor, representing the Liquor Dealer's Association, requested the four days for continuous opening hours as per state law. Motion was made and seconded to allow these four days as requested with all voting in favor.

The first ordinance of the year was introduced by Councilman Bills as Ordinance 79-1, pertaining to the annexation 5.903 acres of land. Sole owners of the property were Painter and Co. and the City of Evanston. This land was near the cemetery and included part of the road going to the Red Mountain Subdivisions. Motion was made and seconded to pass this ordinance on first reading, with all voting in favor. Ordinance 79-1 went on to pass on second and third readings with no opposition.

Ordinance 79-2, introduced by Councilman Megeath, was to amend Section 2-5 of the revised code of the city to provide that regular council meetings were to be held at 7:00 p.m. on the first Wednesday after the first Tuesday of each month. The ordinance was moved and passed on an emergency basis with all voting in favor.

I read a letter of resignation from Assistant Chief of Police Frank Chisholm. He stated that he and his family were moving to California. After the mayor and council expressed their appreciation of Chisholm's fine service to the city and wished them the best in their new venture, it was moved and seconded to accept his letter, with all voting in favor.

More subdivisions, residential and industrial, were presented for approval with some recommended changes. However, final approval would be through ordinances. Also, there was a request to start a gun club. The council stated that they should meet with the Parks and Recreation Board for their ideas and suggestions.

Recreation Director Poppinga proposed a new position for a greens keeper at the golf course and a parks maintenance foreman, with a segment of the wages being paid by the golf club. A motion from the council was made for Poppinga to look for someone to fill these positions and for the city to enter into an agreement with the golf club concerning the wages. The motion was seconded with all voting in favor.

A discussion took place concerning paying tap fees for water and sewer at the time a building permit was issued; also a need for water meters at trailer parks was discussed.

Steve Snyder, representing LUAG, asked for a letter to be written to HUD to guarantee construction if a grant was given for senior housing. It was moved and seconded that a letter be written by the mayor with all voting in favor.

Due to the fact that the traffic was causing a bad problem at the underpass on 9th Street, Councilman Megeath, representing the fire department, made a motion for the city to give the fire department permission to look on the northeast side of the railroad for a location for a substation. The motion was seconded by Fruits, with all voting in favor.

The winter of 1978 and 1979 was a very cold winter. It got so cold that in late January the entire water system of the town of Lyman was frozen up. Mayor Keller of Lyman and some of his council members met with the City of Evanston requesting help by supplying them with some water. They offered to pay for the water, but the Evanston City Council told them they could have whatever water they needed as long as they paid for the transportation getting the water to them.

We told them that the best location to get their water from would be at the east end of Evanston from a fire hydrant just in front of the Prairie Inn, and they could hook up to that hydrant and get whatever water they needed. Lyman hired a company with water tanks to transport the water. There was a steady run of trucks hauling water to the town of Lyman for the next few weeks until Lyman got their system thawed out.

That winter was a very unusual season with off-and-on periods of thaws and freezes, causing the frost to drop deeper and deeper into the ground. This created problems for Evanston with some of the city water lines freezing up, especially in the Anderson Heights area of 18th and 19th Streets.

During the meeting I asked permission from the council to go to Cheyenne using my own vehicle and meet with the Wyoming Highway Department to request that they expedite the proposed overpass, because we were having so many problems with the traffic at the underpass. Considering these problems, the council determined that this would be a good idea and agreed with my request.

Also, downtown parking meters were becoming a big problem. During discussion it was determined that eventually there would have to be some changes made, because the meters were getting old and were hard to keep repaired, but we were still trying to enforce the two-hour parking ordinance.

On February 20th a special emergency meeting was called at 12:00 noon to adopt Resolution 79-5, introduced by Councilman Albrecht, authorizing the city to apply to the Governor's Emergency Fund for the repairing of water and sewer lines that were damaged as a result of extreme temperatures and adverse weather conditions, and authorizing the mayor and city clerk to execute all necessary documents. The motion was made and seconded to adopt Resolution 79-5, with all voting in favor.

# TOWN OF LYMAN

P. O. BOX 315
LYMAN, WYOMING 82937

February 10, 1979

Evanston City Council
Evanston City Hall
Evanston, Wyoming 82930

Gentlemen:

On behalf of the citizens of Lyman I wish to express
our deep feeling of gratitude to your response in our
time of crisis.

You have literally saved our necks. We have a little
water but not enough to sustain our needs. By your
generous offer of giving us water we are now able
to maintain a good pressure and we will be able to
fight a fire if the need arises.

At this time I am unable to tell you how long we
will need the water. Certainly we hope that it
will be a minimal length of time. We will not
impose upon your generosity any longer than
absolutely necessary.

I will keep in touch with Mayor Ottley. Thank you
once again.

Yours truly,

J. Charles Keller Jr.
Mayor

The regular meeting on March 7th was opened up by Ronald Davis, President of the Council, because I was out of town on city business. After the usual business was taken care of, Resolution 79-6 was introduced by Councilman Fruits to accept a grant offer under the Airport and Airway Development Act to develop an airport master plan for the new Evanston Municipal Airport, as well as authorizing the city to enter into an agreement with BRW/Noblitt for the completion of the airport master plan. Motion made for the adoption of Resolution 79-6, with all voting in favor.

It looked like at this time Evanston was finally on the verge of getting a new airport which would be located just west of Evanston near the Wyoming/Utah state line. This would be a great asset for the Evanston area, especially during the boom period.

A public hearing was held on a zone change on the Ellingford Bros. property. This hearing, like others, was recorded and taped and is on file at City Hall. There were some interested citizens present at the hearing who were opposed to the requested zone change of Residential (R-3) to Industrial (I-1).

Following the public hearing, Ordinance 79-4 was introduced by Councilman Rice to authorize the zone change. After a short discussion, a motion was made to pass the ordinance on the first reading, and was seconded. The motion passed with 4 aye votes, 1 no vote, 1 abstaining, and 1 absent. This ordinance passed on second and third readings with all voting in favor.

More ordinances were acted on during the meeting, namely Ordinance 79-5, authorizing the M Bar B residential subdivision (located just south of North Elementary School and Railroad Park); Ordinance 79-6, authorizing the Zumbrennen Light Industrial Park subdivision located where the old drive-in theater used to be and where Freeway Tire is at present); and Ordinance 79-7, dedicating a street in one of the new subdivisions as a city street. All three ordinances were acted on and were all approved, with all voting in favor. This entire year we had several resolutions and ordinances to act on every regular meeting and special meeting. We also had a number of public hearings. The boom was bringing in out-of-town property buyers to subdivide in various locations. New contractors from other states were coming to Evanston in droves, and often causing ordinances, already on the books, to be amended time and time again, and in addition, it caused the city to continuously pass new ordinances. This was causing very long meetings that sometimes lasted past midnight. We discussed the idea of starting our meetings earlier and/or going into regular meetings twice a month if things got worse. And they did.

On March 16th Lynn Richards retired from the fire department and was honored at the annual Fireman's Banquet dinner for his 42 years of distinguished volunteer service to the Evanston Volunteer Fire Department. Speakers were former Mayor Dan South, Fire Chief Jerry Cazin and me. All thanked Richards for his long and continuous service to the department and expressed their appreciation from the City of Evanstonand wished him well in his retirement. He had served since 1937.

A special meeting was called for on March 21st to take care of Ordinance 78-33 on third and final reading. This ordinance was held over from 1978 by the previous administration for more time to do additional research. There was a lengthy discussion because the ordinance concerned property named Schwitzer Court to be dedicated to the city for a street, and additional property for other public uses in the Almy Addition near the cemetery. The dedicated property was from the developers of the Schwitzer Subdivision, George and Mary Schwitzer. Motion was made to pass Ordinance 78-33 on the third and final reading and seconded, with all voting in favor.

During the special meeting, Ordinance 79-8 was introduced by Councilman Albrecht. The ordinance was to approve another subdivision plat for Uinta Meadows. A discussion took place concerning a larger pipe diameter for the sanitary sewer and concerns about the storm sewer. According to the John Proffit, City Engineer, these items did not appear to meet city standards and Proffit requested time to check these items out. The subdividers and their engineer assured us that this would all be corrected by the next meeting, and it was. Therefore it was moved and seconded for approval, and was passed on second and third readings at future meetings with all voting in favor.

Other business to come up during this meeting included the adoption of the following two resolutions:

Resolution 79-10, introduced by Councilman Albrecht, authorized the city to pay overtime to employees working on snow removal and frozen water and sewer lines.

Resolution 79-11, introduced by Councilman Megeath, tendered an agreement with the Union Pacific Resources Corp. to lease a certain piece of property owned by the U.P. This lease was to create a parking lot near the train station. Motions were made and seconded for the adoption of both resolutions, with all voting in favor.

I read a letter from the Stockholders of the S. P. Ditch Company. It was reported that the City of Evanston was one of the stockholders in the company and that we should have a representative present. This concerned a ditch running through Evanston toward the north and northwest, through Almy that the ranchers used for irrigation. After some discussion a motion was made and seconded to authorize Councilman Jim Rice to attend the meeting and represent the city, with all voting in favor.

On April 3rd I attended the monthly meeting of the Evanston Chamber of Commerce to discuss the problems and plans of the City of Evanston. I indicated that, because of the fast growth, Evanston was having some problems trying to keep up with the maintenance on the streets, sewer and water and other infrastructure, but I said; *Evanston's biggest problem is housing.* With the influx of population from the oil and gas industry, there just weren't enough places to rent.

I told them that the city administration was encouraging housing construction, but the city would not get into the construction business. It is not a function that government should compete in. However, by encouraging the much needed housing, it was going to cause more problems down the road concerning other infrastructure of the city, such as water, sewer, streets, police, and so on. I also talked to the group about the fact that we were now forming an Evanston Renewal Agency and an Evanston Housing Authority with HUD to get funding and assistance from them to help Evanston get badly needed senior and low income housing, plus funding to upgrade some of our more blighted areas.

I then said that we were also in the process of receiving a grant for improvements to the sewer plant. I explained to them that the sewer treatment facility was deteriorating, and was getting expensive to keep repaired and upgraded it so it wouldn't dump raw sewage into the Bear River. I told them that it wouldn't be too long before it became completely inadequate, and that plans were being pursued at the present to acquire additional land for a new plant.

In addition I explained to the Chamber that the traffic was getting worse and that the Wyoming Highway Department was scheduling a new overpass with construction to be started in 1981, but that didn't happen until three or four years later. I also told them that we would be enforcing the two-hour parking in downtown Evanston, and that we were also looking at the possibility of one-way streets in the downtown area.

I brought up the fact that we were not only having problems retaining some of the city employees, but we were also having problems hiring new employees to fill their vacancies. This was primarily because of the high paying jobs in the oil industry. I said to the membership that *the city will have no other choice than to take a good look at the upcoming budget and try to instill a pay increase in the budget for the employees.* I went on to say that *the employees haven't had a reasonable increase for quite some time. Therefore, we have no other choice than to include some kind of raise for the employees, plus we have got to look at some benefits, such as retirement and health insurance if we want to retain our employees and not lose them to the high paying jobs in the oil fields.* After a little discussion, the chamber of commerce agreed with me.

At the regular council meeting of April 4th the bid opening for a new cemetery shop building took place. Motion was made to accept the apparent low bid of $18,920 from Harold Newland, seconded with all voting in favor.

In other action during the meeting, Resolution 79-12 was introduced by Councilman Fruits to authorize the city to enter into a water agreement with the Wyoming State Highway Commission to allow them to purchase water from the city for a highway construction project. Motion was made and seconded with all voting in favor.

Ecotek Corporation, owners of the Ramada Inn, were present at the meeting with a resolution for the city to sponsor them to receive Industrial Development Revenue Bonds for an extension to the Ramada Inn property.

Therefore, Resolution 79-15 was introduced by Councilman Bills, but Councilman Fruits made a motion to table this resolution until April 18th when the council had already planned a special meeting. The motion was seconded by Davis, with all voting in favor.

If this resolution passed, it would be the first of many companies that would be requesting sponsorship in the very near future. Industrial Development Revenue Bonds was a program set up by the U.S. Government to provide funding for the construction of new business and industrial buildings. The program was initially implemented to help improve the economy. The bonds would be guaranteed by the government, but would be sold to the public for investment purposes. The program had to be sponsored by a government entity, such as a city or county, to be valid. Any company or individual applying for these bonds would have to have a very good credit rating plus a lot of collateral behind them before getting approved, because it would be hard for the bonds to be sold if the company was not in good standing. Bonds at that time were very much in demand because of the high interest rates set by the banking industry.

Evanston, because of the boom from the oil industry, was a prime location for the use of the Industrial Revenue Bonds. Believe me, we had many companies applying for the bonds to build their buildings, and as mayor, I signed a lot of them, and sometimes I would have to go out of town to do it.

During the meeting we had a few public hearings held for public input concerning zoning changes and annexations. After the public hearings were over, we addressed Ordinance 79-9, pertaining to a zone change from Family Residential (R-3) to Light Industrial (I-1) and fronting China Mary Road; Ordinance 79-10, also pertaining to a zone change from Family Residential (R–3) to Light Industrial (I–1) off China Mary Road: plus Ordinance 79-11, pertaining to an annexation of property beyond the city line on the east end of Bear River Drive and the interchange. All ordinances were properly introduced with motions and seconds on each ordinance, with all passing unanimously on first, second and third readings at various meetings.

I reported on some proposed changes in the Wyoming Association of Municipalities (W.A.M.) health insurance program. After a short discussion, Councilman Bills made the motion to accept these changes in benefits with the city continuing to pay all the premiums for full time employees. The motion was seconded by Megeath, with all voting in favor.

The employees now would have health insurance benefits, something they had never had before, but the city still had to provide the funding by getting it into the upcoming budget.

During this meeting I had two more letters from police officers submitting their letters of resignation, mainly because of the problems we were having and because of the pay. These resignations were accepted by motion by the council, causing a considerable amount of discussion on what we were going to do. It was decided that at budget time there would be a request for a substantial amount of pay increase to all employees.

Police Chief Harvey reported success in obtaining a partial grant for a juvenile officer to start work in July, and he reported that Sherilyn Hernandez had been hired as Animal Control Officer.

In other reports from the different departments and the council members, because of the oil boom and the fast growth, it was reported in all departments that things were getting worse. The problems were getting out of hand. Because of the housing shortage, some oil field workers were living and sleeping in Hamblin Park, under the river bridges, in people's back yards and just about any other place they could find.

Police problems were increasing with more felonies, more bar problems and domestic problems. We were badly in need of more officers and more police cars. Due to the fact that the city was limited in the number of liquor licenses, the local bars and establishments were overcrowded, causing so much commotion and so many fights that the police department couldn't handle them all. It was getting very dangerous for a police officer to enter a bar when there was trouble. We didn't like an officer making any calls responding to trouble, without another officer along, but we didn't have enough personnel to do this on every call. We were getting very worried about our officers and had every reason to be so.

Traffic problems were continually getting worse, and water, sewer and street upkeep was getting bad. Because of the increase in population, our sewer system was overflowing, causing raw sewer to go into the Bear River that once again, and we were starting to get a lot of pressure from environmentalists.

The only thing good we had going for us was the revenues were starting to come in more each year. It was really helping that we could take care of some of these problems, but since we were still growing in population it was hard to keep up.

During a special meeting on April 18th Resolution 79-15, concerning Industrial Revenue Bonds in the maximum aggregate principal amount of $2,000,000 requested by Ecotek (Bonneville Development Company, a Utah corporation) came up for discussion.

The resolution was originally introduced by Councilman Bills, but was tabled until this meeting. Therefore, Councilman Bills made a motion to bring this resolution off the table for discussion purposes, seconded by Albrecht with all voting in favor.

After a considerable amount of discussion, Councilman Bills made a motion to amend the resolution to include the words *pursuant to Section 15-1-801, et. Seq. of the 1977 Republished Edition*. This was added to the second *WHEREAS* of the resolution. The motion was seconded by Davis, with all voting in favor.

After the reading of the resolution, Councilman Bills made a motion to pass the resolution as amended, which was seconded by Davis with 2 ayes, 3 nays and 2 absent. The motion failed.

The council requested that a credit statement and financial report and prospectus on public benefits be provided by Ecotek. When these requirements were met the council would consider a new Industrial Revenue Bond resolution.

In other business, two citizens approached the council in regard to the unsightly garbage and trash in the Walker Trailer Park on County Road. Building Inspector Bill George was directed to investigate the problem and report any violations of the city ordinances to City Attorney Dennis Lancaster. The attorney then was instructed to take appropriate action on any violation reported. The situation was corrected.

Also, Councilman Davis made a motion to give Councilman Bills the authority to write to the Wyoming Highway Department requesting that sidewalks be built at state expense on both sides of Wyoming State Highway 89 and U.S. Highway 30 S when these two highways were reconstructed. The motion died from lack of a second.

The rest of the meeting was spent acting on several ordinances that had previously been introduced and passed on all readings.

During the regular meeting of May 2nd, Rose Hughes and Elissa M. Garofalo, representing LUAG, presented an inventory of city-owned properties and a draft of anticipated capital improvements to the city council. I told the group and the council that these reports were the results of many months of hard work by LUAG, and thanked Hughes and Garofalo for their part.

Ordinance 79-10, authorizing a zone change from R-3 Family Residential to I-1 Light Industrial, came up for third and final reading. Before the motion was voted on, Councilman Bills made a motion to amend the ordinance to read, *No access for heavy truck traffic from this property to "A" Avenue, or Holland Drive,* which was seconded by Davis. After a short discussion, I called for a vote. There was 1 aye vote and 6 no votes, including mine. The motion for the amendment failed. However, the main motion to pass Ordinance 79-10 on third and final reading passed with 6 aye votes, including mine, and 1 no vote.

In the past, some mayors wouldn't vote except to break a tie, but I decided that I would vote on all issues, especially those issues that were controversial. I wanted the folks to know where I stood on every issue.

Ordinance 79-9, authorizing a zone change from R-3 Family Residential and OS Open Space to I-1 Light Industrial, came up for third and final reading. Motion was made and seconded to pass Ordinance 79-9 on third and final reading with a vote of 6 ayes and 1 no. The motion passed by a majority. A new resolution was brought up to approve sponsoring Industrial Revenue Bonds for the Ekotek group in the amount of $2,000,000. The resolution was numbered 79-16 and was introduced by Councilman Bills.

Motion was made by Councilman Fruits and seconded by Bills to adopt this resolution. Because the first resolution on this issue was defeated, I called for a roll call vote. Those voting in favor were me, Davis, Fruits, Rice, and Bills; those voting against were Megeath and Albrecht. The motion carried with 5 aye votes and 2 no votes.

At certain times of the day, the traffic at the underpass was so heavy that sometimes it would be backed up to the north as far as the city limit sign or even farther, causing real traffic problems. Trying to get an emergency vehicle through the underpass was almost impossible. With the police department, the fire department and the ambulance all being on the southwest side of the underpass, we had no emergency services at all on the northeast side, but we were working on a location for an additional firehouse.

Earlier this year Fire Chief Jerry Cazin, some of the city council members and I met with the Uinta County Commission to request their permission to use a piece of the Uinta County Fairgrounds to build a new fire station big enough to house a couple of fire trucks, a car and an ambulance.

The City of Evanston actually owned all the fairgrounds property, but years ago the city leased it to Uinta County to be used for the annual county fair and rodeos. The county commissioners were very much aware of this and, after a bit of discussion, they agreed to a new lease deleting approximately .70 acres, 150' x 200', located at the northwest corner of the property. This would be large enough to take care of the city's needs and would have good access getting to a location on that side of the tracks.

During this regular meeting of May 2nd Councilman Megeath introduced Resolution 79-17, authorizing the city to enter into a partial termination of the lease between the City of Evanston (Lessor) and the County of Uinta (Lessee), and authorizing the mayor and city clerk to execute all necessary documents to effect the same. After the attorney read the resolution in full, a motion was made and seconded, with all voting in favor.

After the execution of all the necessary documents was implemented, the city immediately found the funding and opened bidding for a new fire hall on the fairground property. We considered this project to be an emergency and couldn't waste any more time in getting it underway.

Also during the meeting, Resolution 79-18, declaring the intention of the City of Evanston to vacate certain alleys located in the Hillcrest Park Additions, was introduced by Councilman Bills.

These so-called alleys were deeded to the city, but never used as alleyways and there were no utility easements or right-of-ways; therefore, the city passed on this resolution with Councilman Albrecht making the motion, seconded by Davis, with all voting in favor.

After all the proper documents were completed, the property would be split equally between each adjacent property owner by a deed from the City of Evanston.

Other business during the meeting involved the passage of a few ordinances on first reading that authorized a zone change and dedicated a street, and we acted on ordinances that were not changed in any way except renumbered. This was part of re-codifying the old ordinances. Each ordinance had to be processed as if it were a new ordinance with only numbers being changed. This was part of the re-codification process.

Plus George Schwitzer approached the council to lease the vacant property of the cemetery for haying purposes. The council didn't have any problems with this, so I directed the city attorney to prepare a written agreement or resolution with the leased areas specified.

I reported that we were receiving a lot of complaints about the Eagles Club, especially repeated violations of their operation of the club. After some discussion, Councilman Fruits made a motion that proceedings be started to suspend this license, seconded by Rice with all voting in favor. I directed the city attorney to proceed with whatever action we had to take to suspend a liquor license.

At this time, there was so much action and business going on in bars and lounges holding a full liquor license, that problems were extending over into clubs that held only a limited liquor license, a license for the purpose of their membership and their guests only.

Both the V.F.W. and the Eagles Club held a limited liquor license, but due to the overwhelming business that the bars were doing, it was hard for the private clubs to control the crowds entering their establishments. Therefore, the city was getting a lot of complaints, not just from other bar owners, but also from their own membership.

It was now 12:10 a.m. of the next day. Therefore, I called for a recess for the meeting to be continued that evening, the same day, at 7:00 p.m.

At 7:00 p. m. of May 3rd I called the meeting back to order with all members of the city council present, as well as the city attorney and the city clerk.

Two public hearings were held, both on zone changes. One involved some land above the freeway on the west side of the city. The other was for a zone change requested by the TJG Corporation, owners Jay and Garry Ellingford. These hearings were recorded, with the tapes on file at City Hall.

After reports were given by each councilman on their areas of responsibility, this meeting adjourned by regular motion at 10:15 p.m.

One reason our council meetings were lasting so long was because we were spending so much time re-codifying all of the old ordinances that had been on the books for so many years. We started this program at the request of the attorney late last year, but it should have been done years ago. It took a lot of time because there had been so many new ordinances to act on, in addition to all the amendments to the old ordinances.

We were classifying each ordinance with a different system in numbering at the request of the attorney. The attorney had suggested that rather than number them just 100, 101, 102, and so on, that they be numbered by year, such as 79-1, 79-2 and so forth. To do this, each numbered ordinance, by law needed to go through the three readings. Also, a good number of the old ordinances needed to be repealed, and that sometimes took a little time. The council felt that by having the ordinances all re-codified and re-classified it would be much easier for the general public to identify them and understand them. Also, all resolutions would be numbered in the same manner.

During this meeting I read a letter from the U.P.R.R. regarding the city's annual lease of the corrals from the railroad to be used by the Evanston Cowboy Days Committee to hold the stock producers' stock during the Labor Day weekend celebration. These corrals were located in the vicinity of the 6th Street overpass and where the Jubilee Shopping Center is at present. The railroad never charged for the use.

The council made a motion to execute the lease again this year, because they felt that the committee would need to use it again. The motion was seconded with all voting in favor.

The issue of the sewer plant came up again, and once again we were made aware that we were dumping some raw sewage into the river, and that over time it would get worse. We were looking for a location and funding to build a complete new plant. We knew there was no use to keep trying to mend the old plant, but we did keep it up as best we could. It was just too old and worn out.

John Proffit, representing Uinta Engineering and Surveying, Inc., and Dale Peterson, an engineer recently moving to Evanston, both were present at the meeting to make a proposal on completing E.P.A. steps I, II, and III on a new sewage treatment facility, but no action was taken at this time.

1979 was the year I finally received my real estate broker's license and took over Uinta Realty from Elaine Blakeslee Michaelis. She furnished me with office space in her new Uinta Title and Insurance Co. building and now I had my own firm that I was not only owner of, but I was also the Principle Broker.

Kathy Cue got her real estate sales license the same time I receive my broker's license. So she became the first salesperson that I sponsored to work under me. She stayed with me until 1983, at which time she ran for Uinta County Assessor and won during the election of 1982.

My son, Tib, who was running our store, Ottley's Sports Center, decided that he would like to get into the real estate business and leave the store. I sponsored him for his real estate sales license, and he became the second person in my firm to sell for me. By this time I needed a larger office and Elaine needed more office space, so I moved my office to a larger building.

When Tib quit the store, this left Sandy to run it for a short time, but we did have a couple of employees working for us. Pete Bass and Kathy Barker both worked for us for a while.

Late that summer one of my other sons, David, moved his family to Evanston from Chadron, Nebraska. Dave had attended Chadron State College under a partial football scholarship. He was going with a girl, Kerri, from Crawford, Nebraska. After they both graduated in 1977 they got married, and in July of 1979 they had their first son, Shep.

When Dave and Kerri moved back to Evanston, Kerri got a job teaching school and Dave took over the store. With Sandy and him both running the store, they decided to get out of the hunting and guns business, which Sandy never did like, and they also slacked off on the fishing and camping business. They wanted to get into more of the athletic type merchandise, such as skiing, golfing, athletic clothing and mountain climbing, as well as basketball, football and baseball inventory.

Sandy came up with the idea of changing the name of the store. She thought that as long as I was mayor of Evanston and the Ottley name was attached to the store name that it would hurt our business, because it seemed that a good share of the public just wouldn't trade with us while I was mayor, so we decided to change the name. Sandy came up with the name "Lockeroom, Etc.," but over time it didn't seem to help much, because most folks knew who owned the store.

We had some pretty good business from the newcomers to Evanston, but for some reason or other a good share of locals would not trade with us. I guess when you are mayor and trying to do a good job looking out for the community's best interest, you can't help but step on a lot of toes, because nobody likes change. And, as this story is told, you will see that my administration made a lot of changes due to the increase in growth.

This was the same with Uinta Realty, Inc. Most of my listings came from out-of-state developers and contractors. Some locals stuck by us, but they were mostly close friends and relatives. I don't know why it had to be this way, but it seems to have happened to every business person who held the position of mayor. At least, that was what I had been told. I know it happened with Mayor Bob Burns. People believe that if you were mayor, you were automatically becoming rich. Well, if that's the case I've got news for them, because although I made pretty good money during the boom, it sure didn't last all that long, and Sandy and I got hurt financially in the next few years.

During our regular city council meeting of June 6th one of the first items on the agenda was the introduction of Resolution 79-22 by Councilman Fruits. This was a resolution authorizing the City of Evanston to apply to the Wyoming Recreation Commission for a grant. This would be a grant for the construction of two baseball fields. These fields would be in addition to the present baseball fields located on the corner of 6th Street, Lombard Street and Yellow Creek Roads. Motion was made to adopt Resolution 79-22 and seconded with all voting in favor.

The next order of business was the introduction of Resolution 79-23 by Councilman Davis authorizing the city to assign a portion of the lease for the Evanston landfill to the Uinta County Weed and Pest District. After the reading of the ordinance and some discussion a motion was made to adopt the resolution and was seconded, with all voting in favor.

We then had two gentlemen from Denver, CO, Bob DeMonBrun and James Anderson, who had just purchased land from Evan Reese and J. D. Kindler adjacent to and just west of the city. They approached the council requesting permission to have this land annexed to the city. A plat was presented showing the exact parcel to be annexed.

I, as mayor, disclosed an interest in this property, because Uinta Realty, Inc. would be obtaining the listings. John Proffit, City Engineer

and Dennis Lancaster, City Attorney, both suggested this would con-
stitute a conflict of interest. Therefore, I excused myself from any discussion concerning the property and left, turning my gavel over to
Councilman Davis, President of the Council. The council president
acts in place of the mayor when the mayor is not available.

During the discussion DeMonBrun and Anderson requested the
city's participation in the issuance of industrial revenue bonds to help
finance their project, which would be an industrial subdivision named
the Evanston Industrial Center.

While I was still out of the room because of my conflict of interest,
Resolution 79-24 was introduced by Councilman Rice. This resolution was the City of Evanston agreeing to sponsor in the issuance
of Industrial Development Revenue Bonds to finance the Evanston
Industrial Center project. Motion was made by the council to adopt
the resolution and seconded, with all council members voting in favor.

I returned to the mayor's seat, accepting the gavel from Councilman Davis. The next item of business was a report from Lissa Garofalo,
representing the Lincoln Uinta Association of Governments (LUAG),
suggesting some changes in a capital improvement project concerning
housing she had been working on for Lincoln and Uinta County. She
made her report to the council, and Councilman Rice made a motion
to accept LUAG's project with some suggested changes. It was seconded by Fruits with all voting in favor.

Ordinance 79-23 came up for first reading and was introduced by
Councilman Albrecht. This ordinance was to annex the property that
would be the Evanston Industrial Center, and once again I excused
myself, handing the gavel to Councilman Davis.

After the first reading of Ordinance 79-23 was read, Councilman
Bills made the motion to pass the ordinance on first reading, which
was seconded by Megeath with all voting in favor. The second and
third readings came up in later meetings, and both times the passage
of the ordinance was accepted by motion, with all voting in favor.
I excused myself both times because of my conflict of interest.

At this time, by a previous ordinance, all new construction required
installation of water meters on their buildings because it was getting

too hard to control without them, and we knew that water meters would be eventually required on all residential, business and industrial buildings in the near future. There were just too many people in Evanston that were not paying for water, sewer or garbage, because we had such a poor system of organizing on the billing list. Water meters would not be a popular thing with most of the citizens, but it was something that had to be done, and soon.

Ordinance 79-24 was introduced by Councilman Albrecht. This was an ordinance specifying the tapping charge for new city water connections, increasing the rates for water service on a metered basis and increasing the flat rate water service charge for cleaning and washing down garages, service stations, and so on. The rate increased from $36 per year to $48 per year. Motion was made to pass on first reading and was seconded, but then Councilman Bills made the motion to table Ordinance 79-24 until our special meeting scheduled for June 11th, seconded by Megeath with all voting in favor.

Councilman Megeath then introduced Ordinance 79-25, an ordinance concerning the practice of installing gas piping, appliance installation and venting as the gas installation code required, and providing for inspections and permits, as well as providing penalties for violations.

Councilman Davis made a motion to pass this ordinance on first reading, which was seconded by Fruits, but Councilman Bills made a motion to amend the ordinance deleting the words *City Recorder*, because Evanston doesn't have a city recorder. The motion was seconded by Megeath with all voting in favor as amended. This ordinance went on to pass on second and third readings by motion, with all voting in favor on each reading.

The next order of business was the introduction of Ordinance 79-26 introduced by Councilman Albrecht. This was an ordinance setting forth a new schedule of tapping fees for new sewer connections. Motion was made to table this ordinance until our special meeting scheduled for June 11th and was seconded, with all voting in favor.

Ordinance 79-27 came up and was introduced by Councilman Albrecht. This was an ordinance establishing that a development permit must be obtained before construction or development begins; designating the City Building Inspector as Administrator of this ordinance; setting forth his duties; and providing standards for flood hazard reduction. Motion was made to table this ordinance until the special meeting on June 11th and was seconded with all voting in favor.

The next item was the introduction of Ordinance 79-28 introduced by Councilman Megeath, making it an offense to discharge any firearm within the city limits of Evanston or within one-half mile outside of the city limits. This was one of the old ordinances that had to be amended through our re-codifying process. Motion was made and seconded to pass on first reading with all voting in favor. This ordinance went on to become law by passing on second and third readings with all voting in favor.

Most of these ordinances that we were now acting on were old ordinances being re-enacted, renumbered, and, in some cases, amended, during the process of re-codifying the entire book of city codes. To do this each old ordinance that was worthy of being retained had to be acted on and go through the same process that any new ordinance would have to go through. Most of them would have to be amended to meet the present standards and needs.

In other business during this meeting, Lucie Harris, representing the senior citizens, reported on the problems the Center was having, and requested funding from the city for the coming year. As mayor, I told her that the council would take her request into consideration as they discussed the 1979-1980 budget year.

Denice Wheeler was in attendance representing the Historical Society, and reported on the job they had done cleaning up the Almy Cemetery for Memorial Day. She asked the city to reconsider the acceptance of this cemetery and subsequent care of it. She stated that she thought the deed could be updated and turned over to the city. She was told that her request would be taken under advisement.

We knew in order for the city to be eligible to apply for a grant for E.P.A. Funds for Phase I, II, and III on the waste water treatment facility, the city would have to ask for proposals from at least two engineering firms. These proposals had been received at the previous council meeting from Uinta Engineering and Surveying and from Dale Petersen, of Rocky Mountain Engineering. The city had to choose which firm they wanted to write the grant and engineer this proposed facility.

A motion was made to go into an executive session at this time to discuss the proposals. The motion was seconded with a majority voting in favor, with six aye votes and one no vote.

Coming out of the executive session, I called the meeting back to order. Councilman Megeath made a motion to appoint Dale Petersen of Rocky Mountain Engineering to do the engineering of the E.P.A. Wastewater Treatment Facility Phase I, II, and III, seconded by Rice with all voting in favor.

Councilman Rice made a motion to pay straight time pay for compensation time that had been accumulated in the various departments—that is, the employee could choose to be paid straight pay for overtime, or to take time off based on time-and-a-half, seconded by Albrecht with all voting in favor.

The special meeting that was held on June 11th was to have a public hearing concerning the proposed use of Revenue Sharing Funds that the city had received in the amount of $66,750. The following was the proposed revenue sharing budget:

| | |
|---|---|
| **Public Safety** | $ 4,250.00 |
| **Health** | 9,000.00 |
| **Library** | 750.00 |
| **Social Services** | 16,000.00 |
| **Machinery** | 6,750.00 |
| **Sewer** | 30,000.00 |

Motion was made by Councilman Albrecht to approve the proposed preliminary budget on the Revenue Sharing Funds, and was seconded by Bills. After a short discussion I called for the vote, with all voting in favor.

The proposed budget in the amount of approximately $2.7 million for the fiscal year of 1979-1980 was presented for consideration.

This was the highest budget request to date, and far more than the city's budget was a few years back, but we had a lot to consider, including the employee retirement plan, a new health insurance program for the employees and possibly an increase in pay for them.

City employees had never had a retirement program or health insurance until this year, and they hadn't had a pay increase for quite some time. Giving the employees any amount of an increase in pay would be good, but it didn't happen during this next year's budget. Revenues from the oil and gas production had finally started coming in, plus sales tax revenues and other taxes had increased, but not enough to consider a pay increase at this time.

We were still in need of a new sewer plant and we needed to enlarge the Sulfur Creek Reservoir to upgrade our water capacity, both of which we would start planning in the near future. We were now dumping a portion of raw sewage in the Bear River and it wasn't going to stop until we constructed a completely new sewer plant. However, we were continuously working on the old plant to keep it from dumping too much of the sewage into the river. The E.P.A. was continuously reminding us of the penalty we would have to pay if we didn't do something to correct it soon.

After some discussion and knowing that by the time the final budget is passed there would probably be some amendments, Councilman Bills made a motion to accept the proposed budget, seconded by Fruits, with all voting in favor.

The three ordinances, 79-24, 79-26, and 79-27 that were tabled last meeting and scheduled to come back on the floor to be acted on never were brought up at this meeting, but might be acted on sometime in the near future. The council just wasn't ready to act on them at this time.

The next regular city council meeting was held on July 11th. Councilman Albrecht introduced Resolution 79-27, authorizing the city to enter into an agreement with Dale Petersen and Rocky Mountain Engineering and Surveying, Inc. for engineering the city's proposed sewer treatment facility expansion project. Motion to adopt Resolution 79-27 was made and seconded, with all voting in favor.

Evanston had applied for a grant from the Environmental Protection Agency for the expansion of the existing sewer plant, and now that we had officially contracted with an engineering firm there wasn't any problem getting the grant.

The word got out that Evanston was dumping raw sewage into the Bear River when the mayor of Montpelier, Idaho called me, quite upset that we were dumping raw sewage into the Bear River, which also runs through Montpelier and which was the source of their drinking water.

You wouldn't think that a community over 100 miles away would be too much bothered with something that we were doing, but he was upset and after listening to him, I tried to explain that we were doing all we could to correct the situation. Finally, just joking, I told him to just think of how nice and green his lawn would be from our sewer. He kind of snickered, but still didn't seem satisfied. Before hanging up I apologized and he thanked me for listening and I never heard any more from him.

Councilman Bills introduced Resolution 79-26, directing the mayor and city clerk to apply to the Wyoming State Loan Board for a coal tax grant in the amount of $609,000 for the extension of a sewer trunk line. Motion was made and seconded to adopt Resolution 79-26, with all voting in favor.

Then Councilman Bills introduced Resolution 79-28 declaring the intention of the city to accept the streets of Westview Village and assume responsibility for repair and maintenance. Motion was made and seconded to adopt Resolution 79-28, with all voting in favor. I abstained from any discussion and voting, because the project was started by my brother and Uinta Realty, Inc. would be listing it. So, once again, I left the room.

Westview Village was the first townhouse complex to be built in Evanston. Therefore, what a townhouse project entailed was new to the council. There would be a Home Owners Association (H.O.A.) formed with covenants, and rules and regulations involved, but they would not supersede any city ordinances that pertained to the complex.

During this meeting I read a letter from John Proffit resigning as City Engineer, effective June 30, 1979. Motion was made by Councilman Albrecht to accept this resignation, seconded by Megeath. I, along with each councilman, expressed our thanks and appreciation to Proffit and his staff for their dedication and service to the City of Evanston. The motion passed, with all voting in favor.

In past meetings we had discussed changing meeting dates, and considered having two regularly scheduled meetings a month, because we were having two or three special meetings each month to take care of all the business that kept piling up.

Therefore, under the direction of the council and me, Dennis Lancaster, City Attorney, had prepared Ordinance 79-38 to be acted on at this meeting. The ordinance was introduced by Councilman Bills. Attorney Lancaster read the title, which stated that the Evanston City Council shall have two regular meetings per month, one on the first Thursday following the first Wednesday of each month and one on the Thursday two weeks later. Each meeting would be scheduled to begin at 7:00 p.m.

After a short discussion the motion was made to pass Ordinance 79-38 and was seconded, with the majority voting in favor and one no vote

The rest of the meeting was taken up with the opening of bids for different materials for water and sewer equipment, and action on more ordinances that were being introduced to meet the re-codification project. It was a long and drawn out meeting and adjourned at 2:00 a.m. on the 12th of July.

A special meeting was held July 17th to have a public hearing on the Revenue Sharing Funds and also on the General Budget for the fiscal year of 1979-1980 as advertised in the *Uinta County Herald* issue of July 5th.

After the council held a lengthy discussion with those present concerning the usage and purpose of the budget, the meeting adjourned at 8:25 p.m.

We also held a special meeting on July 18th to give final approval of the budget that had been presented during the public hearing on

July 17th. Motion was made by Councilman Bills for approval of the budget of 1979-1980, seconded by Fruits, with all voting in favor.

Councilman Albrecht then introduced Resolution 79-30, authorizing the approval and adoption of the official city budget for the fiscal year ending June 30, 1980. Motion was made and seconded, with all voting in favor.

Ordinance 79-39 was introduced by Councilman Albrecht, an ordinance titled ANNUAL APPROPRIATION FOR FISCAL YEAR ENDING JULY 30, 1980. This ordinance was passed on an emergency basis with a motion by Councilman Megeath, seconded by Davis, to appropriate over 2.8 million dollars for the next fiscal year. The motion passed, with all voting in favor.

The rest of the meeting was taken up with bid openings for various water and sewer parts and equipment, and the passage of the various ordinances that had already been acted on; plus two new ordinances, #79-33 and #79-36, that were introduced and passed on first reading with all voting in favor.

These two ordinances authorized a subdivision of Red Mountain Mesa, and an area presently not zoned, to be rezoned to light industrial. Both ordinances passed on second and third readings during the next few meetings, with all voting in favor.

Garry Ellingford requested that I call for another special meeting at noon on July 25th, because we had so much business come up during our regular meetings, we were unable to get anything done without continuing into the wee hours of the next day. Ellingford's wife Vivian provided an enjoyable lunch for everyone during the meeting, which the council really appreciated and thanked her for.

Mr. Ellingford called for the meeting to get his Sunset Industrial Park ordinance passed on the third reading so they could get started on the project this summer. This was Ordinance 79-34, previously introduced and passed on first and second readings, and now up for the third and final reading. Councilman Bills made the motion for the final reading, seconded by Albrecht, with all voting in favor.

Other business included a request from Hal McVey, representing Cities Service, to allow another well location in the city limits.

Resolution 79-31 was introduced by Councilman Albrecht, giving Cities Service the right to proceed with their plans to drill. Motion was made to adopt the resolution and was seconded, with all voting in favor.

In past meetings the council had suggested hiring an assistant to the mayor, which was budgeted into this fiscal year of 1979-1980. We had advertised and gotten one application, from Steve Snyder, who had been with LUAG for the past year or so.

Snyder's application and resumé proved him to be well qualified, so I told the council that I would like to appoint Snyder to the position of Administrative Assistant to the Mayor. Councilman Albrecht introduced Resolution 79-32, authorizing the creation of the office of Administrative Assistant to the Mayor and Council as an appointed position, and to appoint Steve Snyder to that position. Motion was made to adopt this resolution and seconded, with all voting in favor.

The Administrative Assistant position would be called up for a re-appointment along with all other appointed positions during the January meeting of each year. So Snyder will have to be re-appointed this next January, but with him on board it would take a load off me and the council. With his experience, he would be an asset to the city—and let's hope so, because things were moving pretty fast at this time.

The rest of the meeting was used for some readings of pending ordinances with the proper motion and seconds being made on each, with each passing on the various readings. Councilman Albrecht made a motion to pay $20,913.33 from the Revenue Sharing Funds to the Evanston Joint Powers Board to cover the outstanding bills on the water distribution project, and in the event the board had an excess of funds, these funds were to be paid back to the Revenue Sharing Account, seconded by Davis with all voting in favor.

During the regular city council meeting of August 2nd, after the regular business was taken care of, Ordinances 79-24, 79-26, 79-27 and 79-29, which were tabled during the June 6th meeting until the special meeting of July 11th, but were not acted on at that particular meeting, were finally taken off the table.

Ordinance 79-24 was originally introduced by Councilman Albrecht and he also made the motion to take the ordinance off the table, seconded by Fruits, with all voting in favor.

Attorney Lancaster read the title of Ordinance 79-24, to provide for the tapping charges for new city water connections, and to provide that all new water connections shall include a water meter. It also provided that all new and replacement service lines shall include a back-flow prevention device, and it increased the flat rate water service charge for cleaning and washing down garages, service stations, and so on, from $36.00 per year to $48.00 per year. The ordinance included increasing the rates for water service on a metered basis. Also, within the body of the ordinance, were listed the metered water rates and connection fees, and associated costs and fees. Motion was made to pass Ordinance 79-24 on first reading, and seconded with all voting in favor.

Councilman Albrecht made the motion to take Ordinance 79-26, also originally introduced by him, off the table. The motion was seconded by Rice with all voting in favor.

The title of Ordinance 79-26, setting forth a schedule of tapping fees for new sewer connections, was read by the city attorney. The ordinance outlined the schedule of fees for the various sizes of sewer lines. Motion was made to pass this ordinance on first reading, and seconded with all voting in favor.

Councilman Albrecht made the motion to take Ordinance 79-27, also originally introduced by him, off the table. The motion was seconded by Davis, with the majority voting in favor and one no vote.

*8/2/79    UCH*

# Administrative Assistant For the City of Evanston

Steve Snyder of Evanston, has been hired by the City of Evanston to fill the newly created position of Administrative Assistant to the Mayor and Council, beginning Aug. 8th, 1979.

His primary responsibility is to assist and aid the mayor and city council in all phases of municipal administration. He also will be working with all departments of the city government in applying for various grants.

Steve came to Evanston in July of 1977 as the Director of Community Development for the Lincoln-Uinta Association of Governments. In April of this year he became the Acting Executive Director of the Lincoln-Uinta Assoc. of Governments.

Prior to coming to Evanston, Mr. Snyder was the City Administrator to the City of Jefferson, Jefferson, Oregon.

His educational background consists of an A.A. Degree from Glendale College in 1970 and a B.A. Degree in Urban Studies and Environmental Design from California State College in 1972.

The following year he received his Masters Degree

Steve Snyder is Evanston's new Administrative Assistant.

at Oregon State in Natural Resource Management and Urban Studies.

Besides the educational expertise he brings to this position, his familiarity with this area and its people should prove to be a valuable asset.

Through his position with Lincoln-Uinta Assoc. of Governments, Steve has worked closely with the City on many of its problems and has helped in the solution to many of them.

*Uinta County Herald,* August 2, 1979.

The title was read by the attorney. This was an ordinance to establish a development permit, which must be obtained prior to beginning any construction or development, and also designating the City Building Inspector as Administrator of this ordinance; setting forth his duties; providing standards for flood hazard reduction; and providing penalties for non–compliance. Motion was made to pass this ordinance on first reading and was seconded. After a short discussion, I called for the vote, but the motion failed with only one aye vote. I voted nay, but I don't recall who voted aye. Therefore, Ordinance 79-27 never became law.

Councilman Fruits made a motion to take Ordinance 79-29 off the table, seconded by Bills, with all voting in favor. This ordinance was introduced by Councilman Megeath at the June 6th meeting.

The title was read by the city attorney. This ordinance regulated the use, sale, consumption, and possession of alcoholic and malt beverages. Also included in this ordinance were licenses, permits and fees, and it included the open container provisions.

Ordinance 79-29 was a very lengthy ordinance and covered every provision concerning alcohol and malt beverages. Motion was made to pass this ordinance and seconded with all voting in favor.

Ordinances 79-24, 79-26, and 79-29, which were all tabled during the June 6th meeting, went on to be moved, seconded and passed on second and third readings in later meetings. Ordinance 79-27 died on first reading and never was brought up again.

Additional business included a resolution petitioning for annexation, which was moved, seconded and passed on with all voting in favor, and a resolution authorizing the city to purchase a parcel of real property to install a sewer line and other utilities. This resolution also passed with the majority voting in favor with one no vote.

We also discussed creating an official seal for the City of Evanston, and we decided to have the students of Miss Dallas's high school art class draw up a seal. We planned to get concepts from the students and design a seal from their ideas. We also decided to offer a cash prize to the top three choices that the city council picked as favorites.

After receiving approximately 15 drawings from the students, and after finally naming our top three choices, we contacted the winners and invited them to a council meeting to receive their prize money. The third-place winner was Wade Stuhr, who received $15.00, second place was Lanette Moon, who received $35.00, and first-place winner was Joe Bright, who received the grand prize of $50.00.

During the meeting the council and I thanked them for their participation and told them that we were going to try to use their ideas for the official city seal. But it didn't turn out that way, because the council wanted something a little less complicated. But everyone appreciated the students' involvement and time. Later we talked to Thomas Muths, the architect that designed the new city hall about the seal, and he offered to try to come up with something that demonstrated what Evanston believed in and what we were all about. Several months later, in 1980, we finally accepted a seal. The seal had three main topics that Evanston was known for: Opportunity, Equality and Friendship, and in the center of the seal would be the image of a hand shake, indicating "You are welcome to Evanston." This was the seal we officially accepted by resolution at a later meeting in 1980 as the Official Seal of the City of Evanston.

Almost everyone appreciated the seal. The majority of the council members accepted it. We had it made up by the Young Electric Sign Company, and put up bronze plaques in the council chambers, on the building, in the hallway and outside the building. We also had a large order of lapel pins made and gave them away as a token from our community.

One person who was elected to serve on the council later, Ms Julie Lehman, said that she just loved the seal and the lapel pin, and she wore that pin all the time. I was also very proud of the seal, because I felt that it had a lot of meaning in trying to achieve our goal of encouraging industry and business to come to Evanston. We had no idea how long the boom was going to last and we wanted to continue our goal of bringing in new industry with good jobs.

There's an old Chinese proverb that says, be *not afraid of going slowly; be only afraid of standing still.* Although the economy was looking good at this time, I was still always thinking of the future. I was a man of vision and was always trying to keep looking forward and keep things moving—never standing still.

During our second regular meeting on August 16th, Attorney Tim Beppler, representing M.A.P.E., Inc., presented a petition and a plat for annexation, including a Uinta County road known as Constitutional Avenue. M.A.P.E., Inc. was the owner of the mobile home park which the annexation included as well as the county street.

City Attorney Lancaster stated that there might be some question whether or not this land was contiguous to the city, and that he would like some time to research this before any action was taken. Also, Councilman Bills stated that he would like public input, not necessarily a public hearing, but that he would at least bring it to the attention of the Evanston Planning and Zoning Commission.

We passed several ordinances on second and third readings that had been previously introduced.

We accepted a bid in the amount of $55,555 for the construction of the new substation for the Evanston Voluntary Fire Department to be located on the acreage that was provided for located at the Uinta County fair ground and rodeo property.

The Old Town Hall building came up for discussion. I reported that there were some business firms that were interested in purchasing it. We discussed whether or not we should put the building up for sale, or whether we should just abandon it and tear it down. The general consensus of the council was that it would be best to put it up for sale and look at bids. By law we would have to advertise for bids, but at this time we decided to just table the matter and get some input from the public.

The City of Evanston had never had a personnel manual until this year. We previously had enlisted the services of the U.S.A. Office of Personnel Management to compile a personnel manual for the city, and during this meeting the manual was presented for acceptance. Each councilman and I had been given a copy of the manual several days earlier to review and make suggestions. We had previously discussed the manual during one of our work sessions and did come up with a few changes.

Councilman Megeath made the motion to accept and adopt the recently completed manual as presented with the following additions: *Compensatory time off be allowed at 1½ times the time worked and each person may accumulate and retain a maximum of three days, or 24 hours past thirty days.* The motion was seconded by Albrecht, but before the vote Councilman Bills requested that the two provisions in the amendment be separated for voting purposes. There were no objections to doing this.

Therefore, I called for the vote to adopt only the first provision: *allowing compensation time off at 1½ times the time worked and each person may accumulate and retain a maximum of three days.* Motion passed with 5 ayes and 1 no vote. I called for the vote on the second provision:

*allowing a holdover of 24 hours past thirty days.* Motion passed with 4 ayes and 2 no votes. Councilman Fruits was absent at this particular meeting for good reason, but we finally had an personnel manual, and the employees seemed to be grateful for it.

Ordinance 79-45 was introduced by Councilman Bills. It was an ordinance providing for a speed limit of 30 miles per hour on Highways 30 S (Bear River Drive, part of Front Street and Harrison Drive), Wyoming State 89 (County Road), and Wyoming State 150 (part of Front Street) within the City of Evanston; and establishing speed limits of 20 miles per hour at all other points within the city.

After the reading of the ordinance by Attorney Lancaster, motion was made to pass on first reading, and was seconded with all voting in favor. Ordinance 79-45 passed on the second and third readings with all voting in favor, and thus became law.

Councilman Bills came up with the idea of dedicating Greek Street as an official city street so that the city could maintain it and remove snow. Some of the residents living on the street had requested the city to consider this. As mayor, I told Bills and Attorney Lancaster to follow up and see if this would be to the city's benefit.

I made a report on a recent Uinta County District One School Board meeting that I had attended. We discussed the possibility trading some more property with the school district. I said that the board would like to trade the property next to the baseball fields for more of the property located at the upper end of 10th Street to build a middle school. The council verbally agreed to do this and directed the attorney to follow up on it.

The Council gave me permission to approach the Wyoming Highway Department for southbound access from the west end interchange. In the past, the highway department had made a ruling that there would be no access off that interchange going south. But after hearing that Amoco, Inc. was planning to build a plant for sweet gas on Yellow Creek Road near the Anschultz Ranch, and knowing that this would cause a lot of heavy truck traffic on 6th and Lombard Streets, which would be the only two routes that would be available for access to their location, I knew we had to do something.

So when I met with a representative from Amoco, he told me that they requested access off the west interchange exit, but were turned down. I told him that Steve Snyder and I would be going to Cheyenne to meet with the Highway Department to request permission to get the access needed, and that after we explained to them why we need it I thought they would come through.

Feeling that this trip was an emergency, Snyder and I took off that week and met with Leno Menghini, Superintendent of the Wyoming Highway Department. After our discussion with him, he told us that we were right, that there would be a lot of heavy traffic on those residential streets, and he said not to worry, that we would get the right to access and open a road up going south (the Overthrust Road).

We had a good meeting with Menghini and talked about some of the other problems in Evanston such as needing an off ramp at Wyoming Highway 150 and Front Street near the Wyoming State Hospital, Highway 89 (County Road), Park Road, City View and other areas that needed more access. I thanked him for meeting with us and especially for his interest in helping us through this mess of a boom.

But when I got back to town and heard that the East Anschultz plant was going to be located across the Wyoming/Utah state line in Summit County I told the council that this could not happen, and I told Snyder that we were going to Denver to talk to Mr. Jim Vanderbeek, Amoco Vice President and Division Manager. So Snyder called and got us an appointment to meet with Vanderbeek.

The Amoco building in Denver was a tall, silver, roundish building that some people referred to as a Coors beer can. I don't recall what floor Mr. Vanderbeek was on, but I do recall it was pretty high up, and when we were invited into his office, I couldn't believe the size of it. It had to be at least 10 times the size of the mayor's office at City Hall, plus it had a wet bar, a rest room and was as comfortable as any living room I had ever been in.

Vanderbeek appeared to be a good guy and he welcomed us into his office as if we were long-lost buddies. I had met him two or three times before, but I had never sat down and had a real talk with him concerning the problems and impact that the oil boom had on

Evanston. He invited us into his office and offered us a nice soft cushioned seat and a drink. Then he thanked me for approaching the Wyoming Highway Department and getting their approval for southbound access to their proposed sweet gas plant. I told him that we had to do something to get that heavy truck traffic off the two residential streets, Lombard and 6th Streets.

After getting acquainted, I told him that our real purpose was to meet and talk with him about the location of the East Anschultz Gas Plant. I explained to him that I understood that they were planning to locate the plant across the state line in Summit County, Utah. He indicated that was their plan, but I explained to him that Evanston and Uinta County were having problems from the boom, and now Evanston would have all the heavy traffic through town, and we would like to see them locate the plant across the state line in Uinta County, Wyoming.

I went on to explain that most of the employees at the plant would probably be living in the Evanston area, causing us more impact. I also explained how much their new gas plant facility would help Uinta County's tax base, giving the county and city more revenue to help overcome the problems we were already having. I also told him that we were grateful that the oil industry had treated the community well so far, and that we wanted to continue to have a good working relationship with them, but would like them to understand that Evanston is the community that is getting the worst impact from the boom. Therefore, we would appreciate whatever help they can give us.

After a few more questions and comments, he said that he would give what I had said a lot of thought and would get back to us. Then after talking about what was happening in the industry and visiting for a while, he seemed to be ready to work with us in any way possible. Our visit lasted for about an hour and I was very glad that we had gotten the opportunity to visit with him, and become more acquainted with him. I thought it was a visit well worth our while. We thanked him for his time and hospitality and left feeling pretty good, hoping that we had done some good.

A few days later we got the good news that we were hoping for. Jim Vanderbeek called, and said to me that the location of the plant _would be located_ in Uinta County. I was so pleased that I couldn't stop thanking him, and when I broke the news to the council they couldn't believe it, but were damn glad.

We had a relatively small police force, mainly because we couldn't pay a reasonable wage, and we had very few vehicles. If we could give them an increase in pay and obtain more police cars we could be in a better position to retain our officers, but we didn't get it into this year's budget. But once again the oil companies came to our rescue.

Owen Murphy, of Chevron, Inc., had told us that the State of Nevada was selling a bunch of their used highway patrol cars to high bidders and that Chevron would be happy to buy several of them for Evanston if we had the drivers to get them back from Carson City, Nevada. We told him that we would be happy to have those cars and that we were really in need of them. So they went ahead and purchased 8 cars from Nevada for the City of Evanston. This gave us a car for every patrolman in the department, and made it a lot more convenient for the police to do their job. Our police officers drove the cars back from Nevada.

8A   Ogden Standard-Examiner, Friday Evening, Sept. 7, 1979

# Evanston Expecting Dramatic Increase in Money, People

By ROBIN TIBBETS
Standard-Examiner Staff

Editor's Note: This is the second in a series of articles dealing with the impact of the oil and gas industry on Evanston, Wyo. This segment deals with the economic impact on the community.

EVANSTON, Wyo. — In three years, tax revenues from oil and gas valuations have increased five-fold in Uinta County, according to J.W. Vanderbeek, vice president and regional manager of Amoco Production Co.

In 1976 revenues were $83,000, rising the following year to $92,000 and in 1978, to $465,000.

Most of this — $356,000 — came from Amoco property in the county, of which Evanston is the seat. Amoco's assessment was $5,775,000.

"As significant as these figures are, they may be dwarfed by future activity," Mr. Vanderbeek said in a letter to Mayor Dennis Ottley.

"Preliminary 1979 assessment will be nearly $15 million."

"The proportion attributable to the oil and gas boom can be readily seen when you consider that the 1978 gross valuation for real and personal property from all sources in Uinta County was about $36,500,000."

Future increases beyond 1979 seem inevitable, the production company official said.

When the Whitney Canyon natural gas field goes on stream in 1981 and 1982, "the level of funding will again show a very substantial increase.

"Thus, Uinta County can expect steady and dramatic increases in oil and gas tax money to better enable the county to cope with

problems connected with rapid oil and gas development," Mr. Vanderbeek said.

"As I see it, progress, rapid development and 'boom town' conditions are bound to have pluses and minuses," he continued.

**BIG PLUS**

The big plus is the establishment of a "secure employment base in your community, as opposed to the continuing dependence on UPRR (Union Pacific Railroad and Route 80 traffic.

"The negative results are obvious to everyone — crowded schools, housing shortages, water, sewer and road problems, etc.," he said.

Noting that some of Evanston's citizens may be pleased about the future, some may not, Mr. Vanderbeek said one thing is sure.

"Energy activities are going to increase, regardless of whether all residents are pleased about it.

"It seems to me that the people of Evanston must become deeply involved in planning efforts so that

they can take advantage of all the favorable aspects of growth and stable employment."

At the same time, he said, they can resolve the "negative, short-term effects of being a boom town."

Although he agrees that the boom town problems have been many, Mayor Ottley thinks the city is in pretty good condition, financially.

During 12 years on the City Council, including the past eight months as mayor, "I've been in on a lot of

city budgets.

"Before, this town was hurting as far as the budget was concerned. Everytime we wanted to do something we had to scrape the bottom of the barrel for money."

**FISCAL YEAR**

Not so in the final year ended July 1.

"We had an excess of almost $500,000. To me, this is a good budget."

Besides that, the tax levy is down to 5.8 mills, well below the 8 or 9 mills maximum that can be as-

sessed.

"The optional 1 percent sales tax has helped, giving the city money," the mayor said.

With the increase in oil and gas and other property valuations, the city has a $2.7 million budget for the current fiscal year — the largest ever.

Although it can't be attributed to the industrial expansion, Evanston has a new city administration building that houses all departments except police.

The latter has offices in Uinta County's Public Safety Building on Main.

The new city hall was built with an Economic Development Agency grant of almost $1 million.

"It was a sudden thing," the mayor said, having come up under the administration of President Ford. The city had 90 days to make all preparations to get the grant and start construction.

The only requirement was that the city own the land. The only piece it owned was at 1200 Main, a block north of the old city hall on 11th.

The odd part about the grant was that it was available to communities with unemployment problems months before.

**PRETTY GOOD**

"By that time we didn't have any unemployment problems so we came out pretty good. The building didn't cost us more than $3,000," and that was for the grant application.

The council now is thinking of hiring an administrative assistant who could take a lot of work off the part time council's shoulders.

DOWNTOWN Evanston, where things are expected to get pretty crowded.

*Ogden Standard-Examiner,* September 7, 1979.

At that same time, Chevron purchased a brand new ambulance with all the equipment for the county, but was for the Evanston area and controlled by the Evanston Voluntary Fire Department. The department had several members that were certified as E.M.T.s (Emergency Medical Technicians), and they were really happy to have a vehicle that they could work with and help do their job. Thanks again to the oil industry for acknowledging our problems.

During the month of August, the Honorable Senator Alan K. Simpson visited Evanston. He came here mainly to check out the problems that he had heard about in our community and county. It was a real pleasure to have him here, especially because I had the opportunity of having lunch with just him and me. We talked about some of our problems, mainly water and sewer, that Evanston was having and how federal funding would be a great help in the enlargement of both systems. We also talked about some other problems and what steps we were taking to resolve them. I really enjoyed having lunch with him. I felt it was a great honor and privilege, *especially when it was on his dime,* I thought jokingly.

Senator Simpson wrote me a letter dated August 27th and thanked me for having lunch with him. In his letter he wrote: *Please know that my office is here to serve and assist the people of Wyoming—not only the citizens but municipal, county and state officials. Do let me know if there is any way I can be of assistance to you in the many problems that confront the Mayor of any growing and progressive Wyoming city. I wish you the very best during your administration of that municipality.* He was always very supportive of us when we were applying for federal and state funding, especially concerning our water and sewer systems.

East Anschutz Gas Plant

All of our congressional delegation made a visit to Evanston during our trying times caused by the boom, sometimes more than once. The Honorable Senator Malcom Wallop and the Honorable Congressman Dick Cheney had both visited Evanston and Uinta County to check out the problems we were having, and at the same time promising us, as Senator Simpson did, that they would give us their 100% support. When it came down to it they all came through, supporting Evanston and Uinta County in a big way.

On August 27th the city council called for a special meeting with the Evanston Planning and Zoning Commission to discuss some differences that the city council and the board had. The meeting lasted almost two hours, but there were a lot of problems solved and a better understanding between both parties.

Rudger Davis, Chairman of the Board, stated that the Planning and Zoning Commission was pleased at what had been accomplished during the meeting, and I, as mayor, encouraged the council members to attend the P & Z Commission meetings once in a while to further develop communications between the two boards.

At this time the boom was getting national and worldwide publicity. On September 6, 1979 the *Ogden Standard Examiner*, Ogden, Utah's largest newspaper, came out with an article in one of their issues titled NATION'S BIGGEST GAS PROVINCE, and added, EVANSTON: A MODERN-DAY ENERGY BOOMTOWN. On September 7th they had an article in the issue titled EVANSTON EXPECTING DRAMATIC INCREASE IN MONEY, PEOPLE, and then another article in Sunday's issue dated September 8th titled BOOM PRESENTS PROBLEMS FOR EVANSTON SCHOOLS.

On September 6th the *Uinta County Herald* came out with an article titled: THE OVERTHRUST BELT IS BOOMING. The *Herald* stated: *this was a copy of an article published in the Wall Street Journal on August 27, 1979, and because it is of such a tremendous interest to the residents of our area, we reprinted it in this week's issue of the Uinta County Herald.*

The Journal's issue was titled: IN THE WEST, A LONG STRIP OF LAND STIRS HOPES AMONG OIL, GAS MEN, with the following added *"Overthrust Belt" is booming. But Tricky Geology, Cost Cause Drilling Problems…*

**The Search for 'Elephants'** by William E. Blundell

The article went on to say: *Three years ago, this town in the wind-swept emptiness of southwest Wyoming had 4,300 people and a case of the economic blahs. Now it has 7,000 people, with more coming every day, and a roaring boom is on its hands.*

*Home prices have doubled and city services are strained. "We've had a water supply problem, a sewer problem, a housing shortage, and the heavy trucks are tearing hell out of our streets. But we're not a depressed area anymore,"* says *Mayor Dennis Ottley.*

The article continued: *That the oil game has come to Evanston. In fact the town is bracketed by the hottest oil and gas action in the United States, an exploration drive that geologists believe is opening an entirely new hydrocarbon province.*

The Journal article was a very long one about Evanston and the boom. It covered a half page of their newspaper; therefore I am not going to print the entire article, but it was an indication that the

Evanston area was starting to get a lot of national recognition.

During the first regular meeting of the city council on September 6th, most of the business was the passing of various ordinances that had previously been acted on. Other action taken was the adoption of Resolution 79-37 approving the annexation of some property on the west end of Evanston, introduced by Councilman Rice.

Attorney Lancaster questioned whether this property would be adjacent to the city limits and if it could legally be annexed. His decision was that the property in a sense could be called legal because of the continuances of the streets. Therefore, after some discussion, a motion was made and seconded. Motion passed with 5 aye votes, 1 no vote, and Albrecht abstaining, because he felt he had a conflict of interest.

During the meeting Debbie Youngman indicated that she would like to bid on the old town hall when the council decides what to do with it. There was some more discussion, but nothing was decided on at this time.

Eugene Martin presented a site plan and plat for a proposed mobile home park on the east end of Evanston. After making his presentation, motion was made that Martin present his plan first to the Planning and Zoning Commission with the tentative approval of the council. Motion was seconded with 6 yes votes and 1 no vote. The motion passed.

Amoco's representative, R. C. Buckley, presented a plat for a proposed oil well site on the golf course land. They stated that they planned to drill during the winter months if permission for drilling could be obtained. They were told that the city council would have to seek permission from the Wyoming Recreation Commission. Permission was never given.

Once again the council entered into a discussion concerning parking, parking meters, two-hour parking and other problems facing the city at this time, such as water pumps at the underpass, the proposed fire station, with the meeting adjourning at 12:35 a.m. on September 7th.

During the second regular city council meeting held on September 20th, the F.O.E. (Eagles) was denied the renewal of their limited liquor license. Motion was made and seconded with all voting in favor.

Private clubs such as the Eagles are permitted to apply for a limited liquor license, which is less expensive than a full liquor license, and it gives them the right to serve only their members and their member's guests, but no one else. After several complaints from some liquor dealers, and several warnings from the city to stop serving people other than their members and guests, the city decided to R their license.

We were very much aware that because of the boom and fast growth we were going through, it was tough for these private clubs to control the patrons that were coming in. But when other bars and liquor establishments start complaining that they were paying ten times the amount of money for a license but that private clubs were competing with them, it just wasn't fair. The city council had no other choice than temporarily pull their license until they could get their place in order. They must obey the state law that allows them to hold a limited license.

It was kind of a bad deal all around because, by state law, the city was limited in how many full liquor licenses they were allowed. Evanston had about 18 full liquor licenses available at this time and all of them were active. There would be no more available until after the new census was taken and all cities and towns were completely satisfied with the 1980 census. It would be at least another two years before any more full liquor licenses would become available to Evanston, unless the city called for a special census and it was approved by the Census Bureau.

The oil and gas boom was causing such fast growth that bars and other full liquor license holders were overcrowded to the point that a lot of them were breaking the law for the number of patrons they could legally have on their premises at any one time, set by the fire department. So the private clubs were having a hard time controlling the crowd they got as overflow.

During this meeting I brought up the subject of an interchange and on/off-ramp to Interstate 80 where the Wyoming State Hospital is located. It would be an interchange between Interstate 80 and Wyoming State Highway 150. I suggested that in the future, if the traffic continues to get worse, another off-ramp would help the situation.

After a considerable amount of discussion, pro and con, Councilman Bills made a motion to direct Steve Snyder, Administrative Assistant, to write a letter to the Wyoming Highway Commission requesting the suggested interchange. The motion was seconded by Fruits with all voting in favor. But shortly after the letter was written, Snyder and I visited the Wyoming Highway Department and also talked to Leno Menghini, superintendent of the department, about it.

Evanston had a good relationship with the Wyoming Highway Commission and had received a lot of help from them. Dave Nelson, former Mayor of Kemmerer and a good friend of mine, was now on the commission, recently appointed by Governor Ed Herschler. Nelson and I became good friends when he and I met at W.A.M. meetings and in Cheyenne for various reasons. He knew our situation because he was having some of the same problems in Kemmerer, but not quite as extreme. Eventually we got the interchange, but it would be a few more years before the highway department could come up with the funds and start construction.

Also, during this council meeting we had a public hearing concerning the annexation of two subdivisions, Aspen Groves I and II. They were both adjacent to the city limits, but when the plat was approved, the developer did not want to be within the city limits so they had their own well for water and septic tanks for sewer. But when the subdivision was almost filled up with residents, they soon found out that the well did not provide enough water for all the people now in the subdivisions. This was the main reason they came to the city for annexation. They also just had gravel roads with drainage ditches, which they had to maintain themselves. The county only took care of snow removal.

These two subdivisions were developed a few years earlier, prior to the oil and gas boom, but now the folks residing in the areas were requesting annexation so they could hook into city services, especially water and sewer, plus they wanted to dedicate the roads to the city for road maintenance and to request an improvement district to get paved roads, but didn't want curb and gutter or sidewalks. Their reason for not wanting the curbing and such was they wanted to retain the more out-in-the-country look.

Following the closing of the public hearing, Councilman Fruits introduced Resolution 79-39 to annex both subdivisions, and were read in full by Attorney Lancaster. A motion was made and seconded to adopt the resolution, with all voting in favor. Following the adoption of Resolution 79-39 Councilman Bills introduced Ordinance 79-53 annexing Aspen Groves I and II. The ordinance was read by the city attorney, followed by a motion to pass on first reading and seconded with all voting in favor. The ordinance went on to be passed on second and third readings with all voting in favor.

Steve Snyder, Administrative Assistant gave a report concerning the Small Cities Programs as it concerned senior housing. No comments were received from the public, but Snyder did make some comments and explanations in seeking funds for senior housing.

A representative from the Eagles club met with the council and asked for permission to be heard at the City of Evanston regular meeting on October 4th. This request was granted.

Allen Kennedy, General Superintendent of Public Works, reported that the water lines in the Hoback Ranches Subdivision in the Uinta Meadows area were not being installed deep enough to prevent freezing problems in wintertime. I, as mayor, directed Kennedy to notify the project engineer to inform the developer of this problem and that they must meet the city specifications.

At this time, because of so many underground freeze-ups over the past few years, the city was in favor of doing feasibility studies on both the water and sewer lines within the city. A motion was made and seconded to appoint Dale Petersen to do the study on the sewer lines, and John Proffit to do the study on the water lines. All voted in favor.

Most of this meeting was taken up acting on various ordinances that had previously been acted on, mostly concerning zone changes, annexations and new subdivisions. Also, a general discussion took place concerning all phases of the city.

Before adjourning, I announced that there would be a meeting with members of the Wyoming Highway Commission on October 2nd at 2:00 p.m., and there would be a Joint Powers Board meeting on October 4th at 6:30 p.m.

At the regular city council meeting on October 4th, Mr. Blaine Welling expressed his objections to an interchange at the Wyoming State Hospital and Wyoming State Highway 150 location. A short discussion was held, but no action was taken on this matter.

The parking problems on Center Street between 9th to 11th Streets were discussed. Mrs. Jesse Monroe, Mr. and Mrs. Ray Voss, Dr. Robert Marquardt and Jerry Parker, all owners of property on this street, opposed the parallel parking proposed by the city.

Mr. Voss offered to make off-street parking for five cars if the city would provide an approach onto his property, and Dr. Marquardt requested parking meters in front of his business. A discussion took place and the group decided to take a good look at the problem and get back to them.

Later in the meeting and after more discussion, Councilman Albrecht made a motion to go with the 40-degree angle parking on that portion of Center Street, and install three parking meters in front of Dr. Marquardt's office at his request, seconded by Fruits, with all voting in favor.

The next meeting in October, Councilman Megeath made a motion for parallel parking, according to city code, on the downhill side of Center Street between 10th and 11th Streets, seconded by Bills, with 6 yes votes and 1 no vote. Motion passed by a majority.

Dale Petersen and Mike Lanning presented some plats taking in the top end of 8th and 10th Streets to No Name Street, an area that had never been platted before.

When John Proffit and his family moved back to Evanston in the mid-1970s, Proffit had purchased an un-platted lot on an unnamed street that was now called "No Name Street". Before he started building his home on the lot, he needed an address. He came to one of the Evanston City Council meetings to explain his problem and requested we give a name to his street. In the discussion a lot of different names were suggested, including the name Proffit, but when it came down to it John Proffit suggested calling it "No Name Street," and the city council agreed. Motion and second were made and all voted in favor, and that was how the name of "No Name Street" came about. Petersen and Lanning were surveyors and engineers of subdividing this area so other lots could be platted and homes could be built on them. Councilman Bills made a motion to authorize the acquisition of these streets so they would be dedicated to the city; this included part of 8th, 9th and 10th Streets, seconded by Davis, with all voting in favor.

Councilman Albrecht introduced Ordinance 79-54. This was an ordinance providing that all builders and contractors include a water meter connected to the water line in all new construction, and to provide for the installation of the meter. Motion was made and seconded to suspend the rules and pass this ordinance on first reading as an emergency, with 6 yes votes and 1 no vote. The motion passed by a majority.

A motion was then made and seconded to pass Ordinance 79-54 on first reading on an emergency basis with 6 yes votes and 1 no vote with the motion passing. I do not recall who the council member that voted against this motion; it was not in the minutes, but the ordinance would go into law immediately.

During the period of the oil/gas boom, there were many companies coming to the Evanston City Council meetings requesting the city's sponsorship on Industrial Revenue Bonds. This was a practical way of funding the construction of industrial properties. And believe me, as mayor, I signed a lot of them. I even went to New York City on a fast overnight trip, paid for by the builders (Dow Chemical), and was back in Evanston for a city council meeting scheduled for that same day. So I didn't get to enjoy N.Y.C. at all or see any of the famous landmarks, such as the Statue of Liberty.

At this time Councilman Bills introduced Ordinance 79-55 providing new boundaries for voting wards for the City of Evanston. This ordinance went on to be passed on first, second and third readings, with all voting in favor.

The reason for passing this Ordinance 79-55 was that the town was growing so fast in many different directions that we had to change the voting districts, Wards 1, 2 and 3.

At the end of the meeting Councilman Bills made the motion that the city put up the Old Town Hall for sale and advertise for bids, seconded by Albrecht, with all voting in favor.

Meeting was adjourned at 12:40 a.m. on October 5th.

The second regular council meeting of the city was held on October 16th, at which time I read a letter from Rick Sather requesting his resignation from the Evanston Planning and Zoning Commission. Motion was made by Councilman Rice to accept the resignation with a vote of thanks for his service, seconded by Megeath, with all voting in favor.

During the meeting, a motion was made and seconded to go into executive session. This was to discuss problems the city was having with Hoback Ranches on their Uinta Meadows Subdivisions. The problems concerned paving the streets, storm sewers, sidewalks, curbing, and so on.

After coming out of executive session no action was taken at this time.

Other business was passing several ordinances that had previously been acted on and the opening of bids on a ¾-ton 4-wheel-drive vehicle and two police cars.

Finally, I made the announcement that there would be a Joint Powers Board meeting on November 8th at 6:00 p.m.

Following the Joint Powers Board of November 8th, I called the first regular meeting of the Evanston City Council to order at 7:00 p.m. with Councilman Fruits being absent.

A public hearing was held during the meeting concerning the annexation of an area west of the city limits. After the public hearing had closed, Ordinance 79-63 was introduced by Councilman Davis.

During the meeting many more ordinances were acted on with all voting in favor, except Ordinance 79-63, annexing property in Section 19 located west of the city limits and including the Centennial

Valley Subdivisions, which was discussed during the public hearing. It failed because of some objections from the property owners.

Mr. Sonny Blakeslee attended the meeting requesting that the city purchase one high-band radio for the ambulance service. A motion was made and seconded to approve his request with all voting in favor. In a previous meeting, Amoco Oil Company had requested to drill an oil well on the golf course property and promised to do it in the winter months, but Councilman Bills made a motion at this meeting to deny their request. I suggested that the motion may be considered a negative motion and, with the attorney agreeing, the motion died from lack of a second. After a short discussion I suggested that the council move on to other business. I don't recall Amoco ever bringing up that particular request again.

Bids had been called for the sale of the Old Town Hall building, but no sealed bids were received at this time. Mr. Evan Reese, who was in attendance, offered an oral bid in the amount of $17,800. A motion was made by Councilman Megeath to accept his bid, but the motion failed from lack of a second. The council decided to continue requesting sealed bids.

Councilman Albrecht introduced Resolution 79-46, a resolution authorizing the city to convey to Uinta County School District No. 1 property now owned by the city for the use of the new middle school. Motion was made and seconded to adopt the resolution. The vote was called for, with 5 yes votes, 1 no vote, and 1 absent, with the motion carried by a majority vote.

Councilman Rice introduced Resolution 79-47, a resolution to make application to the Wyoming Recreation Commission, and the Heritage Conservation and Recreation Service for a grant for the construction of two baseball fields and other related recreation facilities to be located in the City of Evanston. Motion was made and seconded to adopt Resolution 79-47 with 5 yes votes, 1 no vote, 1 absent, with the motion passing by the majority.

Mr. Joe Wheeler, owner of the Jolly Roger Restaurant and Lounge, was in attendance to present an application transferring his liquor license to Shirley Bowman, who was not in attendance. After

Wheeler's explanation the council requested that the new applicant of the license be present when it would be discussed at the next regular council meeting on November 21st.

I read a letter of resignation from another police officer, Denis Layton. Councilman Albrecht made the motion to accept his request with regret and to express a vote of thanks for his service and dedication to the city, seconded by Davis, with all voting in favor.

We were losing police officers quite frequently to the oil and gas industry because of the high wages they could offer. This is something we did not want to see happen because it cost a lot of money to train these officers, sending them to the police academy for training in Douglas, and the city did not have the income to pay higher wages.

This meeting adjourned at 12:35 a.m. on November 9th.

During the second regular meeting on November 21st, a few more ordinances were acted on with all passing on various hearings, and Councilman Fruits made a motion to give all full-time employees a one-time $50.00 cost-of-living bonus for 1979, seconded by Albrecht, with all voting in favor. This would not be paid until the end of the year, probably during the annual Christmas dinner.

Mr. Robert M. Pryor was present to make an oral bid for the old town hall building in the amount of $42,500, much more than the last oral bid by Mr. Reese, but the council said that they would retain the building for the time being, because the bids weren't even close to what the building was appraised for.

This meeting turned out to be much shorter than most of our regular meetings. It adjourned at 9:12 p.m. of the same day.

At the first regular meeting of the Evanston City Council on December 6th, following the approval of the minutes and the payment of the outstanding bills, Ordinance 79-59, pertaining to the water meter rates based on size of water line, and Ordinance 79-62, changing the maximum height for accessory buildings, came up for the third and final reading with all voting in favor, and Ordinance 79-66, approving the second addition to the Evanston Industrial Center, came up for the second reading and passed by motion, with all voting in favor.

Linda Webb, representing Care, Inc. had made a request in a previous meeting for help from the city, but the city attorney had indicated that this may not be a city function and wanted to check it out. During this meeting Linda Webb returned and made a presentation and requested $2,900 for aid for handicapped preschool age children, but City Attorney Dennis Lancaster explained his legal opinion, and told the council that they would have to decide if this program was in the realm of city responsibility. After a lengthy period of questions and answers, Councilman Albrecht made a motion to direct the city attorney to draw up a resolution to enter into a contract with Care, Inc. in order to meet their request, seconded by Rice, with all voting in favor.

By drawing up a resolution, if adopted, it would give the council the legal right to vote on this sort of request from Care, Inc., and it would give the council and attorney more time to look into the program.

Linda Barker, a rancher's wife and a mother of three, accompanied by other folks also concerned with the drug problem, were in attendance to meet with the council concerning the possibility of drawing up an ordinance making it illegal to sell and/or possess drug paraphernalia in Evanston. She said the ordinance *would not solve all the drug problems, but it would be a positive statement,* and that the community did not condone the use of drugs.

After she finished speaking she turned the floor over to Wyoming State Representative Ron Micheli. He labeled the legal sale of drug paraphernalia a "hypocrisy". He said, *Drugs are illegal, but any three year old child can go into a store or on the street and purchase paraphernalia.* He believed this was "more than hypocrisy," as the legal purchase of drug paraphernalia provided "a stamp of approval" on illegal drugs. Other presentations were made by Dr. Earl Condie, Undersheriff Brad "Jonesy" Fearn, and County Commissioner Dan South.

After more comments from other citizens in attendance and from the council I assigned Councilmembers Albrecht and Fruits to work with Mrs. Barker and City Attorney Lancaster to draft an ordinance to be presented to the council as soon as possible.

The *Uinta County Herald* issue of December 13th read, PARA-PHERNALIA BAN TERMED STEP IN THE RIGHT DIREC-TION, and printed a lengthy story of the meeting of December 6th concerning drug paraphernalia.

Resolution 79-49, declaring the need for a housing authority to function in the City of Evanston, was introduced by Councilman Bills.

In past meetings Mrs. Patsy Madia, Director of the Uinta County Senior Citizens Center, and Mrs. Marie Hicks had approached the council to say that residential rentals had increased so much that folks on fixed incomes could no longer afford to rent anywhere in Evanston.

I knew of one old-timer who had lived in Evanston for many years and had done odd jobs for folks for a long time who was evicted from his apartment because the landlord raised the rent on him so high he couldn't even come close to paying it. He was retired and on a fixed income, and his health was too poor to do odd jobs anymore, so he left to live in Utah near his children. He passed away shortly after he left. He was very unhappy about having to leave Evanston where all his friends were.

I was completely in favor of forming a housing authority to get HUD housing assistance so that the City of Evanston could construct housing units that could be rented at a reasonable rate to those folks on fixed and low incomes. The idea was not for the city to compete with the private sector, but with all of the high paying jobs and easy money to come by, no one in the private sector seemed to want to build low income housing for those in need.

After the attorney read Resolution 79-49, a motion was made for the adoption of the resolution and seconded with 6 yes votes and 1 no vote. The motion passed by a majority.

Councilman Fruits introduced Resolution 79-48, a resolution agreeing to issue Industrial Development Revenue Bonds to finance a project for the Independence Partnership #1.

These bonds were to build an industrial building in the Evanston Industrial Park and would be no obligation to the city. The city would be acting as a sponsor of the bonds only. During this time Industrial Revenue Bonds were very popular and were used by many oil companies and oil-affiliated companies during the boom period. Motion was made and seconded to adopt Resolution 79-48, with all voting in favor.

Councilman Bills made a motion to rescind the action taken in the November 8th meeting defeating Ordinance 79-63, which was seconded by Fruits and passed with 4 yes votes and 2 no votes and 1 abstained.

This was an ordinance to annex the M.A.P.E.S. Trailer Park located just outside the city  limits to the west in Section 19, but was defeated on the first reading and now the idea was to bring it back on the floor to be acted on. Councilman Albrecht declared a conflict of interest, because his brother Charles was one of the owners. Motion and second were made to pass Ordinance 79-63 on first reading, but a motion followed to amend Ordinance 79-63, deleting parts of the area. The amended motion was seconded and voted on, with 2 yes votes and 4 no votes and 1 abstaining. Motion did not pass.

Councilman Bills then made a motion to table Ordinance 79-63 until after the first meeting in January, 1980. With a second motion passed with all voting in favor.

The problem with Ordinance 79-63 was that it included the property where Porter's Fireworks Stand was located. At the present there was a city ordinance making the sale and use of fireworks in the City of Evanston illegal. Therefore, Mr. Porter didn't want this ordinance to pass, because it would have put him out of business, since at this time the city wasn't even considering making fireworks legal within the city. The Evanston Voluntary Fire Department was very much against it.

Police of Chief Dennis Harvey reported that the department had hired two new police officers, and that they would be required to attend the Wyoming Police Academy in Douglas before being certified to work on their own.

This meeting of December 6th ended up being another long drawn-out meeting and adjourned at 12:30 a.m. on December 7th.

It was unbelievable, all the attention and publicity that Evanston, Wyoming was getting throughout the nation. A newspaper reporter, James Foster, had published a two-part story article in late December in two different newspapers: the *Evansville Press* (I'm not sure where that's from) and *Rocky Mountain News* out of Denver, Colorado.

The first part of the story went like this:

*Evanston, Wyo. – As snow swirls about at 7,300 feet in the Rocky Mountains, G. D. Eckerdt stops his pickup truck uncomfortably close to the edge of a cliff.*

*"Just look at that," exclaims Eckerdt, an oil man for most of his 49 years. "Isn't that a pretty sight?" Eckerdt is gazing at four giant drilling rigs spread out over about a mile and a half of desolation known as Painter Reservoir.*

*Over the ridges in every direction are more rigs—40 in all in this immediate area—operated under contract to Chevron U.S.A., Inc. and Amoco Production Co., the two leaders, and a handful of other big oil companies and independents.*

*"IF THERE IS AN oil frontier in this country, this has got to be it," says Eckerdt, Chevron's area foreman, "We just don't know yet how big it is."*

*He's referring to what is known as the Overthrust Belt, a 60 mile-wide ribbon of geologic nightmare that runs from Canada to Mexico right down the backbone of the nation under the Rocky Mountains.*

*The Overthrust Belt represents what may be the last big onshore oil find in the "Lower 48" United States.*

*Proven reserves in the Overthrust Belt, perhaps 500 million barrels of oil and 6 trillion cubic feet of gas, but estimates of total potential are as high as 15 billion barrels and 100 trillion cubic feet of gas.*

The article went on about how big this discovery of the Overthrust Belt could be and a lot of the oil experts said that this oil boom could last as many as 25 years. But that didn't happen.

The second part of Foster's article went like this:

*Evanston, Wyo. – The sign at the city limits of this town stuck tight in the southwest corner of the state is sadly out of date.*

*The sign should read Population 7,000-going-on-15,000—and eight oil wells. Evanston is booming, with the population expected to reach 15,000 in 1983. It is a rowdy, free-spending convention of truckers, geologists, roughnecks and construction hands, all of whom, it seems, rode hell-bent into town in four-wheel drive pickups and wide-load semis.*

*They've been drawn by the frantic drilling activity in the Overthrust Belt, a rich oil and gas formation.*

*"Everybody thinks he's going to get an oil well in his backyard." says Mayor Dennis J. Ottley, 47, summing up the spirit that penetrates like the wind.*

*"We're small but have big-city problems," declares City's Administrative Assistant Stephen Snyder, 32. "We're not frightened, but we're concerned," Snyder continues.*

*"All these single-status men coming in, making fantastic salaries, with no families, hanging out in bars."*

*Ottley and Snyder both agreed that housing is the city's biggest problem. The average price of a home here has doubled in the past three years, and new construction is getting higher and higher.*

Again, this second part of Foster's article went on about the problems we were experiencing at this time, especially housing and police problems.

An article by William Kittredge was published in *OUTSIDE* magazine titled, *Evanston, Wyoming, Another Boomtown, Another Bonanza, and An American Conflict That Won't Go Away. OVERTHRUST DREAMS…*

It seemed that every time we turned around Evanston was receiving publicity quite often from popular and well known newspapers and magazines concerning the boom. The December, 1980 issue of *TIME* magazine's cover feature was titled, *Rocky Mountain High*. The article was capped *as Life In "Oil City, U.S.A."* Within the article, Bob Blaycock, 25, a roughneck who makes $1,300 per week installing oil rigging equipment said, *This is Oil City, U.S.A. and you can put up with a lot.*

An article by Craig Vetter was even published in *PLAYBOY* magazine with the title, *Against The Wind*. The author added the caption under the picture: *Some things get better,* and stated in his article that *the best moment he ever had in Evanston, Wyoming, was leaving it. I'd spent a couple of months there in the summer and fall of 1981, roughnecking on the oil rigs, living with other guys who had somehow become desperate enough to go looking for work in a boom town; and very soon, it was clear that I was in over my head, again.*

Evanston and Southwestern Wyoming was in a big boom at this time, and it seemed to be the only area in the United States where any jobs were to be had, because most of the nation was in a recession at this time. This was bringing a lot of single men from all over the country to Evanston and the area to find a job, making a living and surviving the best they could.

During the second regular city council meeting on December 20th, Mr. Ken Williams, representing the Elks Club, asked about the status of the Old Town Hall building. I believe he was inquiring about it with the idea that it may make a good lodge for the Elks Club.

I, as mayor, explained to him that some of the council members had a desire to retain the property, and that it had also been considered as a site for senior housing, but at the present time we were not prepared to sell the building.

City Attorney Lancaster had drawn up a resolution authorizing the City of Evanston to enter into an agreement with Care, Inc. for providing special education services for children who are developmentally disabled.

Therefore, Resolution 79-50 was introduced by Councilman Albrecht. Motion was made and seconded, with all voting in favor.

During the meeting more ordinances were introduced and acted on, referring to annexations of various areas, and Ordinance 79-64 was introduced by Councilman Fruits. The title was read by Lancaster.

This ordinance provided for more issuance and sale of an Industrial Development Revenue Bond for the Evanston Industrial Center Project, in the principal amount of $950,000; and of certain documents related to it, but because my business of Uinta Realty, Inc. was involved, I abstained from all discussion and voting and left the chambers, turning the meeting over to the president of the council, Ron Davis.

But first the following paragraph was read by City Attorney Lancaster and printed in the minutes for record purposes:

"*The City Clerk-Treasurer reported that although it is prohibited by state law for any member of the governing body of the City to be interested in any contract or the performance of any work in the making or letting of which such officer may be called upon to act or vote, if said member shall disclose the nature of the interest and extent thereof to all the contracting parties concerned therewith and shall absent himself during the considerations and vote thereon and not attempt to influence any of the contracting parties and not act directly or indirectly for the governing body in inspection, operation, administration or performance of any such contract, then the said acts shall not be unlawful. The Mayor of the City, Dennis J. Ottley, has a contractual relationship with the Evanston Industrial Center Partnership, a Wyoming partnership, as an agent for the sale of the real estate of the partnership, and may benefit directly or indirectly from the decisions of the Governing body of the City. The City Clerk-Treasurer further reported that Mr. Ottley has disclosed the nature of his interests and the extent thereof, that he did not take any part in the action of passing Ordinance No. 79-64 in its first or second readings and that he shall absent himself during further consideration and vote upon said Ordinance. Thereupon the following proceedings, among others, were had and taken.*"

After I had left the chambers and turned the gavel over to Council President Ron Davis, during the discussion on Ordinance 79-64 there were some amendments suggested and a motion to adopt the amendments was made by Councilman Fruits and seconded by Albrecht. A roll call vote was requested by Davis, with all voting in favor, including Davis.

Therefore, Councilman Fruits moved that the foregoing Ordinance 79-64, as amended, previously passed on first and second readings and read by title only at this meeting, be passed, adopted and approved on final reading, as amended, that thereafter it shall be published in full in the *Uinta County Herald*, a newspaper of general circulation in the City of Evanston, in its edition dated December 27, 1979, and that said Ordinance, as amended, shall take effect after its publication as aforesaid, seconded by Councilman Megeath, with a roll call vote of 6 yes votes, all voting in favor.

The president of the council, as presiding officer, declared that all members of the city council had passed, adopted and approved Ordinance 79-64.

At that time I was asked to return to the chambers and take my position as mayor back from Councilman Davis.

During the rest of my term as mayor, I declared a conflict of interest many times because of being the owner of Uinta Realty, Inc. Many developers and contractors came from out of state and some were listing their properties with my real estate firm. Local developers and builders did not work with my firm in selling their properties. Most of them sold their own product or went with another real estate agency.

I was told years ago that if I ran for mayor and won the election that I would lose a lot of business, because when you are mayor and do anything to improve the community you can't help but step on toes, and when you do that you lose business because people hold things against you. Well, I found this to be true, both in my real estate firm as well as in my sporting goods store.

However, I did not run for mayor to make any particular person or group of people happy, I ran to help build a clean and proud community. My interest in every decision I made, in my mind, was for the best interest of Evanston as a whole. I have always tried to be fair and up front with everything I had done for Evanston. I never favored anyone in particular and if it ever appeared to anyone that I had it was purely unintentional.

I knew that this particular year of 1979 and the next three years, the peak of the boom would be crucial and very difficult for the city, and that there would be a lot of problems to overcome. My only interest was in trying very hard to keep everything under control and not let things get too far out of hand. The entire city council was concerned; they wanted to keep Evanston in the best order possible, and that was why we were so concerned about the enforcement of planning and zoning. Without that, the community might not have turned out as well as it did. We simply wanted to make sure that the City of Evanston remained a community worthy of a good place to raise a family.

Other business that came up during the last meeting of the year was a report from Allen Kennedy, General Superintendent of Public

Works, that a wastewater treatment plant operator with a class 3 licenses had been hired, taking the place of Fay Riebennacht, who had left the area. The new operator would be Mr. Thomas Edwards. Kennedy also reported that most of the parts for the plant and some water meters had arrived. City Attorney Lancaster reported on reducing utility rates for the elderly. He said that the Attorney General had ruled that it was illegal to give reduced rates to anyone, but eventually we found a way of doing just that, but it wouldn't be for a while.

Steve Snyder, Administrative Assistant, reported that the E.P.A. had given their approval for Evanston to go ahead with Step 1 of the wastewater study.

I reported on the meeting that Snyder and I had with the Wyoming Highway Department, telling the council that the department was still planning a 6th Street overpass with the possibility of repairing the present underpass, and that the on-off ramp, or interchange, at the Wyoming State Hospital was still a possibility in the future.

I also announced that Snyder and I would be attending the Wyoming Association of Municipalities (W.A.M.) winter meeting on December 27 and 28, 1979.

My first year as mayor, in 1979, was a very busy year for the entire city. We, the city council, were especially busy with all the changes and amendments made in our ordinances, and with trying to keep up with the need for improving the city's infrastructure and other departments of the city. We changed our meetings to two regular meetings a month so that our meetings wouldn't last so long, but even with that, most of our meetings were still lasting beyond midnight.

We expected 1980 to be even busier and more challenging. Evanston was still growing and hadn't peaked yet, so there would be more problems, and more and more developers and contractors to contend with. This would not be a bad thing, but it would give us a busy and interesting year. City revenues should increase again in 1980, which would help a lot. Hopefully!

*"The greatest thing in this world is not so much where we are, but in what direction we are moving."* – quote by Oliver Wendell Holmes

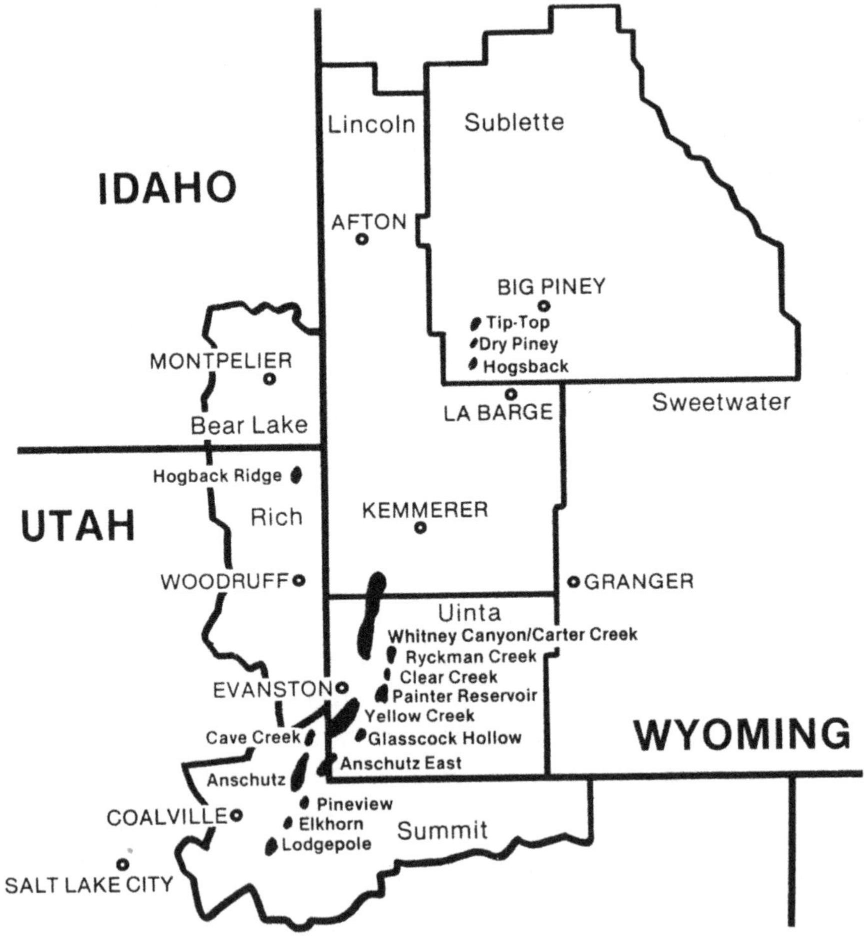
IDAHO
Lincoln
Sublette
AFTON
BIG PINEY
Tip-Top
Dry Piney
Hogsback
MONTPELIER
Bear Lake
LA BARGE
Sweetwater
Hogback Ridge
UTAH
Rich
KEMMERER
WOODRUFF
GRANGER
Uinta
Whitney Canyon/Carter Creek
Ryckman Creek
Clear Creek
EVANSTON
Painter Reservoir
Yellow Creek
Cave Creek
Glasscock Hollow
WYOMING
Anschutz East
Anschutz
Pineview
COALVILLE
Elkhorn
Lodgepole
Summit
SALT LAKE CITY

1980....The year of 1979 is now over and the one thing that I found out was that there is a lot more to being mayor than just signing Proclamations. It was a very busy but interesting year, and now we are going into 1980, my second year as mayor. We hoped to get through the year without too much trouble, but we were expecting another very busy year. Our community was still moving and growing fast. Our growth increase now, more than ever, included more permanent families, causing the city's housing to be even more in demand.

However, outside developers and contractors were coming in as well and buying up various areas and in some instances buying "already developed" subdivisions. Affordable single family housing was the most needed, housing that would qualify under the HUD and Federal Housing programs at that time. Interest rates were very high during the early 1980s. They were running anywhere from 18% to 22% and in some cases more, so it wasn't easy for someone to afford or even to qualify for financing.

This past year we had talked about separating the offices of the city clerk and the city treasurer, primarily because it seemed that the Clerk/Treasure, Don Welling, was getting overloaded by the busy and late meetings, the increasing budget, and all the other duties of the two offices. It was decided that selecting someone, temporarily, from the existing employees would be the way to go, at least until the new budget was approved. The council left it up to me, as mayor, to make that decision. I indicated that I would be appointing a new treasurer at the first meeting in January, 1980.

Therefore, during our first regular meeting on January 3rd, I first gave my annual report and spoke of the progress of the previous year and of our accomplishments. Speaking to members of the city council, all appointed officials and members of the various boards and commissions, and all employees, I said, *Although the year was extremely busy with some pretty difficult problems, all of you should feel very proud at what has been accomplished, and I especially want to thank each and every one of you for your assistance, cooperation and dedication and for the hard work you have given in getting things done, especially with what we had to work with.*

*However,* I continued, *we are still looking at some big problems ahead of us, with the fast growth and so called "boom" that we are now facing, we still have some problems to think about and to look forward to such as housing, water and sewer, traffic, subdivisions and annexations, police and many others, but I'm sure that together we will get things done, and I thank you again for all your assistance and hard work.*

Although there were some extremely important things to work on, it seemed that everyone agreed that housing was the most serious, but I was just as concerned with our sewer problem, and our overall infrastructure problems. I was concerned about the fact that we were, at times, dumping raw sewage into the Bear River. This bothered me an awful lot and I know that most of the council was concerned, but we were doing everything we could to keep the present sewer plant in good operating order. We were in bad need of a new sewer plant. We had the location taken care of, but it was a matter of getting the funding, plus easements and right-of-ways. The funding wouldn't be available for a couple more years.

One of the first orders of business, following my annual talk, was the swearing in of the new treasurer. Phyllis Martin had been the assistant to Don Welling as clerk/treasurer, and I felt that it was only fair that the council give her an opportunity to prove she could handle it. Therefore, I told the council that I was appointing Phyllis Martin as the city treasurer. After a short discussion and giving my reasons, a motion to confirm was made and seconded, with all voting in favor.

Martin was congratulated by me, the members of the council, and all other city officials present. We now had Don Welling as City

Clerk and Phyllis Martin as City Treasurer. It was the feeling of the council that both could and would work together for the betterment of the community.

During this meeting Resolution 80-1, concerning the need for increased return of revenues to cities and towns, was introduced by Councilman Fruits. The resolution stated that the Evanston City Council supported legislation that would return an additional one-third of the 3% state sales tax back to the cities, towns and counties, and urged our entire state legislative delegation to support the passage of such a bill as well. A motion was made to adopt Resolution 80-1 and seconded, with all voting in favor.

Other business included a request for city water from those residing outside the limits of the city, re-appointments to the Parks and Recreation Board and the Airport Board, and a letter from the Evanston Liquor Dealers requesting the four extended days for 1980, which were approved by motion and seconded with all voting in favor.

Next, I read three letters: one from the Census Bureau on a city limits map; one from the National Flood Insurance program; and one from the U.S. Army Corps of Engineers concerning clean water and pollution of the Bear River. A lengthy discussion of these letters followed, but no action was taken at that time.

Allen Kennedy, General Superintendent of Public Works, reported that the city's water well, located near the high school football field (now the Evanston Middle School's field), was having pump problems. He suggested that the city replace the pump, which was approved, and he also reported that as of that date there were still some annexations and some subdivisions that had not transferred their water rights to the city as required by ordinance. Dennis Lancaster, City Attorney, was directed to look into this.

Also, since the Aspen Grove subdivisions were annexed, the roads that were under the county needed to be changed. It was suggested by Councilman Bills that we dedicate the county road as the Aspen Grove Road. The name was accepted by resolution, and the city council members assigned to the streets and alleys were directed to see that this change was shown on the city map.

At one time we had as many as a dozen oil wells drilled within the city limits and a lot of property owners were receiving royalties from them, which was a good thing, and the city council and Planning and Zoning Commission was very careful where the wells were located, which was also good. We were all concerned with how our community would have looked if we had allowed drilling everywhere the oil companies wanted to. But they were very understanding. One time Champlin Oil, the oil and gas company of the Union Pacific Corporation approached me for permission to drill an oil well in the North Evanston area near the Bear River. The only access to it would be through 1st and 2nd Avenues, either crossing over Holland Drive Bridge, or going around China Mary Road, which wasn't even a dedicaded road at the time. However, in our conversation I told them that we couldn't afford to have that heavy traffic going across the bridge, which wasn't built for it, and it wouldn't be fair to the residents to have heavy traffic going through their neighborhoods. The company was very good about it and said they understood and never brought the subject up again. They found another route through private property off County Road.

The second regular city council meeting on January 17th started off, after the usual business was taken care of, with the introduction of Ordinance 80-1, introduced by Councilman Fruits, amending and creating a new section of the code of the City of Evanston concerning "Drug Paraphernalia," and making it unlawful to possess, to manufacture or deliver, or place advertisement to promote the sale of objects designed for use as "Drug Paraphernalia."

Ordinance 80-2 was introduced by Councilman Rice, amending and creating a new section concerning the policy to reimburse subdividers for extensions of water, sewer, and storm sewers when hooking onto city mains.

Over the next few months, these ordinances were passed by regular motion with a second, with all voting in favor on all three readings. Some of these ordinances were already on the books, but it was still part of the project of getting our city codes re-codified and brought up to date. This project should be complete in the very near future and took up a lot of the council's time through the past few years.

Other business concerned the passage of other ordinances, mostly pertaining to new subdivisions, zone changes, annexations, and permits for construction and development purposes. Again, all these ordinances passed on all three readings and became law.

Resolution 80-2 was introduced by Councilman Davis concerning the issuance of more Industrial Development Revenue Bonds. Motion was made for adoption and seconded with all voting in favor. During this month, including both meetings, I had to dismiss myself again from the bench and turn the gavel over to Councilman Davis, President of the Council, because of the possibility of a conflict of interest concerning my real estate agency, and the possibility that my company might benefit from the project in question. This happened quite often, and some of the other council members also had to abstain, because they might have had a relative or someone closely involved in a project. New subdivisions, annexations, zone changes, and requests for industrial bonds, where someone had a conflict or thought they might have, seemed to come up at every meeting.

Another request that came up during the meeting was for additional trailer spaces in the Willow Park Trailer Park, to increase their capacity from 81 spaces to 117 spaces. This request was sent back to the P & Z Commission for their consideration.

As mayor, new appointments were made by me to the Planning and Zoning Commission and the Evanston Joint Powers Board. Appointments to the P & Z Commission were Larry Wilson – 3 years; Nancy Dawson – 3 years; and Pat Fosher – 3 years. Appointments to the Evanston Joint Powers Board were: Councilmembers Russell "Bub" Albrecht – 1 year; Jimmie Rice – 1 year; Ronald Davis – 1 year; David Bills – 3 years; Roy Fruits – 3 years; Russell Megeath – 3 years, plus City Clerk Don Welling for 2 years and me for 2 years.

All the above appointments were approved and confirmed by regular motion and seconded, with the majority voting in favor.

I also formed a new board with the following appointments to the Evanston Housing Authority: Marie Hicks – 1 year; Art Ortego – 2 years; Gene Smith – 3 years; Patsy Madia – 4 years; and Reverend William Ellington – 5 years.

These appointments were also confirmed by motion and seconded, with all voting in favor.

At this time the subject of employee vacations came up. Apparently some employees had not used all their vacation time up in 1979. In the past, the policy had been that if an employee did not use their vacation time during the year they had it coming, then they automatically lost it, but after a little discussion it was suggested that employees would be allowed to use whatever vacation time they had coming in 1979 only if they used it within the first quarter of 1980. Motion was made by Councilman Megeath to allow the suggested time, seconded by Fruits, with all voting in favor.

The Evanston City Council discussed and expressed their concern about the enforcement of the two-hour parking limit in downtown, plus the merit system evaluation program for the employees.

Councilman Bills reported on some of the activities of a new committee that was formed, the Downtown Improvement Committee. He stated that they would like to form a corporation with the city's help, but City Attorney Dennis Lancaster stated that he didn't think the city should fund this plan. A lengthy discussion took place and it was decided that if a corporation is to be formed that the committee, not being an official city-appointed commission, should sell memberships to the downtown merchants that are willing and form their corporation through their own funding.

A few days later the Downtown Improvement Committee met with the Evanston Chamber of Commerce concerning their tentative plans for the beautification and improvement of downtown Evanston. Making the presentation were committee members John Deru and Gary Coles.

This committee was formed to improve the downtown area and keep it as an attractive business district. Other shopping areas being developed in other locations of the city caused a lot of concern for the merchants that downtown would eventually be deserted, and the City of Evanston would lose the original heart of the community.

Deru and Coles also reported to the Chamber of Commerce that they were in the process of incorporating the committee. They stated that the committee felt that, by doing this, it would show that they were more sincere in what they were trying to do, and they thought that it would be best to obtain membership.

Just before adjournment I reported on a meeting that I had attended with the county commissioners and the mayors of Lyman and Mountain View. I stated that Wyoming State Representative Ron Micheli was in attendance and that he had endorsed the bill that would return a greater portion of the sales tax revenues to the cities and counties, which would be a great help to the communities.

One of the first orders of business that came up during our first regular monthly meeting on February 7th was the re-introduction by Councilman Fruits of Ordinance 79-69 providing for the issuance and sale of Industrial Development Revenue Bonds to the Evanston Industrial Center Group. This ordinance had been tabled on the third reading for additional time to study it and was now brought back on the floor for the third and final reading.

Because of Uinta Realty's involvement with the group as the listing and selling agency of their properties I felt that I had a conflict. Therefore, once again I turned that portion of the meeting over to Council President Ron Davis, and excused myself by leaving the chambers. The third and final reading of the ordinance was passed by motion and seconded, with all voting in favor.

Prior to excusing myself I read two letters of resignation from Robert Pryor and Marla Smith, both from the police department. In accepting the resignations, the council members and I wished them both well and thanked them for their past service to the community. Motions were made and seconded to accept the resignation, with all voting in favor.

A good share of this meeting was taken up by acting on previously introduced ordinances on second and third readings. These ordinances concerned drug paraphernalia, re-imbursements to subdividers, additional subdivisions, establishing development and construction permits, and providing the issuance of revenue bonds to the

Ramada Inn owners. All these ordinances passed on all three readings by motion and were seconded, with all voting in favor.

Resolution 80-11 defining the City of Evanston's policy concerning Industrial Development Revenue Bonds was introduced by Councilman Fruits. Following the reading of the resolution by City Attorney Lancaster and after some discussion and an amendment, it was moved for adoption as amended and seconded, with all voting in favor.

These industrial bonds were beginning to get very popular and more and more developers and contractors were requesting the issuance of them. This bonding program seemed to be a very practical and feasible way of funding construction. I know it was helping the city because the city had no obligation for them, but the community was benefiting by allowing fast growth and industry. It was a program that was helping us to keep up with all the needs during the boom.

Resolution 80-5 was introduced by Councilman Albrecht to issue revenue bonds to a project in the Red Mountain Subdivision to an entity called the Red Mountain Partners. This resolution was adopted by motion and seconded with all voting in favor.

Uinta County Commissioner Dan South, a partner in the Red Mountain Partners, was present at the meeting representing them. While there, he asked the city council if we had any extra room in the new City Hall. He said they needed office space for the Deputy County Attorney. I told him that the council would discuss this and get word back to him. The new City Hall was pretty much filled up with not only the administration, but the Police Department, the City Judge Office, the Recreation Department and later on, the Planning Department.

Later in the meeting, the council and I brought Commissioner South's request back on the floor for discussion. It was decided that we could not afford to give up any space in the new City Hall, but would offer space in the old town hall building.

More resolutions and ordinances were introduced and acted on pertaining to   subdivisions, annexations, zoning and more requests for revenue bonds.

Resolution 80-6 was introduced by Councilman Albrecht. After the resolution was read by the attorney the motion for adoption was made and seconded with all voting in favor. This resolution gave the city the right to approve any land use, subdivision, zoning, water and sewer inspections and fees, plus any other requirement or modification that may have an effect within the service area in conformance with the general plan of the city. At that time I believe that the service area included any property within one half mile of the city limits. Resolution 80-7 was introduced by Councilman Albrecht to request another grant from the Wyoming Recreation Commission and the Heritage Conservation and Recreation Service of the United States Department of Interior for a grant for the construction of two softball fields and related recreation facilities. This was a matching fund grant for which the city would participate in part of the funding. Motion was made for the adoption of Resolution 80-7 and seconded, with all voting in favor.

Another resolution came up to lease a parcel of ground on the railroad company's right-of-way for a roadway, park and free public parking. These properties pertained to the railroad property along Front Street where Martin Park and Depot Square are now located. This resolution was passed and adopted by regular motion and seconded, with all voting in favor.

Updating and re-codifying the city code was discussed with a report given by City Attorney Lancaster that the project was almost finished. Councilman Albrecht made the motion for the city attorney to follow through and do whatever was necessary to complete the work on the city code, seconded by Bills, with all voting in favor. It looked like we were almost finished getting the ordinances finally brought up to date.

Other business that came up during this meeting was Steve Snyder, Administrative Assistant, reported on meeting with officials of the Utah Power and Light Company about getting service to new areas. They suggested that those wanting service to sign up early.

Snyder also made a report on an estimate for drilling a one hundred foot water well at the cemetery with 10" casing. He stated that the cost would be approximately $22,000, and looking at another dry year we knew we had to drill more wells to keep up with the water demand, especially through the summer months. The water well was approved by motion and seconded, with all voting in favor.

Also, concerning our water situation, John Proffit of Uinta Engineering and Surveying was working on the transfer of all the water rights to the city from new annexed subdivisions. He stated that he was making good progress.

Page 10 UINTA COUNTY HERALD Evanston, Wyo.
THURSDAY, FEBRUARY 28, 1980

# Instant Traffic Tie-Up At Underpass

A slight mishap at the "busy bottleneck" at the Front Street underpass can create an instant traffic tie-up as seen above. Both Highway 30 and Highway 89 are instantly affected. As shown in the photo below, Front Street also feels the same effect. As the impact increases in Evanston, the situation could become critical this summer.

Because of the heavy traffic in downtown Evanston, the problems at the underpass had been discussed quite often the past few months. To help correct the problem I, as mayor, had appointed Councilman Bills to look into locating a capable company to do a traffic study concerning this problem. He stated, during this meeting, that he had contacted Leigh, Scott and Cleary, Inc., traffic planning engineers, to do a traffic and street plan study for the city. After his report he made a motion to accept their offer, seconded by Albrecht, with all voting in favor.

City Attorney Lancaster was requested to draw up the proper documents to have subdividers furnish a title search on their property to insure clear title. We had problems in the past where we or the subdivider had to go back and correct problems that came up after the approval of the subdivision.

Councilman Megeath reported on the progress of the new fire department's substation at the Uinta County Fair Grounds and attended a meeting with state officials and others concerning the possibility of forming a fire district. He stated that only unincorporated areas could be included in a fire district. Apparently the only way we could name a fire district was if we went countywide and became the Uinta County Fire District. This didn't happen until a few years later.

The city was very concerned, at this time, about the sour gas ($H_2S$) wells that were being drilled in the area, so Councilman Fruits volunteered to send for some copies of ordinances from other cities that had this problem and would get them to us as soon as he received anything.

On February 14th the *Uinta County Herald* issue headlined: OIL BOOM BRINGS PROBLEMS AND MONEY TO THE EVANSTON AREA. It said: *both the size of the city and the number of residents have doubled in the last three years, and according to projections, the number of residents will again double in the next five years. The city had already annexed 800 acres, was now considering annexing another 170 to 500 additional acres.*

In addition, the column went on to say that Mayor Ottley stated *that the city was not standing still, and numerous plans are underway so the city will be able to handle the growth.* He added that *one of the major problems was housing and that the average price of a home has doubled in the past three years. Most of the people moving in cannot find the financial backing to secure a house.* He continued, *Trailer spaces and rentals are of prime importance to the area. As these are also limited, many people are permanently residing in motels.*

The news article went on to say that, according to me, *Problems of providing services crop up in all areas. The present sewer system was designed for 10,000 and was constructed 13 years ago. Since that time, the facility has become outdated.*

*Ottley* also stated that the town was planning the construction of a $4 million sewer project which will be constructed with state and federal funds. Phase 1 of the three phase project has already been completed. The project would include the relocation of the plant and two or three new trunk lines. The new system would be designed to handle a population of 25,000 to 30,000 and should be completed in approximately three years.

The *Herald* went on, with Ottley saying, *Evanston has a considerable number of older residents that are living on fixed income, and they are feeling an economic squeeze accelerated by the boom town conditions.* He continued, *The city is very concerned about their welfare and has now developed a Housing Authority Board. The primary purpose of that board is to develop housing for the elderly, and that present conditions include a 40 unit housing complex close to the downtown area.*

The second regular city council meeting was on February 21st with most of the meeting consisting of passing more ordinances and resolutions on new subdivisions, annexations, zone changes and industrial revenue bonds, plus a number of requests from several citizens concerning garbage removal, house inspections, grading and draining of certain streets.

Councilmembers Ron Davis and Jimmie Rice were absent, plus Administrative Assistant Steve Snyder and City Attorney Dennis Lancaster had been excused.

Ordinance 80-5 was brought up for second reading. This was a very controversial ordinance that would allow Multiple Family Residential (R-4 zoning) in an area across Wyoming State Highway 150 from the high-density housing area of Aspen Groves I and II. A number of the folks residing in Aspen Groves I and II were against the ordinance, because it would affect their view of the Bear River Valley and the mountains, and maybe house values.

Councilman Albrecht made the motion to pass Ordinance 80-5 on the second reading, seconded by Bills. A short discussion for questions and answers was held for several people in attendance before I called for the vote. The vote was a tie, 2 ayes and 2 nays, with two of the council members absent. Therefore I, as mayor, had to break the tie and I voted in favor of passing the ordinance on second reading, but there would be a third and final reading at the next council meeting, and there was no telling how that would end up.

I voted in favor because the Aspen Grove subdivisions sat far above the highway on the hill and the residents would still have the view of the valley and the mountains, and also this zone was on the east side of Wyoming State Highway 150, a fair distance from the subdivisions. I couldn't see where it was going to bother the folks residing in the of Aspen Grove area, but there was still one more reading of the ordinance and no telling what might happen if we have a full council.

Before the meeting adjourned we had several reports from various committees and assignments, plus the resignation of John Deru from the P & Z Commission, and the appointment of Anita Maioran to fill the unexpired term of Mr. Deru.

Councilman Albrecht made a motion for the State Oil and Gas Commission to be notified about a sour gas well at the edge of the city, seconded by Bills, with all voting in favor. City Clerk Welling was directed to notify the commission.

Councilman Fruits made a motion that the City of Evanston request the Wyoming State Highway Department do a study of relocating the new State Highway 89 to pass by the new fire substation. The motion was seconded by Albrecht, with all voting in favor. When the new overpass or viaduct was built off of 6th Street that would be exactly where the new route of Highway 89 would go.

At this time I suggested that the city start thinking of appointing a full time engineer, because we were paying a lot of money for engineering services from local companies. It was decided that we would talk about this later, and then start advertising for one. We also had been talking about hiring a city planner, but both would have to be budgeted for, and that wouldn't be until June.

Councilman Fruits made a motion to postpone the next regular city council meeting until March 11th, seconded by Bills with 3 yes and 1 no vote. The motion passed by a majority.

On March 11th the city held its first regular city council meeting acting on the third and final reading of Ordinance 80-1, pertaining to the selling and usage of "Drug Paraphernalia." Motion was made by Albrecht, seconded by Rice, with all voting in favor.

Page 9 UINTA COUNTY HERALD Evanston, Wyo.
THURSDAY, JULY 10, 1980

# Chief Says City Crime 'Is Up'

He's the man behind the badge, heading the 17-man strong force of blue-uniformed officers charged with enforcing Evanston's laws.

Chief Dennis Harvey is charged with administering the police department—sitting in on city council meetings, preparing the department's budget, listening to long-winded salesmen trying to sell him cleaning chemicals for the dog pound, pacifying irate taxpayers...

Harvey heads Wyoming's only unionized police force. Evanston's police department "is the only one (unionized) in Wyoming as far as I know," Harvey said.

Evanston Police Department officers are members of the International Brotherhood of Police Officers Number 504.

EPD joined the national union Feb. 18, 1975.

Sgt. Forest Bright has served two of his four years with the EPD as president of the local IBPO chapter.

Evanston's police department is separated into two divisions, one concentrating on investigations and the other, patrol.

Patrolmen respond to complaints relayed through the dispatcher's office while investigators follow up reports detailed through the patrol.

Directly under Harvey in the chain of command is Lt. Dean Foreman.

Foreman has been with the force since March 16, 1970.

Heading the investigation department is Sgt. Bruce Waters, who will complete his fifth year with EPD this December.

Bright is the patrol sergeant.

Under Bright is Corp. J.R. Dean, Investigator, Frank Maioran serves below Waters.

Investigator Kevin Smith serves as juvenile officer.

Patrolmen operate on three 10-hour shifts with two overlapping during the busiest hours for policemen, 9 p.m. to 3 a.m.

Family problems, bar problems, thefts and burglaries are more prevalent during these hours, Harvey said.

Crime in the city, Harvey said, "is up."

Officers issued a total of 424 speeding tickets last year. From Jan. 1 through April 31 this year, 326 traffic citations have been issued.

Harvey also revealed the number of times the EPD responds to requests for assistance at bars has increased dramatically.

A total of 304 bar incidents were investigated in 1979, with 41 arrests being made.

This year's total through May 31 is 216 calls, 35 arrests.

The area covered by the department has "increased one-third from what it was last year."

Harvey hopes to hire six new officers this year. Two have already been added to the force. "We're hiring two at a time so my sergeants can go out and train them," related Harvey.

A new officer will ride with the sergeant one week. Then the sergeant takes the passenger seat while the recruit drives.

When the sergeant feels the newcomers "can go out and ride by themselves, he'll just give them a car and let them patrol by themselves."

## Police Chief Dennis Harvey

All officers receive five weeks of basic training in Douglas with 40 additional hours of instruction per year.

Harvey said more equipment is needed. Smith is currently preparing documents requesting a grant for two more radar guns.

A box of unused night clubs is against the wall of Harvey's office. He is currently trying to get an instructor from Salt Lake City to teach an eight-hour training course for the sticks.

More patrol cars are also needed, Harvey said.

Harvey, a nine-year EPD veteran, said "When I joined (the force) they expanded it one (officer)."

This year he hopes to expand the department by a total of six.

Harvey, 33, has been police chief two-and-a-half years.

Ordinances 80-2, 80-6, 80-7, 80-8, 80-9, 80-10, and 80-11 all came up for third and final readings, ordinances that pertained to the reimbursement to subdividers for extension of water and sewer hookups, authorizing the new Aspen Grove III subdivision, the annexation of certain lands, approving more Industrial Revenue Bonds, and the name change to Aspen Grove Drive. All were passed by regular motion and seconded with all voting in favor.

The controversial Ordinance 80-5, pertaining to the zoning of certain properties to Multiple Family Residential (R-4) came up for third and final reading. Councilman Albrecht made the motion, seconded by Davis. Because there were several folks in attendance and some opposition to the ordinance I opened the floor up for discussion.

Attorney Harry L. Harris, representing the Home Owner's Association of Aspen Groves I and II, was in attendance to make a presentation on their behalf in opposition to the ordinance, and Mr. Calvin Ragsdale, representing the property owners, Broken Circle Cattle Company, to speak in favor of the ordinance.

After a considerable amount of discussion on the pros and cons, I called for the vote to pass Ordinance 80-5 on third and final reading. The final vote came out with 5 ayes, 1 no and 1 absent. Motion passed by a majority of the council. I did not have to break any ties, but I voted anyway and voted aye. I have always felt that the folks needed to know how the mayor stood on issues.

Following the passing of the ordinances, Chief of Police Dennis Harvey made a report of the increase of police calls from bars and liquor establishments at night and the need for additional officers. Some discussion followed, but we informed the chief that we really couldn't do any more hiring until budget time, and at that time we would take a good look at it.

I told the council that I would like to have a meeting with all of the liquor dealers and discuss the problems that they were having as well as the problems that the police were having in trying to keep order. I made the comment that *although we must be very concerned with all the police calls and over fights and rowdiness happening in the bars, we are not going to provide bouncers for them.* I continued, *We also must be concerned with the size of crowds that are in the bars at any one time.* I then reminded the council that the fire department sets the number of occupants allowed in an establishment, and they do this for the safety of everyone in case of fire or other disasters. I also stated that I did not want to see any of our officers harmed while trying to break up any commotions caused at the bars, inside or outside, and I didn't want to see anyone else hurt, as far as that goes.

At this time we started looking for property for a new city public works building, or to buy additional property where we were, which meant relocating the neighbor, Mrs. Mildred Condos, because the shop on Front Street between 11th and 12th Streets was too small for the additional equipment we were obtaining, and the city crews were gaining more employees.

City Attorney Lancaster reported on a meeting he and Allen Kennedy, General Superintendent of Public Works, had with Mr. Dennis Kirscher of the Union Tank Car Company about using some property that the company was leasing from the city. Kirscher indicated at the time that there may be a possibility of releasing a parcel of land to the city, but months later the city found a better location.

Also, Lancaster reported that the property owners along Greek Street were willing to deed the street to the city, but only if they could retain the mineral rights, and have the city appraise the property.

Greek Street was not an official city street, but was named because a long-time Evanston citizen, originally from Greece, named Rudy, lived there and owned property on Greek street. Rudy also had a small grocery store on County Road next to the river that was called "Rudy's," but later was purchased by Rip Bruce and his family. At that time it was called "Rip's." Later Rip's moved across the street, where they are at the present.

Councilman Bills from Ward 3 reported that he had met with the property owners at their request, asking if the city would possibly include Greek Street as one of the city's streets. After some discussion Councilman Bills made a motion to have Greek Street appraised and claim it as a city street, and let the property owners retain the mineral rights. The motion was seconded by Fruits, with all voting in favor.

Councilman Megeath reported that the Evanston Recreation and Parks Board was working on a resolution to permit drinking in certain areas of Hamblin Park during special occasions.

Councilman Rice reported that B.R.W. Noblitt Company was still looking for a new airport site, and traffic at the present airport had doubled, which is much more than was predicted by this time.

The second regular city council meeting held on March 20th had more ordinances acted on, and Resolution 80-9 to issue Industrial Development Revenue Bonds to Tom Brown, Inc. was introduced by Councilman Davis. After City Attorney Lancaster read the resolution, a motion was made for adoption and seconded, with all voting in favor. An ordinance would be introduced in regard to this resolution next meeting.

Resolution 80-10 was introduced by Councilman Megeath directing the mayor and city clerk to apply to the Wyoming Farm Loan Board for a coal tax grant of $172,900 for construction of a frontage road on the south side of highway I-80 between Yellow Creek Road and Wyoming State Highway 150, now known as Cheyenne Drive. A motion was made for adoption of the resolution and seconded, with all voting in favor.

City Treasurer Phyllis Martin presented the audit report from the Wyoming State Examiner's office which included the period of March 1, 1978 through June 30, 1978. A motion was made and seconded to accept the report, with all voting in favor.

Resolution 80-14 was introduced by Councilman Megeath, designating Hamblin City Park and the Purple Sage Golf Course areas where alcoholic or malt beverages may be consumed or carried in an open container. A motion was made for adoption and was seconded with all voting in favor.

At this time a motion was made for the City of Evanston to advertise for a full-time engineer to start work by May 1, 1980, and was seconded with all voting in favor. City Clerk Welling was directed to start the process of advertising.

I reported that the Evanston Housing Authority sent notice that the city must come up with some kind of an option or lease between the city and Uinta County Senior Citizens, Inc. prior to March 31, 1980 to meet HUD requirements. Therefore, I announced that there would be a special meeting to introduce a resolution concerning a land location for senior housing on March 27th at 8:00 p.m.

The special meeting of the Evanston City Council was held on March 27th. Councilman Rice and City Attorney Lancaster were both excused. I called the meeting to order to adopt Resolution 80-18, which was introduced by Councilman Albrecht and read by me, due to the absence of the attorney.

The City of Evanston was applying for full funding for senior housing for the construction of 40 units. The deadline for the HUD grant was March 31st, requiring that we name a location where the housing project would be constructed. Therefore, we had to come up with a resolution fast for a proposed location in order to meet the deadline.

Resolution 80-18 was introduced and motion was made to use property already owned by the city on 3rd Street next to the new armory. It was seconded and voted on, with all voting in favor.

The location named above was not where the senior housing project would be constructed, but we had to name a location to meet the deadline for the grant. There were several other locations that were being considered.

The first location suggested was the old Clark School building on Summit Street between 12th and 13th Streets, because it was close to the downtown where all the stores and utility companies were, making it easier for the elderly folks. But the Uinta County School District voted against the idea; therefore the idea of using that location was dropped.

Other locations looked at included Dean Richins' property on Elm Street, but none of the properties that were considered were ever leased or purchased for the senior housing project. Mr. John Galeotos, director of the Cheyenne Housing Authority, was hired by the Evanston City Council temporarily as a consultant.

Galeotos stated that there would be funds for 94 units for the entire State of Wyoming, and Evanston would be eligible for 40 of them, but it would be a while before any definite location was decided on or any construction was started.

In a recent work session with the city council, Police Chief Harvey reported that the department needed to increase their budgetary needs to $120,000 over the previous year's budget of $351,000. He stated that the department would be asking for six additional patrolmen, two patrol cars and additional equipment such as bulletproof vests.

At the first regular city council meeting of the month held on April 3rd, Mr. Mark Zimmerman, a representative from  Amoco Production Company, met with the council to answer any questions about Amoco's plans in the Evanston area. He stated that the company would financially assist the city in alleviating the impact brought about by recent oil and gas activity in the area.

# New Fire Station Will Eliminate Fire Fighting Problem In North Evanston

By Virginia Giorgis

Evanston - Firestation #2 is nearly complete according to Firechief Gerald Cazin.

Cazin said it will be only two or three weeks before utilities are completed in the new station.

The 40 man department is comprised of all volunteers according to Cazin. He said the department is in the process of building up to 50 men as a larger department

will be needed in the next five years.

Cazin said the new station will provide better protection to north Evanston as the department will have trucks on that end of town. In addition, the new station eliminates the problems of providing fire protection to the north end of town if the underpass is closed or clogged up due to the increased amount of traffic.

Firestation #1 is on Eighth

and Center St. according to Cazin. All eight of the department's trucks had been stored in this station even though it only had five stalls. Half of the trucks will be moved to station #2, a five stall station. In addition, the men will be divided and report to both stations.

The impact has also created an increase in fires according to Cazin. The department responded to 118 fires last

year. Before that there were only 45-50 fires per year.

In line with the national trend, Cazin said, arson is also on the rise in Evanston. He said two of the fires last year were "definitely arson, with a possibility of four or five."

He also said Evanston had no child-oriented false alarms. He credited this to the department's work and educational programs in the community.

# Cazin Honored For 50 Yrs.

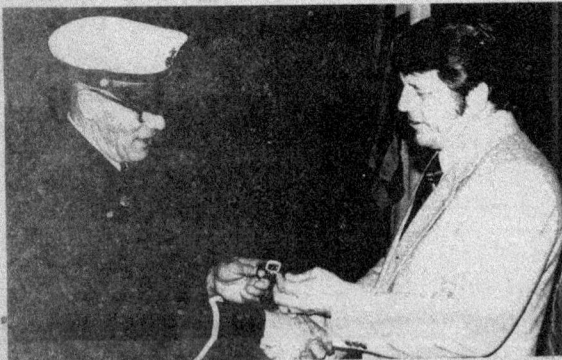

Fire Chief Gerald Cazin is presented a watch was presented to Cazin by the Evanston City Council for the past 50 years of service he has given the Evanston Fire Department. Chief Cazin joined the Evanston Fire Department on April 3, 1931.

*Uinta County Herald,* April 17, 1980.

*We're going to give our fair share or more,* Zimmerman told the council during the meeting. *I don't think we're very far away from some concrete action,* he continued.

He also announced that in spring, Amoco planned to begin construction of a Whitney Canyon gas facility to remove hydrogen sulfide and liquid hydrocarbons from natural gas taken from the fields.

Some of the council members voiced their concern that bad smells would be produced in the area, but Zimmerman stated that *there should be no bad smells at all emanating from the facility. Although,* he said, *some minor odors may be emitted during the start-up.*

Fire Chief Jerry Cazin was honored for his 50 years of dedicated service to the Evanston Volunteer Fire Department. He was presented with a gold watch and a standing ovation showing the city's appreciation. I stated that *there has been no other person that had done more for the Evanston Fire Department than Chief Cazin, and on behalf of the City I say thank you and congratulations for all your time and service that you have given to the City. We all wish you well.*

Chief Cazin thanked the council and everyone for their show of appreciation given to him for his fifty years of service to the community and the fire department.

Ordinance 80–18, introduced by Councilman Bills pertained to the re-platting of certain lots in the Evanston Industrial Center, and once again I had to abstain and leave the chambers, turning the gavel over to Council President Davis. Motion was made to pass the ordinance on first reading and seconded, with all voting in favor.

Ordinance 80–18 went on to pass on second and third readings by regular motion and second, and I abstained from each reading and left the room, turning the meeting over to Councilman Davis.

Ordinance 80–15, introduced by Councilman Megeath was an ordinance establishing districts in which storage of explosives and blasting agents would be allowed within the city limits. Motion was made to pass Ordinance 80–15 on first reading and was seconded with all voting in favor. This ordinance was also passed on second and third readings during future meetings by regular motion and second with all voting in favor.

Following the passage of Ordinance 80-15 on the first reading, the council continued to discuss the issue and ended up agreeing that the responsibility of issuing permits for explosives storage should be given to Fire Chief Cazin and his department.

At this time the Evanston City Council, acting as the Board of Adjustments to the Evanston Planning and Zoning Commission, had a zoning appeal concerning a recent denial of a Conditional Use Permit by the commission. The appeal was filed by Big K Corporation on residences in light industrial (I-1) zone. After an attorney for Marion and Melody Kessler requested that they wait until next meeting, Councilman Bills made a motion to continue this appeal until April 17th at 8:30 p.m. The motion was seconded by Albrecht, with all voting in favor. This appeal was recorded by an electronic device and the tape was held on file at City Hall.

Administrative Assistant Steve Snyder reported that application for a grant for senior housing had been made, and that a parcel of land was available for sale for the project. The land in question was owned by Mr. Dean Richins and Mrs. Gwen Johnson.

Councilman Bills made a motion to authorize Snyder to enter into negotiations with Richins and Johnson to acquire the property, seconded by Megeath, with a vote of 5 yes, 1 no, and 1 absent. The motion passed by a majority.

A general discussion took place concerning lights in various areas: the sidewalk under the Yellow Creek Road underpass, the fire department's new substation, Aspen Grove Park, and some of the Aspen Grove area streets. Allen Kennedy was directed to look into this.

On April 13, 1980 the *Denver Post* came out with their Sunday addition with three large articles. The first was a headline article that read: WYO. OIL SECRETS BEING UNLOCKED, (Overthrust Belt tagged "Last Frontier in the 48")… The article ran, *It also looks like heartening news to Evanston, Wyo. – population 7,500. Salaries are good, unemployment is virtually non-existent, and cash registers daily ring out a song of prosperity. The expected recession of 1980 appears ready to by-pass Evanston.*

The second article had the headline OVERTHRUST BELT (Wyo. Oil Secrets Being Unlocked). The article went on to say: *Evanston, Wyo. – Oil fever, the like of which some say hasn't been seen since a decade ago when Alaska's Prudhoe Bay oil field was discovered, is rife in Southwestern Wyoming. Officials say the city needs more than $10 million for sewer improvements, a new police and fire building, a new hospital and pay increases to keep municipal employees from joining the rush to the oil fields.*

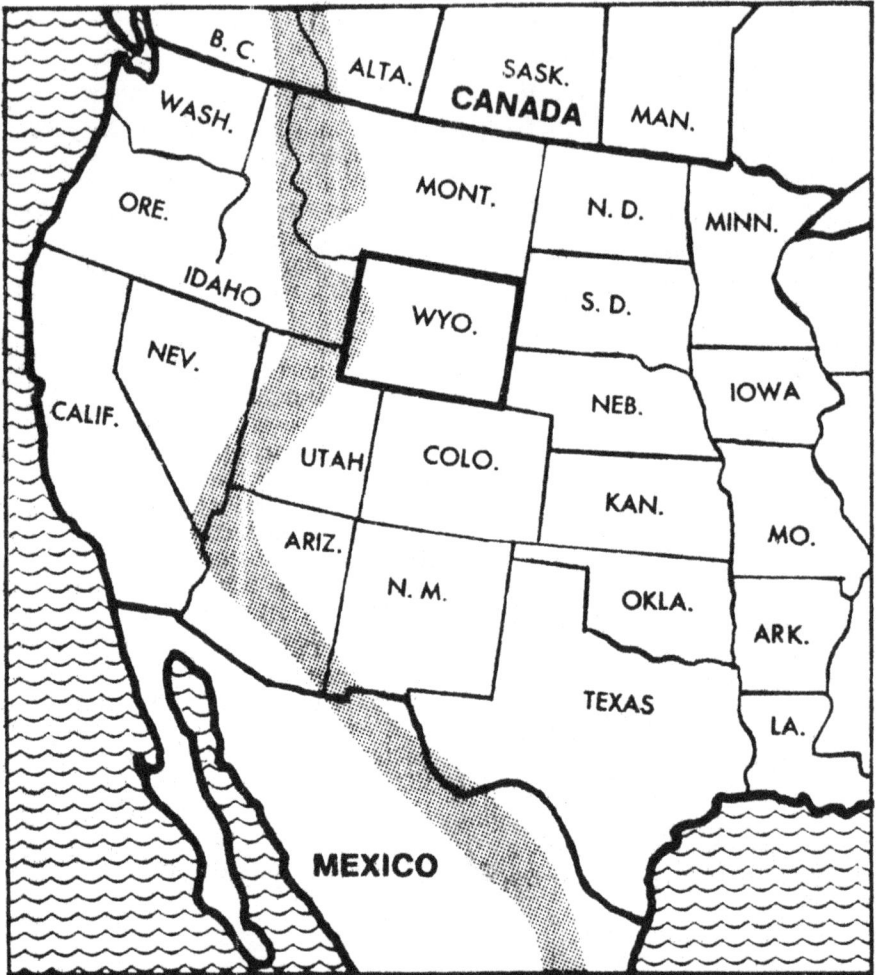

**OVERTHRUST BELT IS INDICATED BY GRAY**
Canada has been getting natural gas from the belt since the 1920s.

The third article was titled: OIL HUNT AT FEVER PITCH IN WYO. OVERTHRUST BELT with two sub-titles: *Booming Evanston's Needs Awesome,* and *It's The Hottest Place In Country—Now.* There's no doubt that Evanston and Southwestern Wyoming is the hottest area in the country, because we are getting all kinds of publicity, not only nationally, but also worldwide.

The second regular council meeting for the month was held on April 17th. Councilman Albrecht was excused. The first order of business, after the approval of the minutes, was the introduction by Councilman Bills of Ordinance 80-14. This ordinance was an amendment to a previous bill to prohibit parking of certain trucks and/or trailers within the city on arterial streets, streets followed by the U.S. and State highways, and streets in or adjacent to residential districts.

Because the boom brought large trucks and trailers into town, we started having problems with them parking on our residential street. We were not only having traffic and residential parking problems, but also problems cleaning the streets and removing snow. Sometimes these big truck and trailers would park where some residents couldn't even get into their driveways. Therefore, the council had to act on an ordinance restricting where that type of vehicle could park.

The ordinance read in paragraph (b) that all overnight parking of the class of vehicles designated in paragraph (a), *(the paragraph describing the type and size of the trucks and trailers),* [of this section] is prohibited on any public street in or adjacent to a residential district as defined.

This ordinance had a correctional amendment to it, but the amendment did not affect the ordinance in any way. Therefore, Councilman Megeath made the motion to pass Ordinance 80-14 as amended, which was seconded by Fruits, with all voting in favor. This ordinance went on to pass on second and third readings by regular motion, and was seconded, with all voting in favor.

Resolution 80-15, introduced by Councilman Megeath, and read by City Attorney Lancaster, was a resolution authorizing the City of Evanston to enter into an option agreement for the purchase of real property from Dean F. Richins and Alice L. Richins for the total purchase price of $120,000. Motion was made to adopt Resolution 80-15 and seconded, but the motion failed with a vote of 2 yes and 4 no.

General Superintendent of Public Works Allen Kennedy reported that the pump station project on Red Mountain was finally completed. It was inspected and accepted by regular motion and seconded by the council.

During this meeting the bid for the Holland Drive sidewalk and street work and asphalt resurfacing on 10th Street was opened and read. The only bid was from Parson Asphalt for $40,010. Motion was made to accept the bid of Parson Asphalt and seconded with 5 yes votes and 1 no vote. Motion was declared passed by a majority vote.

More ordinances were introduced and acted on pertaining to zone changes, establishing commercial and industrial sewer tapping fees for the different size services, and Resolution 80-17, authorizing the city to accept a grant from Amoco Production Company in the amount of $100,000, was introduced by Councilman Fruits. This grant was to be used for the benefit of the Evanston Police Department as authorized by the Evanston City Council.

Councilman Davis moved to adopt the resolution, seconded by Bills, with all voting in favor. Members of the council and I stated our appreciation for the generous gift and assured Amoco that funds would be utilized in the best possible way.

Also, Uinta Title and Insurance, Inc., and The First Wyoming Bank had made sizable donations to the city to be used for the police department. The city council and I gave a special thanks to them, expressing our appreciation for their generous donations. This was a good indication that some of the businesses of Evanston were also very concerned and wanting to help in any way possible.

At that time Chief Dennis Harvey was given permission to advertise for three police cars, and he gave his report on the activities of the department and also asked permission to purchase bulletproof vests among other equipment. His request was granted.

City Treasurer Phyllis Martin reported that the W.A.M. (Wyoming Association of Municipalities) convention was being held on

June 11th, 12th and 13th, and asked how many would be attending. She also reminded us that any and all budget requests should be turned in as soon as possible.

During the regular city council meeting of May 8th there were more ongoing ordinances that had been acted on second and third readings by regular motion and second with all voting in favor.

The city had leased the old city dumps to Don Rutner for his use and to salvage the larger items of junk. At this time I reported that the city received a check from Don Rutner in the amount of $645 for the city's portion of what junk he had salvaged and sold, but we still had to have the dumps cleaned up and this was not part of his lease.

A petition from James and Elaine Harris was presented to the city council concerning the garbage and trash that had accumulated around the Sherman Way Apartments, located on 2nd and Center Streets. The Harrises lived on Center across the street from the apartments. The city attorney was directed to send a letter to the property owners concerning the matter.

Mrs. Arnold Reid was present at the meeting and told of her concern about a tree near the intersection of 11th and Summit Streets that she felt was posing a hazard and that the city should take a look at it and prevent any problems. City Attorney Lancaster and General Superintendent Allen Kennedy were directed to check into her concern and report back to the mayor and council.

A public hearing was held concerning some extra unanticipated revenue in the amount of $30,957 and $10,000 that would be used for administrative and engineering costs for a sewer study. The hearing was advertised by law, but no one showed up to comment on this unanticipated income and so the hearing was closed. Therefore, a motion was made by Councilman Fruits to use the funds for the purposes indicated, seconded by Albrecht, with all voting in favor.

Councilman Bills introduced Ordinance 80-16 to create new sections in the revised code of the City of Evanston to adopt engineering standards and specifications for construction of public works in the city, and provide for filing of said standards and specifications with the city clerk. Motion was made to pass Ordinance 80-16 on first reading and was seconded with all voting in favor. This ordinance went on to pass on second and third readings by regular motion and was seconded with all voting in favor. Ordinance 80-20 came on the floor for first reading and was introduced by Councilman Megeath. This was an ordinance to provide for the issuance and sale of Industrial Development Revenue Bonds for the Oncor Corporation Project in the principal amount of $4,000,000, and approving the form and authorizing the execution of certain documents related to. The motion was made to pass the ordinance on first reading, and was seconded with all voting in favor. This ordinance also went on to pass on second and third readings by regular motion and was seconded with all voting in favor.

It seemed like we were getting more and more requests for these industrial bonds. But as I said before, it is a good feasible way for these big companies to get funding for the construction of their facilities and there is no obligation to the city. The city is merely a sponsor, but by the county and city agreeing to participate it means an increase in the Uinta County tax base.

Terry Davis and Sonny Blakeslee made a presentation requesting $10,000 from city funds for equipment for the ambulance service. The council and I complimented this fine service and told them that their request would be highly considered at budget time.

Donna Davison, Executive Director for LUAG, made a presentation requesting $7,000 from city funds to supplement LUAG's budget for the coming year. Ms Davidson was also told that her request would be considered in next year's budget.

Mr. Doyle Child, owner of Hoback Ranches, Inc. approached me one day about the City of Evanston purchasing 40 acres of property from him. He knew we were looking at property for some of the projects we were working on, such as senior housing, a human service facility, and a recreation center. After talking with him for a while he said he would sell the 40 acres to the city for $220,000, which I thought was reasonable during a period where property values were increasing every day.

I had brought this up to the council members earlier, and they all agreed that it would be a good buy, but we would not be able to do it at this moment because of budget restraints, but could pass a resolution giving us the option to buy the property. Therefore, City Attorney Lancaster drew up Resolution 80-19, introduced by Councilman Megeath.

The resolution authorized the city to enter into an option agreement to purchase 40 acres of real property from Hoback Ranches, Inc. for $220,000. Motion was made for the adoption of Resolution 80-19, and seconded with all voting in favor.

In other business, Councilman Bills made a motion for the Personnel Board to review the resumés of applications for city engineer and make recommendations to the mayor. The motion was seconded by Fruits, with all voting in favor. The engineer's position would be an appointed position by the mayor and confirmed by the council.

A general discussion took place with General Superintendent of Public Works Allen Kennedy and the council concerning fire hydrants, the Spaulding Grove property owned by the city, final plats of subdivisions, the Union Tank Car Company and the new fire hall. Questions, answers and suggestions were made on the various concerns, but no action was taken, other than Kennedy's request that before a final plan on a subdivision was accepted, that he have maps of all water lines and sewer lines, and locations of all shut-off valves.

Resolution 80-21 was introduced by Councilman Albrecht authorizing the city to enter into an agreement with Muir, Chong, and Associates to provide consulting services to develop a preliminary plan for the revitalization of the downtown area of Evanston. This firm was recommended by the Downtown Improvement Corporation, recently formed for the benefit of improving the downtown area and making it more attractive for shopping. Motion was made for the adoption of Resolution 80-21 and was seconded with all voting in favor.

By adopting this resolution, the city showed that it supported the revitalization of downtown Evanston, would do whatever was possible to make the area more attractive, and the mayor and council would consider the plans provided by the Downtown Improvement Corp.

This was another long and tiresome meeting, adjourning at 12:55 a.m. on May 9th.

According to the news article put out by the *Uinta County Herald* on May 22nd, downtown parking was the number one concern of the Downtown Improvement Corporation.

The article went on to say that the Downtown Improvement Corporation held a well publicized public meeting on May 21st, which was sparsely attended. The meeting was to provide a forum to discuss progress and plans of the Corporation and the options open to those interested in the beautification of downtown Evanston.

Corporation members Rick Sather and John Deru were critical of the appraisal of the downtown district, which was defined as the area bounded by Front and Center Streets, and 6th and 12th Streets.

Mr. Deru stated that about 50% of Evanston's earned dollars go out of town for shopping. He indicated that we must try to make downtown a nicer place to shop. Mr. Sather stated that there were 96 business licenses in the downtown district, and if we didn't start going forward, we would be hurting pretty quick.

The hypothesis of the Corporation is that if the shops and stores of the downtown area were more pleasant and parking more available, the business community could compete for dollars now going to outside communities in Utah. The Corporation, which had already received $3,000 from the City of Evanston, indicated that the city council was also very concerned about the future of the downtown business area.

The Corporation proposed to sell membership at $5.00 a share to the business property owners, business license holders and resident property owners within the limits of the described downtown area.

*We don't want to force anyone to do anything,* stated Rick Sather. *If we were bonded, say for $300,000, we could have low interest money available to the corporation members for improvements.*

*All we're trying to do is to make it possible for people to improve the outlooks of their stores,* he continued. He went on to announce that there will be another meeting scheduled for June 4th.

During the second city council meeting of the month on May 22nd, Councilman Bills made a motion to approve voucher number 839 to the Wyoming Land Commissioner for a lifetime lease in the amount of $4,175.60 at the location of the water treatment and filtration plant and storage tanks, seconded by Albrecht, with all voting in favor.

Again time was taken up to act on many pending ordinances to be passed on second and third readings. These ordinances were acted upon by regular motion and seconded with all voting in favor.

Jerry Parker, Superintendent of Uinta County School District No. 1, made a presentation and a request for the use of 7 acres of land owned by the city in the Uinta Meadows area for a new elementary school. Councilman Fruits moved that the city grant Parker's request and direct City Attorney Lancaster to prepare a resolution including the legal description and purpose of the land in Uinta Meadows that had been requested for a site for a new school. The motion was seconded by Albrecht, with all voting in favor.

After the closing of the public hearing, Councilman Rice made a motion to approve the appeal by Mr. and Mrs. Madrid, which was seconded by Albrecht. A roll call vote was called for, with these results: Albrecht, yes; Rice, no; Fruits, no; Bills, no; Megeath, no. I voted yes, and Morgan was absent. The motion failed with 2 yes and 4 no votes.

I read a letter for the resignation of another police officer, Dan Harris. I said we had to do something about losing all these officers to the oil patch, because it was costing the city a lot of money to train these officers and put them through the police academy at Douglas, Wyoming. After a few comments from the council, Councilman Bills made the motion to accept the resignation with regret, and with good wishes and good luck for Harris in the future, seconded by Megeath with all voting in favor.

Following that resignation, I appointed Mark Lynn Fazio to be a member of the Evanston Police Department, with Councilman Fruits making the motion to confirm my appointment, seconded by Rice, with all voting in favor. All police officers were appointed by the mayor and confirmed by the city council.

The city had received only one application for the position of engineer previous to this meeting; therefore, after discussing it with all city council members, I appointed the lone applicant, Wayne Shephard, to the position of Evanston City Engineer. Councilman Bills made the motion to confirm my appointment of Shephard, seconded by Fruits, with all voting in favor.

In a previous meeting Chief Harvey had reported that people had set up permanent residence at the Spaulding Grove camping area, owned by the City of Evanston. They were in the area working in the oil patch and were creating a big mess and dumping trash in the river. The city instructed Harvey to give notice that they must vacate the area.

This sort of thing was very serious for Evanston, because it was happening all over the area. People were camping in Hamblin Park, under the Bear River bridges, using water from the river and dumping human waste and other garbage into the river. They also often camped in people's backyards, sometimes without the owners' permission. Many of them were camping on vacant properties all over the area, most of the time without the property owner even knowing about it. Some would have a small camper, some would only have their pickup or some kind of a vehicle, and some would just have a sleeping bag or some kind of bedding. These were people coming into Evanston and the area to work in the oil industry, because the rest of the country was in a recession at this time.

During this meeting Chief Harvey reported that the folks camping at Spalding Grove Camping Grounds had been served with an eviction notice and must vacate the property immediately. He said they asked for a few days but were told no longer than the coming Sunday.

I reported to the council that there would be a meeting with our U.S. Senator, Malcolm Wallop, on June 6th at City Hall and that all city council members were invited.

Councilman David Bills reported on the Evanston Planning and Zoning Commission meeting, and stated that there was a lot of discussion on the City of Evanston jurisdiction concerning the half-mile perimeter outside the city limits.

Other things discussed were the dog problems, the water tank at Red Mountain, fencing between the fairgrounds and the Hamblin Park area, Downtown Improvement Corporation's project, the fire substation at the fairgrounds, and the underpass, among many other problems, plus reports from the various departments were also given.

Evanston was in a very big boom period at this time and I don't think there was a single problem that hadn't come up in one of our meetings. Many interested people were getting involved in their own concerns and programs. This community was starting to come together to work out all these problems, and as far as I was concerned, it was great to see the entire community showing this much interest. And, as mayor, I was grateful for all the support the city was getting, and I'm sure all the city council members and staff were glad also.

There were some disagreements on how to handle the projects and set priorities, but the results pretty much turned out for the best. Still, it was great to have so many Evanston citizens involved and showing their interest in the city during this period. It was a tough period, but everyone in Evanston was starting to show a lot of civic pride.

On June 3rd a special city council meeting was held in the form of a public hearing to receive input from the public for the proposed budget for Revenue Sharing Funds in the amount of $112,424.18. The proposed use of these funds would be as follows: Mental Health – $8,000; Senior Citizens – $12,000; LUAG – $7,000; Library – $5,500; Public Safety – $16,000; Water Well – $50,000; and Water Plant Repair – $13,924.18. These items were discussed as to need and priority, and it was noted that these expenditures would be allowed if the optional sales tax passed and became effective.

**Sleepy Evanston goes from room to boom**

Debbie, Andy Romanski, son Mike, stray dog they adopted, took a chance on oil rig job | In Evanston. Until they've saved enough money for a trailer down payment, the | Romanskis live in tent behind them. They share impromptu camp site with other oil | work families who haven't money, can't find any housing around Evanston.

*Salt Lake Tribune,* September 7, 1980 Lifestyle.

Star-Tribune/VIRGINIA GIORGIS

## Roughing it

Campers are common sights in the area surrounding Evanston. They include camper shells and trailers. Some are located close to streams, and others are perched on dry ground. Workers in the area hve resorted to campers and tents in order to have a place to stay. Many say they can't find any places in town.

# Evanston housing shortage causes difficulties for new mineral workers

*Casper Star-Tribune,* October 5, 1980.

Also during this meeting, City Treasurer Phyllis Martin presented to the city council a list of proposed expenditures for the budget for the fiscal year of 1980–1981 in a total amount of just over $4 million.

On May 2nd the *Uinta County Herald* published an article headed HUMAN SERVICE COMPLEX FOR COUNTY DISCUSSED. It went on to say that the Uinta County Human Services Confederation held its monthly meeting with Mr. Joe Golden from the Wyoming Department of Health and Social Services Planning Administration, and Mr. Robert Novotny from the Wyoming Department of Administration and Fiscal Control, to discuss the proposed Human Service Complex. They said that the state could not assist in financing a Human Service Building project, but state representatives were willing to make a commitment to lease office space if such a complex would be built, because the state was also having problems finding office space in the area.

Apparently there were several other state, county and city agencies in attendance, including the Evanston Police Department and the Wyoming State Hospital. Kevin Smith, Investigator/Youth Program Officer of the Evanston Police Department and a member of the County Confederation noted, *A lot of problems here are simply from not belonging.* That included newcomers and also old-time residents.

He went on to say, *We have been wanting a place to house battered wives, neglected children—on a temporary basis. The problems are here and we have a need for such a facility. It's awful hard to find the money and political backing to get something like this started and off the ground.* A halfway house or a safe house for those neglected folks was part of the program that was included in the senior housing project as well as the Human Service Building.

During the first city council meeting on June 5th Mr. John Deru, a downtown businessman, presented his plans for a proposed canopy or a cover over the sidewalk in front of his store building, Deru's Glass.

He stated that he wanted to improve his building to give it a little more of the western look. He said that this would be going along with the ideas and plans that the Downtown Improvement Corporation had been talking about to help improve the downtown area. Deru was a member of corporation and he said that he thought by doing something to his own building it may encourage other down-town merchants also to do something to improve their stores.

*City Treasurer Considers*

# City's Growth a Challenge

**THIRD IN A SERIES**

**EDITORS NOTE: In an effort to introduce our readers to various city staff members and the departments they work in, the Uinta County Herald is in the process of featuring each week an employee and the work he or she does for the City of Evanston.**

Be it if they are pulling in an hourly wage or guaranteed salary, many employees are content to go about their work in a laid back, low key way. With the attitude of whatever happens, happens.

Not so for city treasurer Phyllis Martin. One won't overhear her humming the tune "Whatever Will Be, Will Be--Que Sera, Que Sera."

A five-year veteran with the city, four as assistant city clerk-treasurer, Martin recalls, "When I first started with the city, things were not that hectic. There was some breathing time. It's not that way anymore--now you're busy."

That she is. Evanston, due to recent annexations, and the impact of oil activity in the area, has seen a rapid-fire growth as of late. Does it bother Martin? It does not.

She said, "I have a tendency to get terribly excited about what's happening to us. It's a challenge--and it's nice to be a part of it."

Prior to January, 1980, the office of treasurer and clerk was a combined responsibility, but due to the increase in workload, the office was split with Martin being assigned the treasurer role while Don Welling, formerly the treasurer-clerk, was named city clerk.

Sharon Comer serves as assistant clerk-treasurer for the two.

A primary duty for Martin as treasurer is "being accountable for all funds of the city. In simple terms--it involves a lot of time."

That it does. Especially at this time of year as the city is in the process of preparing its 1980-81 budget which will be finalized in July.

As the city has grown, almost double in population, so has the operating budget. It is anticipated this year's fiscal budget will exceed $5 million.

Last year's budget was $2.5 million, but much of the increase in this year's figure is due to inflation (especially in cost of materials), additional equipment, and more extensive maintenance crews, along with federal and state grants.

Martin said, "All budgets have been presented to me from the various departments. There is definitely an increase, but we are anticipating a large sum of money in grants and this will be reflected in the budget. Hopefully, people will understand that a great deal of this money will be in grants. Approximately $1.5 million of it."

When Martin initially started with the city, the budget was $506,553.

She adds, "The budget is increasing because of our needs, and to provide services, it just takes money."

Martin, a 13-year resident of Evanston, noted grant money, in part, has been earmarked to expand or build a new sewer plant and expansion of lines, the airport board receiving a $240,000 grant, $.5 million in site acquisition, and water lines.

Increased expenses in the budget are reflected in salaries, large equipment item purchases for upkeep including an impacter for the sanitary landfill that will increase eight years to the life expectancy, and police department needs and officers.

In addition to working closely with city administrator Steve Snyder, Martin also handles payroll, and all reporting to the state, along with presenting the council with a monthly balance sheet.

She feels her office suffers through no abnormal problems. "The council and departments are very careful on expenditures."

Of the impact, Martin said, "It's a shot in the arm (for Evanston), however, changes sometime come a little faster than we like to see."

But, she adds, the "council has prepared for what's happened. I'd like the general public to see what's happening here. The council and mayor are staying with the trend of our needs."

**PHYLLIS MARTIN**

*Uinta County Herald,* Evanston, Wyo. Thursday, May 8, 1980.

Deru was told that the city would have City Attorney Lancaster research the uniform building code and existing fire codes to see if a permit can be issued. He was told that the city would get back to him as soon as Lancaster could come up with a report.

When Lancaster looked into the ordinances concerning permanent awnings, he reported back to the mayor and council that there was an ordinance on the books banning permanent awnings and porticoes over sidewalks extending from building fronts.

When Mr. Deru was made aware of this, he was assured that the city would look into having that section of the old ordinance repealed, and what it would take to consider his request again in the near future.

Again, this was a meeting where several ordinances and resolutions were acted on. All of them were adopted and passed on various readings by regular motion and seconded with all voting in favor.

Subdivision plats were presented by Jeff Carlton, surveyor of properties outside the city limits west of Evanston: Crane Creek Subdivision owned by Clarence Lowham, and Centennial Valley owned by J. D. Kindler. Although these sub-divisions were outside the city limits but within the half-mile authority, the city still had the right to have input and give their approval. Both subdivisions were approved by the city with a few suggestions.

I made another appointment to the police department. Thomas McCafferty was appointed and confirmed by the council by motion, and seconded with all voting in favor. I then read a letter from the Department of Environmental Quality, Water Quality Division, telling the council that some of the city employees successfully completed the test that qualified Thomas Whittaker as a Class 4 water operator and Arvel "Bud" Eastman, Frank Sheets, and Allen "Oop" Hansen as Class 1. The council and I congratulated them for their diligence, dedication and learning expertise.

At this time Councilman Bills made a motion for Steve Snyder, Administrative Assistant to the City, to amend the FHA (Federal Housing Administration) grant application to include a Human Resource Center, seconded by Megeath, with all voting in favor.

In a June issue of the *Uinta County Herald*, there was an article headed EVANSTON MAY BE THE FIRST TO HAVE A COMPLETE HUMAN RESOURCES COMPLEX. The paper went on to say that Evanston might have a senior citizens housing complex, a recreation facility, and a human resources agency complex all housed on a 40-acre parcel of land contingent on the city's acquisition of the land from Doyle Childs of Hoback Ranches, Inc. Denice Wheeler, spokeswoman for Uinta Health Services Confederation said at Wednesday's meeting, *Tonight is going to be a history-making event. There has never been, to my knowledge, another complex with all of these ingredients in one site.*

She emphasized, *We are not asking for money,* but rather we are offering to *give our time, our experience, our dedication in an effort to make Evanston a model.*

I said, *I think this is a program that we, as a city, cannot afford not to pursue. I think the idea is great.* I went on to say that *a 601 grant has been applied for by the city to obtain the 40 acres.*

On June 19th, the second city council meeting of the month, we held a public hearing to transfer funds: $24,000 from the General Fund to be distributed: Attorney, $4,000; Sanitation, $15,000; Engineering, $5,000. Councilman Bills made a motion that this transfer of funds be permitted, which was seconded by Rice with all voting in favor.

During the meeting several more ordinances came up for second and third readings with motions and seconds being made as required. Although there was a period of discussion on some, there were no objections. They all passed by a unanimous vote.

The request by Superintendent Jerry Parker of Uinta County School District No. 1 concerning their need for additional property for the new elementary school site in Uinta Meadows was acted on by resolution at this meeting.

Resolution 80-28 was introduced by Councilman Megeath, declaring the intention of the mayor and city council to vacate property within the Uinta Meadows Addition meant for public use and previously dedicated to parks and playgrounds. This property would be deeded to School District No. 1 to construct a new elementary school. The motion was made to adopt the resolution and was seconded, with all voting in favor.

Mr. Steven Bell, representing Hanifen, Imhoff, and Samford, made a presentation and offer of financial advice to the City of Evanston on a continuing basis. I thanked them for their interest and told them that their offer will be taken under advisement with the city attorney and legal counsel before any decision was made.

Bell's offer was never considered, because the city council and I determined that we already had good advice from various sources. It seemed like we were getting some kind of offer from different companies during every meeting. Almost all of these offers were from firms outside of Evanston and some were even out of state, so we were being very careful not to accept any offer without researching them first.

The city council finally made the decision to sell the old town hall building and advertise for bids on it. Therefore, Councilman Megeath made the motion that the City of Evanston proceed with advertising for bids on the old building, and that bids were to be opened during the first city council meeting in August. Davis seconded the motion.

But Councilman Rice amended the motion to include that all bids must exceed the appraised value of $65,000, seconded by Bills. All voted in favor of the motion as amended to proceed with the bidding.

Former Mayor Dan South, representing South and Jones Timber Company, a large sawmill presently located in the City of Evanston near where the Bear Project and ponds are now located. South had expressed his views on the proposal of the new overpass and the re-routing of Wyoming State Highway 89 and requested that his company be given at least one year notification by the city and/or the highway department. His concern was that with the new overpass going in where they were located, it would completely eliminate their timber company because the overpass would be going right through their operation and they needed time to relocate.

When all was said and done, the Wyoming Highway Department got South and Jones relocated several miles north of Evanston on County Road 103, with some assistance. I'm not sure how much or in what way the state assisted them, but I know, from what Dan South had told me, they did get some help.

I felt that the State of Wyoming should have to pay the complete cost of relocating them. They had been a great asset to the City of Evanston and Uinta County for a long time and deserved whatever help they received from the state.

We had two timber sawmills located in the city at that time: South and Jones, and a company out of Idaho called Price Valley Timber, which was located where the Walmart Super Store is at the present. Both companies were burning waste wood particles and the city was getting complaints from a lot of citizens about the pollution caused by the smokestacks, but my feeling was that they were at least creating jobs; but eventually South and Jones was relocated and Price Valley just shut down and left the area, because of the new viaduct that was to be built off 6th Street.

The proposal of the new route for Highway 89 was on the agenda later in the meeting, at which time I presented the proposed re-alignment and an aerial photo of the city showing the proposed route outline, north and around the cemetery to the east side, then southeasterly to where it would connect to U.S. Highway 30 S, now known as Bear River Drive, and passing across the river over the new overpass to the intersection of Front Street, and connecting into 6th Street.

Councilman Davis made the motion to approve the proposed re-alignment of the route as proposed by the Wyoming Highway Department. The motion was seconded by Rice, with all voting in favor.

The flow of the traffic on the westerly side of the underpass was discussed. Councilman Bills made a motion for a free flowing right turn, no left turn, a straight ahead flow of traffic to Center Street then left to 6th Street, then a left turn to Front Street. This plan would be on a trial basis only. The motion was seconded by Rice with all voting in favor. This proposal only lasted until the city went to one-way streets in the downtown area, which was very near in the future.

During this meeting more ordinances were introduced. Councilman Albrecht introduced Ordinance 80-32, an ordinance amending a previous ordinance providing for a seven-day notice before public hearings on variance requests or Conditional Use Permits. Motion was made to pass ordinance 80-32 on first reading and seconded with all voting in favor.

Ordinance 80-29 was introduced by Councilman Albrecht, also amending a previous ordinance to expand the uses permitted in a Highway Commercial (C-3) Zone. Albrecht made the motion to pass Ordinance 80-29 on first reading, seconded by Megeath, but then, after considerable discussion, Albrecht made the motion to table this ordinance until the first regular meeting in July, which was seconded by Bills with all voting in favor.

Following that action, Councilman Davis introduced Ordinance 80-28, an amended ordinance providing that title reports and the filing of final plats by subdividers be within ten days from date of approval by the city. The motion was amended but passed on first reading, and went on to pass on second and third readings by motion and seconded.

Thursday, June 12, 1980     Star-Tribune, Casper, Wyo.

photo/VIRGINIA GIORGIS

## Hurry up and wait

Vehicles line up on Highway 89 at Evanston as they wait their turn for a shot at the railroad underpass which is the only access to the south side of town from the north. Mayor Dennis Ottley said plans call for rerouting 89 east and connecting it to the proposed overpass and Sixth Street.

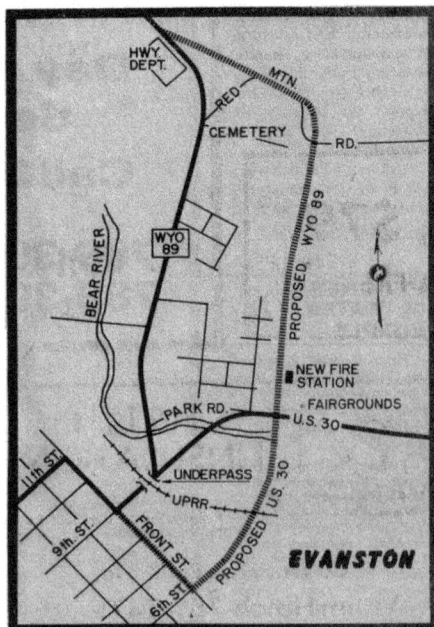

Surveyor Jeff Carlton, representing Painter and Company, presented a plat for a proposed site for a temporary trailer house to be located near the Red Mountain Road that would be hooked into city services. After some discussion, Councilman Bills made the motion for the city to enter into an agreement with Painter and Company to allow the request, but only until January 31, 1981, at which time it would need to be removed. The motion was seconded by Albrecht with all voting in favor.

Councilman Albrecht introduced Resolution 80-31, a resolution to amend the inducement resolution for the Dow Chemical Company. Motion was made to adopt the resolution and seconded with all voting in favor.

This resolution concerned more Industrial Development Revenue Bonds. Every time an ordinance to approve a company receiving Industrial Revenue Bonds was passed, there was always an inducement resolution that followed. I believe this was by law.

After the announcements from Amoco Production Company and Chevron Oil Company that they had started building man-camps for their employees on sites where their processing gas plants would be located, I told the council that we should appreciate the fact that these man-camps were being built, because it was going to help the housing shortage problem in the City of Evanston.

Both companies, Chevron and Amoco, had announced that sour gas processing plants would be scheduled for construction in locations several miles north of the city. The Chevron plant would be in the Ryckman Creek area and the Amoco plant would be located at Whitney Canyon. Completion date of both plants would be either late 1982 or in 1983. Man-camps would be constructed for the benefit of the employees. These camps would provide housing and boarding.

In the process of building these man-camps, a Mr. Duke Jones of Jones Refuse Service from Morgan, Utah approached the city council with a request to use the new Evanston landfill. He stated that he had been asked by some of the oil company camps to provide garbage service for them. Jones also asked if the city would be interested in contracting with his firm to haul city garbage. The city council requested that Jones and his company present a proposal for the city to look at and consider, and a proposal to use the city landfill. Nothing ever came of his proposal to haul garbage for the city because the council decided that they would continue to haul their own garbage, but he was permitted to use the landfill for a fee as per ordinance.

Resolution 80-30 was introduced by Councilman Megeath, and Ordinance 80-30 was introduced by Councilman Bills, with both resolution and ordinance referring to the annexation of certain parcels owned by the Broken Circle Cattle Company. Resolution and ordinance were both moved seconded for adoption with all voting in favor.

At this time I appointed Mr. Robert Pryor to the police department with a motion by Councilman Bills to confirm the appointment, seconded by Davis, with all voting in favor.

The rest of the meeting concerned some recommendations from the Personnel Board to change some policies and procedures. One of the changes was to allow department heads to issue purchase orders for their own departments not to exceed $200.00. Motions were made on these changes and seconded, with all voting in favor.

Councilman Bills made a motion for the mayor to call for a special city council meeting on June 30th at 7:00 p.m. to deal with some general business, seconded by Megeath, with all voting in favor.

This meeting was another long and drawn-out meeting adjourning in the wee hours of the next day. One reason the city council elected to have a special meeting was to get some business out of the way so our regular meetings wouldn't last so long. It wasn't good keeping people at a meeting that late, but with so much going on we were pretty much forced into having special meetings quite often.

During the special meeting of June 30th, we passed several ordinances on second and third readings with all voting in favor, and I read a letter of resignation from Rudger Davis resigning from the Evanston Planning and Zoning Commission. Motion was made and seconded that the council accept his resignation, with all voting in favor. The mayor and council gave him a vote of thanks for the many years of his faithful and excellent service.

After a short discussion concerning Overthrust Road, the new fire substation, the grant application for senior housing, and so on, the meeting adjourned at 10:00 p.m.

The regular city council meeting of July 3rd was called to order with the regular business properly taken care of first, followed by the passing on third reading of Ordinances 80-26, 80-28, 80-30, 80-31 and 80-32, with all voting in favor.

The above ordinances pertained to the vacating of certain streets; providing for title reports and filing of final plats by subdividers; annexation of Broken Circle Cattle Company land; new subdivisions in the Red Mountain Mesa area; and providing for a 7-day notice before public hearings concerning variance requests or Conditional Use Permits.

Councilman Davis introduced Ordinance 80-33, an ordinance concerning the vacating of an irrigation easement located within the Evanston Industrial Center Addition. Motion was made to pass Ordinance 80-33 on first reading and seconded with all voting in favor. The ordinance was passed on the next two readings by regular motion with all voting in favor.

Councilman Megeath made a motion for the city to look into changing from the present I.R.A. plan to a pension plan, and to have a committee appointed and assigned to study the plans, and make a report of their recommendations to the council at the regular meeting on July 17th. The motion was seconded by Bills. There was considerable discussion of why the sudden change was proposed when the city had just come up with the present plan a year ago. This is the first time the city employees had ever had a retirement plan. However, the vote on the motion was called for by me with all voting in favor.

I appointed the following to the committee to study the pension plan: Steve Snyder, Administrative Assistant; Russell Megeath, City Council Member; David Bills, City Council Member; Bruce Waters, Police Department; Phyllis Martin, City Treasurer; Allen Kennedy, General Superintendent of Public Works; and Allen "Oop" Hansen, Street Foreman. We would just have to see what they came up with before we took any further action.

Mr. Mike Stevens and Mr. Richard Adams, representing Contour Development Company, made a presentation of their plans for a shopping center that would include a grocery, a department store, and a variety and a drug store. They described their financial plans and said their project would be completed by the end of 1981. Their location would be on some of the U.P.R.R. property on Front Street.

We all showed a lot of interest, and there was no doubt that, with the influx of people, the city could handle the addition, but the way things were going we were also concerned how all these new stores and centers were going to affect those stores and shops that had been in business in Evanston for so many years, especially the downtown area; but over time most seemed to have survived.

At this time Ordinance 80-34 was introduced by Councilman Megeath to repeal Section 6-43 of the revised code of the City of Evanston, 1977 which banned permanent awnings and porticoes. After the city attorney read the ordinance, a motion was made to pass on first reading and was seconded, with all voting in favor.

Ordinance 80-35 to provide for a permitting process for and a fee on home occupations was introduced by Councilman Bills. A motion was made to pass on first reading and seconded, with all voting in favor.

Another demand caused by the boom was for home occupations that the City of Evanston never had before, except occasional requests for home beauty shops and the like, but now a lot of homeowners were requesting to turn part of their homes into commercial businesses such as gift shops, day care centers, and so on. So the city felt that there had to be a procedure by ordinance passed to help control the matter.

After a considerable amount of complaints concerning the noise of the large trucks, motor bikes and other loud vehicles, and other sources, a noise ordinance numbered 80-36 was brought up and passed by regular motion, with all voting in favor on the first reading.

A new ordinance numbered 80-37 providing for two residential suburban zones (RS-1 and RS-2) was introduced by Councilman Bills. The motion was made to pass on first reading and seconded, but after some discussion, Councilman Bills moved to table Ordinance 80-37 until later in the meeting, with all voting in favor.

At this time Councilman Bills introduced Ordinance 80-38 providing for general rules of procedure, which stated that the city council must follow the procedures established in *Robert's Rules of Order.* Motion was made to pass on first reading and seconded with all voting in favor.

Councilman Bills then introduced Ordinance 80-39, which was an ordinance providing that a motion to reconsider, after being tabled, need not be seconded by a member who voted in the majority. However, a motion to reconsider must be made by a member who voted in the majority.

I questioned why we needed this after we passed an ordinance stating that the city would follow *Robert's Rules of Order*, but City Attorney Lancaster explained that it might be necessary, so I called for a motion. Motion was made and seconded with all voting in favor.

Other action that came up in the meeting prior to adjournment included the opening of several bids for new vehicles. Motion was made by Megeath to accept the low bids on each provided they all meet bid specifications, seconded by Fruits with all voting in favor. Also discussed were standards and specifications for trailer parks, and an announcement by the city treasurer that there would be a public hearing at City Hall on July 15th at 8:00 p.m. concerning the 1980-1981 budget.

After my administration's first budget of 1979-1980 was approved we had a small carryover, giving the city some reserve, besides those funds that were already earmarked for certain projects and enterprise departments. "Enterprise Departments" are those that collect funds for services rendered, such as the water department. Those funds that are earmarked for those departments could only be used for that purpose.

When you have a carryover from your budget you are not, by law, allowed to use those funds in your anticipated revenues. Carryover funds remained in what we considered a reserve fund, which could be used for any department by council action unless earmarked for a particular item or department. Therefore, when you have a carryover it can add to your reserve, giving the city a nice cushion to work with.

After the last budget was approved for the previous year I had a meeting with City Treasurer Martin and City Clerk Welling on what I thought a city budget should be based on. *As a suggestion, I told them, I would like to see all future budgets be considered and based on the previous year's revenues.* Addressing Martin, I said, *I would like to see you base the upcoming budgets on the previous year's revenues less 15 to 25%. That way I think we will end up with a carry-over every year unless the city has an economic downfall that would affect the city's revenue in a very negative way.* Every year I was mayor they took my suggestion, and at the end of the next fiscal year we had an attractive carryover.

Therefore, on July 15th we held the public hearing concerning the budget for the fiscal year of 1980-1981. The tentative fiscal year budget was almost $3.9 million, which would exceed last year's budget by $1 million. City Treasurer Martin explained some adjustments had been made to the budget, and nearly $1.5 million was in grants. These grants would include funds for airport improvement, recreation, the first phase of the E.P.A. sewer grant, land acquisition and extension of the water system.

I stated that there was a 70% increase in the amount of grants and a 30% increase in non-grant items. I also stated that the biggest increase in the general budget was in wages, and that the city's 65 employees will be given a 15% increase in pay.

A question and answer period followed, and Walter Jones, Uinta County Librarian, expressed his thanks and appreciation to the council for their consideration of the needs of the library.

The second city council meeting in July was held on the 17th. This was another long and tiresome meeting that adjourned at midnight. But one of the first orders of business was to move to take Ordinance 80-29, introduced by Councilman Albrecht, off the table. The motion was seconded and passed with 4 yes and 1 no vote.

Ordinance 80-29 was to amend and expand the uses permitted in a highway commercial (C-3) zone. After a lengthy discussion Councilman Bills again made a motion to table the ordinance indefinitely, seconded by Davis, with all voting in favor.

Ordinances 80-33, 80-34, 80-35, 80-36, 80-37, 80-38 and 80-39 came up for second reading. They were all passed by regular motion and seconded with all voting in favor. All these ordinances would be acted on third and final reading at the next regular meeting. I expected them all to pass unanimously.

A public hearing was held at this time concerning the vacating of some property owned by the city for public use. In question was the property that the school district requested to be added to the site of the Uinta Meadows Elementary School. The hearing was recorded and the tape would be on file at the City Hall.

Following the hearing, Councilman Davis introduced Ordinance 80-40 to vacate property owned by the city that was previously dedicated for parks and playgrounds. This ordinance would permit the city to deed the property to the school district for the purpose mentioned above. Motion was made to pass Ordinance 80-40 on first reading and was seconded, with all voting in favor.

Councilman Albrecht introduced Ordinance 80-41 dedicating a street going to and within the Red Mountain Mesa subdivision area as Red Mountain Road. Motion was made to pass the ordinance on first reading and was seconded, with all voting in favor.

Two more ordinances were introduced in the meeting establishing a mobile home park (M-P) zone and subdivision requirements, and adding the definition of a mobile home park. Both ordinances passed by regular motion and were seconded with all voting in favor.

Ordinance 80-44 was introduced by Councilman Davis to change an unzoned parcel of land owned by Jack (Dub) W. Mills to be a highway commercial (C-3) zone. However, because the property in question was adjacent to residential property and had no frontage to the highway, a lengthy discussion was held. After I called for the question to be voted on, Councilman Albrecht made the motion to pass Ordinance 80-44 on first reading, seconded by Fruits. The motion failed with 5 no votes. Two of the council members were absent.

Resolution 80-36 accepting the city budget for the 1980-1981 fiscal year ending June 30, 1981 was introduced by Councilman Fruits. Motion was made to adopt Resolution 80-36 and was seconded with all voting in favor.

On the next ten ordinances, City Attorney Lancaster disclosed that he may have a conflict of interest and requested that Attorney Tim Beppler be appointed as a special city attorney for the consideration of these ordinances, as well as for a hearing scheduled for August 7th.

Attorney James Phillips, representing the Broken Circle Cattle Company, and from the same firm as City Attorney Lancaster, made a lengthy presentation for the cattle company on Ordinances 80-48, 80-49, 80-50, 80-51, 80-52, 80-53, 80-54, 80-55, 80-56 and 80-57. Each of these ordinances pertained to zoning in properties near or across the highway from the Aspen Grove subdivisions and had no definite plans on the use of each parcel described in the ordinances. Each ordinance was properly introduced, with a motion and a second made.

Ordinances 80-48, 80-49, 80-50, 80-51, 80-53, 80-54 and 80-56 all passed on first reading by a majority vote. Ordinance 80-52 asking for a light industrial (I-1) zone failed with 7 no votes; Ordinance 80-55 asking for a highway commercial (C-3) zone failed by 3 yes and 4 no votes. I, as mayor, had to vote to break the tie on this ordinance. I voted no, because I was concerned that the property mentioned had no definite plans of how it would fit in with the area. Finally, Ordinance 80-57 asking for multiple family residential (R-4) zoning failed by 7 no votes.

Other business consisted of Resolution 80-35 being introduced by Councilman Fruits. This was a resolution vacating some sewer and drainage easements in the Red Mountain Subdivision areas. Motion was made for adoption and seconded with all voting in favor.

Resolution 80-37 was introduced by Councilman Davis. This resolution declared the intention of the city to vacate some streets, alleys and roads located within a subdivision known as the Uinta View Ranchettes, owned by my brother Robert "Bob" Ottley. It was a 20-acre parcel of land where he wanted to build a home for himself and his son Parke. This was one of those times I had a conflict and turned the meeting over to Council President Ron Davis and left the chambrs. Motion was made to adopt resolution and seconded with all 6 council members voting in favor.

Before adjournment a proposed pension plan was discussed, with Councilman Megeath reporting that the committee would like to accept sealed proposals, and have the Wyoming State Insurance Commission or the Wyoming Association of Municipalities (W.A.M.) or some other independent agency make recommendations. Megeath was directed to follow through.

General Superintendent of Public Works Allen Kennedy requested that all street-name signs be furnished and paid for by developers of subdivisions. He stated that with so many subdivisions being developed at this time and with so many streets having to be named, it was becoming very expensive for the city, and was having an effect on the budget. No action took place at this time, but it appeared that the council was in agreement with him.

A recent article in the *Uinta County Herald* reporting on a Downtown Improvement Corporation meeting, read that Mr. Richard Chong of Muir, Chong and Associates reported that Front Street may be a stumbling block to the downtown economic vitality because of its high crime rate, many transients, history of rough bars and marginal businesses.

Mr. Bob Leigh from the Denver planning firm, Leigh, Scott and Cleary, Inc., hired by the City of Evanston in April of 1980 to study Evanston's transportation problems said, *I agree with your (Chong's) conclusion that lack of parking facilities is the worst problem, even more than circulation. The underpass, however, is one of the worst I've seen. It's a big city problem. It hurts the downtown because it hurts the accessibility.* He continued, *The concentration should be on developing parking areas that look nice on Front Street.*

*There is no guessing with redevelopment planning,* said Mr. Chong. *Your redevelopment plan will make it or break it with downtown. It's that serious. You can't afford to make any mistakes.*

After more comments from Mr. Chong and additional discussion from the downtown group, Mr. Rick Sather, Chairman of the Corporation said, *Now it's time for action, but where do we go from here?*

When the railroad property southeast of the underpass started developing with shopping centers, banks and dealerships, and the proposed overpass, there had been two lumber companies, Tri-State and Evanston Lumber, a few homes, the old Becker's Brewery building, which was being leased at the time by Luke Lym, owner of Western Beverages and a meat cutting business, and there were stockyards, three gasoline bulk plants, and a saw mill. All businesses had to be relocated, evicted or just went out of business, because all structures were torn down.

Now, at the present time, you see all new businesses, including a Walmart's Super Center, a Murdock's, a MacDonald's, a Wendy's, plus a strip mall and several other businesses. This development of the U.P.R.R.'s properties made a tremendous change to the city and probably hurt a good number of retail stores in the downtown area. It put Cornets Variety Store on the corner of Harrison and Main completely out of business. It was good for Evanston in some ways, especially in the increase in revenues from sales tax, property taxes, and so on, but it did affect the community in a lot of other ways. Evanston was no longer a bedroom community to Utah's Wasatch Front. Evanston was now a community of its own. Good or bad, that's the way it was. Some citizens disapproved of the change while others approved and accepted it. It was all in how you looked at it.

Although it was not legal, there was a report that Evanston even had its own house of ill repute during the boom. But it wasn't just a report—it was actually happening. The house in question was called "The House of the Rising Sun," and was operated by a young woman who called herself Falyene, but also went by a nickname of "Bambi." She had just recently moved to Evanston, and had been a prostitute in Las Vegas prior to moving here. She was only 21 years of age, but apparently she had been around a bit and knew her business. It was reported that she kept her "product girls" very clean and kept a strict house.

Uinta County Herald –Thursday, July 10, 1980

# Mel-O-Tones

## ...and Discords

### by Mel Baldwin

This fat printer has had four letters to the editor and about a dozen calls since we published an article June 26 entitled "Fallyene Operates Oldest Business." All four letters were from indignant residents. The calls were about equal in number from those who disapproved and those who approved of the article. All were from longtime local residents — none from newcomers.

We printed two letters last week and are printing the other two this week. Unless I have a change of heart. These will be the final letters printed about this particular article.

I have appreciated receiving the letters and hearing the opinions expressed. I've also appreciated having others drop in or call to tell me their thoughts on the matter.

I partly agree with all of them, and partly disagree.

For instance, I can't agree with several good and longtime friends who say that, under the present circumstances, a house of prostitution is a necessity in town. They have expressed some convincing arguments, but I just can't agree. There's

something so repulsive and degrading about the whole filthy business that it outweighs any arguments for its necessary presence.

On the other hand, I'm not entirely sympathetic with others whose main concern doesn't seem to be that we have prostitution but only that we dared to publicly report it.

The fact of the matter is that Evanston does have prostitution, fully established and apparently flourishing. We felt (and still strongly feel) that it needed to be reported to the people. This we did.

It was investigated, as best we could do so, by a trained, experienced and very talented reporter. She obtained firsthand information at some physical risk to herself, and definitely at risk to her reputation in meeting with such a person.

I am immensely pleased that people read the article and were interested enough to express themselves, one way or another. I respect their opinions and welcome both favorable and unfavorable responses about anything we publish. Keep them coming!

I did not, however, appreciate the very

personal references to Deb Cunningham. She did a remarkably good job of reporting. She gave no opinions of her own, and did not editorialize on the subject. Her quotes were firsthand, directly from the woman whom she interviewed.

Rather than castigating her or the publishers for having the audacity to report what's happening, a good course of action might be to organize a group to put pressure on those in authority to rid Evanston of this insidious malignancy before it gets any worse. You might even thank Deb for having the courage to investigate, learn the facts and let you know its happening.

Incidently, for those who wondered: Deb hasn't taken over the editorial duties of the paper (even though she is qualified to do so). Everything she, or anyone else on the staff, writes is approved by me before it is printed.

—O—

JUST A RUMOR - We may not always agree but it's just as important to me for you to have your say as for me to have mine.

*A New Evanston Resident,*

# Falyene Operates Oldest Business

By Deb Cunningham

NOTE: With the oil industry fueling an economic boom in Evanston, rapid growth has brought more than housing problems to the area. Money is spent more easily. Crime is increasing. Men outnumber women. An inevitable additon to a "boom" town is now established in Evanston.

Falyene is the name she goes by.

Falyene--Bambi's lover.

Operating on the philosophy of supply and demand, she found her way to Evanston and set up her business.

Falyene wrote October 27, 1979, "As nothing is for here we only hope for a free path along a highway of fortune."

"Her path led here. And I've done" reminiscing "fortunate" she says she's been.

Falyene felt there was a need in this growing city, and she met it.

Other jobs were also tackled by the 21-year-old blond, waitressing and construction.

But her main contribution to Evanston is frowned on in self-righteous indignation by most elements of society.

Falyene is about five foot seven. Some would call her

a bit overweight.

Eyes wide and large as the deer from which she took her name, dart around the room sending messages.

Snickers, low-keyed talk, heads nod her way, pointing her out, saying "I know who she is."

Her house is frequented by men.

In it reside three women and a cook. Falyene lives elsewhere.

The house is sometimes referred to as 'The House of the Rising Sun' as immortalized by Dylan, or a house of ill repute.

Falyene says, "There's a lot of money to be made here--the people that come here are not from here."

Falyene talks of "the things I've seen--the things that have run that lonely highway."

As a child of nine she found herself vulnerable to a stepfather who exercised his pleasure with her.

At 13, Falyene was "framed for smack" and spent "18 months in a federal penitentiary in California" with six months parole.

In 1977, she gave her two children to two sets of parents.

"I'm happy for them--

they both have brothers and sisters."

One boy was one and a-half months old, the other, 22 months at the time of adoption.

Casper welcomed her when she was 17. There her "black pimp" ("You might classify him as a Rolling Heights pimp") taught her "all the basic principals of being a lady."

She also worked Las Vegas. In a "legal house."

Here, she's careful. She retains a lawyer. And sends her "ladies" to a doctor once a week. Falyene taught them the necessities of cleanliness.

And how to check the customers for crabs and lice and diseases associated with her trade.

Of herself, Falyene says, "I'm a very clean immaculate person."

Falyene relates, "I'm totally against street walking and if I find my girls in a bar - they'll be canned."

"As far as walking the streets--that's trash."

Her employees are "all ladies--they act like ladies. I wouldn't have anything but."

Drugs are banned in the house and profanity is frowned on.

"Profanity is used on

occasion, but they hold that back."

In addition to her three ladies, Falyene also utilizes the services of two bartenders in town and a man who operates a car service, chauffering men to the house.

Her cook shares the duties of madam with Falyene.

Falyene says her house is "a place where a man can have his pleasure if he can't have it at home."

Her defense against complaints of townfolk, "The township itself is safe because Mom and Dad's little girl isn't running

around getting pregnant."

Falyene was discovered in Casper while playing pool in a bar. She says she is "one of the top 10 semi-pros in the women's tournament league, sixth in the U.S."

Of her work now--"I like what I'm doing."

Poetry fills her spare time.

The following was written Christmas Day, 1979:

"I have thought myself my own discipline throughout the years, going through my tears as though a mountain's stream...as the tears show the reflection of the rain."

Page 2 UINTA COUNTY HERALD Evanston, Wyo.
THURSDAY, JULY 10, 1980

# Letters

We welcolme expressions of all view-points from readers. Letters should be kept brief as possible and are subject to editing. Letters must include signature and valid mailing address. Unsigned letters will not be printed.

# A 'Lifelong Resident' is Upset

# With Cunninghams, Both of 'Em

Dear Mel:

As a life-long resident of Evanston, I have been upset and concerned for some time about various happenings in our community under the guise of progress and prosperity; but the most startling is to find a half-page advertisement in the Uinta County Herald for a house of prostitution. What is even more amazing is the rationalization that this is an act of mercy for the women and girls in the community, when, in fact, molesters have no interest in this type of service.

If this business has been admitted into our City, I am extremely disappointed in our officials. I am also disappointed in the fact that you have relinquished your right as editor of your newspaper. I sincerely hope that Deb will be more discrete in the future. As for Mr. Cunningham, if he is disenchanted with the City of Evanston, there is a very simple solution.

Sincerely,
Luella Horne

# Deb Still Gets No Respect

Dear Mel,

I just happened to be in Ogden at the hospital with my little boy when the article on Faylene came out in your paper. That is the reason that I am so late writing this.

I've never been impressed with any of the articles by Deb Cunningham, but this is an all time low. I realize that some people think of this as modern and liberated, but in my opinion it is in bad taste, and if the reason we need two papers a week is to print this type of thing, maybe we can get by with one. For people who want to read this sort of thing there are many magazines etc., on the news stands, but please not our town paper!

Sincerely,
Ilene Matthews

At the time it was reported to the police, but things were moving so fast and our department was still quite small. Besides, to be honest, we didn't think too much about it because, with all the young single workers coming into the area, we thought it might help the situation, if you know what I mean.

Our police officers were so busy on other problems, such as a shooting at the Ramada Inn that involved a police officer and frequent violent, domestic and unruly crimes, including murder/suicide. To tell the truth, we had about five years of hell in the area, but we were all doing the best we could controlling crime and keeping the peace.

The *Uinta County Herald* came out with an article in July headed, SHARP RISE IN DOMESTIC VIOLENCE...GRIM SPECTOR OF BOOM TOWN. This article spoke of the increase in domestic violence and the need for a Human Service facility and a safe house for battered women and neglected children.

There was no question that all these things were needed and eventually in a few years they would be a reality, but in the meantime we also had some very big problems with our infrastructure, such as sewer, water and streets.

After we were able to lease the Front Street property between 9th and 10th Streets from the railroad there was a group of local citizens that wanted to preserve the Beeman-Mercantile Company building that at that time was located and stored on a piece of railroad property near where Cazin's is at the present, but was still intact and could easily be moved without damaging it.

The Beeman-Cashin Building had been a local company that sold farm and ranch equipment and hardware, and feed and grain during the late 1800s and early 1900s. I believe it was also a blacksmith shop. It was originally located on the corner of Main and 10th Street.

Moving the Beeman-Cashin Building to its present location was the first historic building of Evanston to be moved near the train depot, creating what is now known as Evanston's Depot Square. Thanks belong to a lot of long-time residents of Evanston and those historians that wanted to help keep the downtown a historic area. I don't recall

all who were involved, but it showed a lot of love and care for the heart of an old and proud community.

The *Uinta County Herald* ran an article in the July 26th issue headed CITY AND COUNTY INVESTED IN CHAMBER OF COMMERCE. The article read that at the Evanston Chamber of Commerce meeting, Executive Director Bert Roberge reported that both the City of Evanston and Uinta County had *"made investments in the chamber. The city gave $6,000.00 and the county gave $1,500.00,"* he said.

The article went on to say that Mayor Ottley discussed plans for the new overpass, which would take a load off the Front Street underpass. The Chamber of Commerce would urge the Wyoming Highway Department to speed up plans for the construction. *"We will urge them (meaning the highway department) to give it their immediate attention,"* Roberge said.

The overpass off 6th Street was frowned on by a lot of folks. The residents of 6th Street were worried about the traffic, and the downtown merchants were worried about its effect on their business. Therefore, the opposition sarcastically named the project "Ottley's Folly." I guess it was because I was probably the most instrumental person to push for that location, but I also had a lot of folks behind me. I guess you couldn't blame people for their concern. The *Minneapolis Star* newspaper, out of Minneapolis, Minnesota printed an article on July 25th noting that Evanston's population had more than doubled since 1977, when gas and oil companies swarmed into town.

1980 was another election year, and three of the city council members would be up for re-election: Russell "Bub" Albrecht of Ward 1, Jimmie Rice of Ward 2, and David A. Bills of Ward 3. Filing date was from June 27th through July 11th, with the primary election to be held on September 9th.

In late June, at a special press conference, the formation of the Overthrust Industrial Association (O.I.A.) was announced, citing the desire *to be good neighbors and good citizens and of a benefit to the community.*

According to Robert Bizal, Amoco's western area director, the founding members of the O.I.A. were Amoco Production Company, Chevron U.S.A, Inc., and Champlin Petroleum Co., an affiliation of the U.P.R.R. The certificate of incorporation had been filed on June 24th with the Secretary of State. Bizal said, *Any company whose actions may have an impact on the Overthrust area will be eligible to join.* Members will be required "to commit" resources to assist the O.I.A. and the community.

Bizal said the O.I.A. would assist local governments in *maintaining the quality of life in the Overthrust area.* This would include assisting local communities in planning for energy-related growth before tax increases are realized, assisting local governmental units in meeting growth demands for public services, educating the public about the development of the Overthrust Belt and performing studies to collect data concerning the future growth of the communities.

The O.I.A. would be governed by a board of directors ranging from three to nine members, the size of the board to be determined by the number of companies belonging. The initial board would be A. M. Roney, Amoco production manager; Owen F. Murphy, Chevron public affairs manager; and Robert L. Gordon, Champlin employee relations district representative.

The City of Evanston and Uinta County were growing so fast, with more and more problems that just kept creeping up on us. The lack of revenues that were badly needed wasn't helping much. It seemed like the past several months Steve Snyder and I were going either to Cheyenne or Denver at least twice a month. We went together most of the time, but sometimes one of us would go alone. County Commissioner John Fanos also would travel with us at times, because there were problems in the county as well.

When we went to Cheyenne we would often meet with Governor Ed Herschler. When discussing our problems with him, he always seemed to be supportive of what we were trying to do. Of all the programs that we talked about with him, he always seemed to be 100% in favor and gave us a lot of support.

Most of the time when we went to Cheyenne, we would be there to meet with the Wyoming Highway Department, the Wyoming

Water Commission or the Wyoming Department of Environmental Quality (D.E.Q.). While there we would sometimes meet with Secretary of State Thyra Thompson. She also was a great supporter of Evanston and Uinta County.

Everyone in the state offices knew of the problems we were having, because most of the state was in a recession, like the rest of the country. We were overwhelmed by one of the biggest booms that the State of Wyoming had ever experienced, and everyone in Cheyenne knew that we were in a bad situation and in need of a lot of help, not only from the State of Wyoming, but also from the federal government, as well as the oil companies.

We made a lot of trips to Denver because that was where the Amoco and Chevron regional offices were, and after they formed the O.I.A., we had cause to go there even more: that was where the company that O.I.A. hired, The Denver Research Group, as consultants to help us through our mitigation plans.

Also, we had to travel to Omaha to meet with the Union Pacific Corporation companies once in a while, such as Upland Industries, the land company; Champlin Production, the oil and gas company; Rocky Mountain Energy, the mining company; and of course U.P.R.R., the railroad company of the corporation. They all played a big part in helping us with our problems. Over the years we gained a lot of property from the Union Pacific Corporation, which helped make Evanston an extraordinary community, a model community admired throughout the country.

I was absent during the first city council meeting on August 7th, because I was out of town meeting with those in Cheyenne or elsewhere trying to get some help. Councilman Rice was absent at the beginning of the meeting, but he came in later. Therefore the meeting was conducted by Council President Ron Davis.

During this meeting more ordinances came up for second and third readings, and resolutions pertaining to more annexations, right-of-way and easements, and additional requests for Industrial Development Revenue Bonds for constructing more facilities. All passed and were adopted by regular motion and seconded, with all voting in favor.

Bids for the purchase of the old town hall building were opened and read as follows: Bixland Corporation of Lafayette, California – $87,950, accompanied by a check in the amount of $10,000; and Ken Robison and Richard Sather of Evanston, Wyoming –$67,000, accompanied by a check in the amount of $6,700.

Motion was made by Councilman Albrecht to take this matter under advisement, seconded by Bills, with all voting in favor.

A bid in the amount of $107,760 from Parson Asphalt for resurfacing streets came up for acceptance. Motion was made by Councilman Bills to award the contract to the sole bidder pursuant to the terms and specifications being met, seconded by Megeath, with all voting in favor.

Ordinance 80-60 was introduced by Councilman Albrecht to vacate streets, alleys and roads located within the Uinta View Ranchettes Subdivision that were no longer in use. The streets, alleys and roads within the subdivision were described in the body of the ordinance. Motion was made to pass the ordinance and seconded, with all voting in favor.

The Uinta View Ranchettes Subdivision was owned by my brother, Bob Ottley, so if I had been present at this meeting I would have had to declare a conflict and excuse myself from the chambers, but luckily I was absent.

Ordinance 80-65 was introduced by Councilman Albrecht, authorizing a zone change, and Ordinance 80-66 was introduced by Councilman Bills, authorizing more land on the west end to be annexed. Ordinance 80-65 was passed on first reading by motion and seconded with all voting in favor, but Ordinance 80-66 was tabled until the next regular council meeting. Motion to table was made and seconded, with all voting in favor.

More ordinances, numbers 80-67, 80-68, and 80-69 were introduced. These ordinances authorized other subdivisions and some zone changes with all being properly passed by motion and seconded, all voting in favor on first reading.

A letter of resignation was read by Council President Davis from Elsie Crompton stating she was resigning from the Planning and

Zoning Commission. Motion was made to accept her resignation with a vote of thanks and commending her for her service, and was seconded with all voting in favor.

Before adjourning, Councilman Megeath made a motion for the mayor to have permission to appoint an assistant chief to the fire department, seconded by Bills, with all voting in favor.

A special city council meeting was held on August 14th to act on some ordinances that were pending so that construction could begin, especially Ordinance 80-40 vacating public land for the new Uinta Meadows Elementary School that was so badly needed.

Other ordinances that came up for second and third readings were all passed by regular motion, except Ordinances 80-48 and 80-51, both pertaining to the zoning of highway commercial (C-3), which failed on a 2 yes, 4 no vote and 1 absent (me), causing both ordinances to fail.

Ordinance 80-66 was introduced by Councilman Bills at the last meeting, but tabled for additional study. This ordinance pertained to the annexation of a parcel of land near the Centennial Valley Sub-division, which at this time was not in the city limits. There was a question of whether the land to be annexed was adjacent to the city. After the city engineer's inspection, it was found to be adjacent and eligible for annexation. Therefore, motion was made to pass 80-66 on first reading and was seconded with all voting in favor.

Resolution 80-42 was introduced by Councilman Albrecht. This resolution authorized the city to enter into a contract with Alexander Grant and Company to provide audit services to the City of Evanston, Evanston Joint Powers Board, Evanston Airport Board and the Evanston Parks and Recreation Board. Motion was made to adopt Resolution 80-42 and seconded, with all voting in favor.

Every year, by law, the City of Evanston and its boards had to be audited by a reputable accounting firm, and the city council had to introduce a resolution pertaining to that firm to do the audit. The cities and towns always, again by law, had to retain a balanced budget.

Other business to come up was that Councilman Albrecht made a motion to accept the high bid of $87,950 for the old town hall building from Bixland Corporation, seconded by Bills, with all voting in favor.

This was one of those issues that some of the locals didn't take a liking to and held it against me, as mayor, but the only other bid of $67,000 by a local group was more than $20,000 less than the high bid of $87,950. The council voted for the highest bid, which I too was in favor of, mainly because of the city's need of more finances, and it was in fairness to not only the high bidder, but also to the citizens of Evanston as well.

I believe some of the hardest and most controversial ordinances to act on for me and the city council members were the zoning and re-zoning ordinances. It didn't seem we could ever satisfy anyone; there were always those that were in opposition. Being on the city council during these years of fast growth was a tough time to be a council member. Anyone that ran for that position had to be either very patriotic or damn stupid, because the pay wasn't very good, but at least the mayor and council members would receive health insurance if they needed it. Some of the members were already getting insurance through their employer and didn't need the city insurance.

Speaking of zoning, the Downtown Improvement Corporation came up with a plan for the downtown zoning during their recent meeting. These plans would be acted on by the city as the various zones came up. Other business acted on was a motion from the Beautification Committee to suggest to the city council a change regarding the Cowboy Days celebration. The group proposed three alternate locations for booths. Instead of the old traditional area of downtown, the booths could be set up in the park next to the train depot, or the street section of Center to Main on 9th Street, or Center to Main on 10th Street. The evening dance could be in the parking lot next to the Uinta County Library, whose property at this time was only leased to the city from the railroad for certain purposes and would have to be checked whether or not it was allowed. This was still railroad property at the time.

The city council had discussed the possibility of removing all the parking meters in the downtown area and enforcing the two-hour parking ordinance, but at this downtown meeting there were objections to that idea. The city council was very concerned in saving the downtown area and we were available to listen to any groups with reasonable ideas.

According to an article in the August 16th issue of the *Uinta County Herald*, there were a lot of unsatisfied people in attendance at the Downtown Improvement Corporation meeting. The article said that other than zoning of the downtown area and the discussion of Cowboy Days, there was opposition to the removal of parking meters. One of the founders of the corporation said the removal of the parking meters was not the solution. Other small towns, he claimed, that had tried to enforce the two-hour parking limit had found enforcement difficult and time consuming.

However, we, the city council, were aware of the downtown problems. The parking was a big problem, we were very much aware of that, but a lot of it was caused by the merchants themselves. Some of their own employees would park in front of the stores.

The merchants needed to talk to them about where they should park, and the answer was not in front of another person's business. This wasn't just a city council problem. It was also a problem for the merchants as well. They had to also come up with solutions. The Evanston City Council had the entire community to worry about. The local paper reporting on the Downtown Improvement Corporation meeting said in the same article: One of the charter members of the corporation, Debbie Youngman, declared that the city had hired a traffic study by a Denver firm that had been deemed privileged information, and she had been denied access to it.

I personally don't recall this happening, but if it was true there must have been good reasons for not releasing it at that time. There's a possibility that it was because the city council hadn't even had a chance to look at it yet.

The article continued to say that the members expressed general dissatisfaction with the use of taxpayers' money for crowning of the streets. They indicated that it would have been better just to grade the streets rather than continuous crowning.

*If this board is going to survive we're going to have to go to these meetings of City Government and find out where our tax dollars are going,* Young-man stated.

It was well known that anyone was always welcome to any of the city council meetings or work sessions, and they could be put on the agenda any time they wished to discuss something with the council. Nobody was ever denied that opportunity, but that does not mean that the council would always agree with them. The council generally makes the final decision, and that decision is always based on what is best for the city overall, and not for any particular person or group.

My office was right up front in City Hall, and if anyone wanted to talk to me personally, I was generally very handy as long as I was in town. I would always visit with anyone that wanted to. Sharon Constantine, the receptionist and my secretary, was always there to set up appointments if necessary. My administration was very transparent and had never tried to hide anything from the public. Sometimes we might have held back information for a short period of time, but it would always be with good reason.

I recall a few years ago when I was a member of the city council, the subject of bribes came up. One of the previous council members made a statement that he had been offered a bribe many times (it was unknown if he accepted any of them). The rest of us looked at each other, wondering if he was telling us the truth or if maybe we just didn't know what a bribe looked like.

Well, I can tell you that in my 12 years as a councilman, I never knowingly was bribed by anyone. Someone might have bought me a lunch, a drink or gave me some little gadget to get on the best side of me, but no one ever offered me anything of value to do something for them…until earlier this year.

A local businessman owned some land with his partner on the west end near the city limits of Evanston. One day this man called me while I was at the mayor's office and asked me if I had time to go for a ride with him. About 15 minutes later he came into my office to get me. When we left the office we got in his truck and went for a ride. He drove out to a site which he and his partner owned and told me that they had signed an oil lease agreement on this property with Amoco Production Company Their lease was going to expire soon, and Amoco was going to have to apply for a drilling permit from the city soon and start drilling. If they didn't, they would lose their lease.

We sat and talked for a short while then started back to City Hall. On the way back I asked him what he expected me to do. He said he would like me to use my influence with the council to deny Amoco a permit at this time and delay giving them a permit until their lease ran out, at which time they would have to negotiate a new lease. He said that he and his partner would have the opportunity to negotiate a better deal for them from Amoco, and that they would make it right with me. This kind of took me aback, because I had never had anyone take me aside and talk to me about something like that. We were both pretty quiet at this time.

But after reaching City Hall we sat in the truck for a few minutes and I told him that there was no way I would do something like that. He indicated that there would be a good payoff to me, making it well worth my time, but we never got to a figure amount. I just told him that I wouldn't do something like that for myself or anyone else. His last remark to me was, *Well, Mayor, you'll never get rich that way.* My last comment to him was, *Well, I had never planned on being rich in the first place, especially by accepting bribes like that.* It shook me up so badly that I just slammed the truck door and walked back to my office, not saying a word about what happened to anyone. This was the first time I had ever been approached with what I knew damn well was a bribe, and I didn't appreciate it one bit. I was Mayor of Evanston for another 10 years with a four-year break, and never had that happen again.

The second city council meeting for the month was on August 21st with, once again, a full agenda. The big items on the agenda were the several ordinances that were up for second and third readings, and several more that were introduced.

All the ordinances that were up for second and third readings were passed by motion and seconded, with all voting in favor. There were no objections to any of them.

But Ordinance 80-48 was brought back on the floor to be reconsidered on second reading. Motion was made for passage on second reading and seconded with 6 yes votes and 1 no vote. The motion passed by a majority vote.

Ordinance 80-48 had failed earlier. It described property along Wyoming State Highway 150 to be zoned highway commercial (C-3). This property was located across from Aspen Grove I and II, areas considered to be high-value residential areas, and the zoning proposal had been heavily opposed by residents of the two subdivisions.

A presentation and discussion in favor of the ordinance was made by James Phillips, Attorney, representing the Broken Circle Cattle Company, owners of the property along Highway 150. After a general discussion, the motion to pass Ordinance 80-48 on second reading was made and seconded. The motion passed by a majority with a vote of 6 yes and 1 no.

Also, the motion to reconsider Ordinance 80-51 was made, which had also failed earlier. It was seconded with a 6 yes votes and 1 no vote. The motion passed by a majority.

Ordinance 80-51 also pertained to property owned by Broken Circle Cattle Company, located along State Highway 150, and had also met with a lot of opposition from the residents of Aspen Grove I and II.

The motion was made to pass Ordinance 80-51 on second reading and was seconded again with 6 yes votes and 1 no vote, with the motion passing by a majority.

During the meeting there were six new ordinances introduced. Ordinance 80-61 was introduced by Councilman Fruits, providing that fire hydrants in subdivisions and mobile home parks must be purchased by the subdivider from the City of Evanston, and providing for subdividers to also purchase street signs under the direction of the city engineer. Motion was made to pass on first reading and seconded with all voting in favor.

Ordinance 80-62 providing for two industrial zones, light industrial (L-I) zone and heavy industrial (H-I) zone, was introduced by Councilman Albrecht. After several proposed amendments were considered, a motion was made to table Ordinance 80-62 until the second regular meeting in September and was seconded. Motion passed by a majority with 4 yes votes, 2 no votes and 1 abstaining.

Ordinance 80-63, adopting the uniform fire code, was introduced by Councilman Davis. Motion was made to pass on first reading and seconded, with all voting in favor.

Ordinance 80-64, setting the procedure for the establishment of Planned Unit Developments, was introduced by Councilman Davis. Motion was made to pass on first reading and was seconded with all voting in favor.

Ordinance 80-70, providing for regulations of home occupations and deleting home occupations as permitted uses in certain areas was introduced by Councilman Albrecht. Motion was made to pass on first reading and seconded, with all voting in favor.

Ordinance 80-71, approving the Evanston Heights Addition, was introduced by Councilman Bills. Motion was made to pass on first reading, with all voting in favor.

In other business, I read a letter of resignation from Dale Davenport of the Planning and Zoning Commission. Councilman Bills made the motion to accept with a vote of thanks, seconded by Fruits, with all voting in favor.

At this time I appointed Jon M. Lunsford as Assistant Fire Chief and as a full-time employee. He would be one of the very few full-time employees of the fire department. Motion was made by Councilman Fruits to confirm the appointment, seconded by Albrecht, with 5 yes votes and 1 no vote, motion passed.

I also appointed Dan Christen to the police department as an officer. Councilman Fruits made the motion to confirm, seconded by Bills, with all voting in favor.

After a general discussion concerning street lighting, traffic control, Yellow Creek sidewalks, a heliport, stop signs, garbage ordinance and other items, the meeting was adjourned at 11:00 p.m.

During the first monthly city council meeting held on September 4th, there were two ordinances that came up for third and final readings. They were Ordinance 80-37, providing for two Residential

Subdivision (RS-1) and (RS-2) zones, and Ordinance 80-46, defining mobile home parks and establishing requirements for them.

Both of these ordinances had been passed previously on first and second readings with all voting in favor, but Councilman Bills, for some reason I don't recall, made a motion to table these two ordinances, seconded by Fruits, with all voting in favor to table.

The only reason I can imagine for tabling the two ordinances was either to give the council or someone else more time to look into the ordinances, or to see what other ordinances pertaining to zone changes were coming up in the future. They might come off the table at a later date for the third reading if council moves to bring them up again.

Next, the very controversial Ordinance 80-48 came up for the third and final hearing. Mr. James Phillips, the attorney representing the Broken Circle Cattle Company property owners, presented an outline usage proposal and plat of suggesting buildings for a shopping center to be named "Winterwood."

Judy Hatch, a supporter of the ordinance, presented a petition in favor of the C-3 zone, while Stephen Feingold, Fred Zeigler, Dr. James Morse and Conrad Michaelson voiced their opinions in opposition to the C-3 zone.

Gary Coles and Leonard Cook, representing the downtown area, each made presentations explaining how additional commercial zones throughout the city would negatively affect the already depressed downtown area.

In the *Uinta County Herald* issue of September 9th was a Letter to the Editor from Dr. James A. Morse. The letter was quite lengthy but part of his letter said, *"I have pointed out to the City Council that if another major shopping center is allowed in the area, the drain from downtown Evanston will be tremendous, essentially neglecting that area. It is my feeling that the time, energy, and money being spent for this effort could much better be used to alleviate the problems of downtown Evanston so as to preserve that already established commercial area."*

Well, the letter was all well and good and was discussed during the meeting, but I made it clear to the council and those present that the downtown area was not the only area in Evanston that we were having trouble with. We were very concerned with the future of the downtown area, and we were in the process of doing what we could to keep the downtown area active as the heart of the city.

However, it was not the place of the city council to try to control competition. We don't do it in the housing industry and we shouldn't do it in the commercial/business industry. But it is our job to make sure the city is properly zoned and we should look at every ordinance that may have an effect on the city very closely to do what we could to help the entire community.

I said that I could understand why Dr. Morse was concerned about the zone change because he resides in Aspen Grove II and the change could affect his neighborhood and possibly the value of his house, but I also pointed out that Highway 150 was a state highway and the frontage should be considered to be highway commercial (C-3); but that was up to this council and I would go along with however they decide.

The discussion continued until I asked the council members if they would like to respond or if they had any more questions. Councilmembers Albrecht and Megeath responded with a few words, but then I called for a ten-minute recess and told everyone that we would bring up Ordinance 80-48 again for discussion later in the evening.

To get some of our other business taken care of we opened the bids concerning the sidewalks under the Yellow Creek Road underpass. The bids were opened as follows: Harold Newland ............... ........................................................................................ ...... $19,777.........Clegg Construction ................................... ..................................................................... $20,919

Councilman Fruits made a motion to award the bid to the low bidder, seconded by Bills, with 6 yes votes and 1 no vote. The motion passed by a majority vote, but I don't recall who the dissenting vote was or why.

Ordinance 80-66 came up for third and final reading, but was tabled by a motion made by Councilman Fruits, seconded by Megeath, with 5 yes and 2 no votes. The motion to table passed by a majority.

Other bids were opened for new vehicles of different types, such as police cars, dump trucks and heavy equipment vehicles. Motions were made and seconded to award all bids to the low bidders, providing all bids met the proper specifications. All voted in favor.

At this time I opened the floor back up for more discussion on Ordinance 80-48. After a short discussion Councilman Megeath made a motion to table Ordinance 80-48 until the September 18th city council meeting, seconded by Bills, with all voting in favor.

Ordinance 80-72, authorizing a zone change from Family Residential (R-3) zone to Highway Commercial (C-3), was introduced by Councilman Megeath. A motion was made to pass Ordinance 80-72 on first reading and seconded. It was defeated with 6 no votes to 1 yes.

John Leiber, from Wyoming Job Service, with the support of Bert Roberge, Evanston Chamber of Commerce Executive, approached the city council requesting assistance in locating some land or an office area for the agency. Roberge said that they would like it to be in Evanston. The council wholeheartedly agreed, and offered the possibility of some land in the 40-acre parcel the city was in the process of purchasing. However, the Wyoming Job Service did not want to wait that long and decided to purchase a lot in the Centennial Valley area on Wasatch Drive and build an office building there.

Resolution 80-44 was introduced to pay $6,000 this fiscal year to the Evanston Chamber of Commerce for the services they provided to the city. A motion was made and seconded to table this resolution until the November 6th city council meeting. The motion to table passed by a majority with 5 yes and 2 no votes. However, later in the meeting, Councilman Bills made a motion to reconsider Resolution 80-44, seconded by Fruits, with 6 yes votes and 1 no, with the motion passing by a majority. Then motion was made by Bills, seconded by Albrecht, to adopt the resolution with all voting in favor.

I then appointed Tuffy Liverman to the Evanston Planning and Zoning Commission to replace Dale Davenport who had recently resigned. Motion was made to confirm this appointment and seconded, with all voting in favor.

The council also accepted the resignation of Kevin VanSyoc as Animal Control Officer. Motion was made to accept his resignation with a vote of thanks for the service he rendered to the city. Motion was seconded with all voting in favor.

Councilman Fruits made a motion that "No Truck Traffic" signs be installed on Main Street from 6th Street through 12th Street, seconded by Davis, with all voting in favor.

Councilman Albrecht made a motion to change the two city council meetings in October. He moved that the first meeting would be on October 9th, and the second meeting on October 23rd. It was seconded by Bills with all voting in favor. Why this was necessary I don't recall!

Before adjourning, Councilman Albrecht made a motion to authorize the mayor to make application for the Women's Correctional Center to stay located in Evanston. The Women's Center had been at the Wyoming State Hospital for the past few years until they could come up with a better location.

Although I did apply to keep the center in Evanston with Steve Snyder's help, the State of Wyoming selected Lusk, Wyoming as the location. At the time, Lusk was facing some pretty depressed and disheartening times and needed the boost in their community to help get their economy moving. I told the council that I thought the state did the right thing, and that I didn't feel too bad about not getting to keep the center in Evanston.

This meeting adjourned at 12:05 a.m. of the next day, another lengthy meeting.

The second city council meeting of September was held on the 18th with another full agenda. Ordinance 80-48 and 80-51, both very controversial, concerning the zoning of Highway 150 to a commercial zone (C-3), came up early in the evening for the third and final reading. A group of people were in attendance, both pro and con. The folks from Aspen Grove I and II subdivisions were in attendance again to express their opposition to the two ordinances, because the area in question was directly across the highway from their homes. The Broken Circle folks, owners of the property to be zoned, and their attorney, James Phillips, were also in attendance, speaking in favor of the two ordinances.

With respect to the group and thinking there might be something new to come up I opened the floor for more discussion, but told them that I would be limiting the time of debate, because both of these ordinances had already been passed on first and second readings, at which times we had already heard all the pros and cons. Also, we had a large agenda this evening and we didn't want to be there all night.

So when I opened the floor for discussion I did give those that wanted to say something the opportunity to speak their mind, but it was all the same old stuff on both sides. Therefore, thinking we had heard enough of the same, I ended the debate and called for a motion from the council.

Councilman Davis made the first motion to pass Ordinance 80-48 on third and final reading, seconded by Albrecht, with 5 yes votes and 2 no votes. The motion passed by a majority vote.

Councilman Rice made the second motion to pass Ordinance 80-51 on third and final reading, seconded by Albrecht, with 5 yes votes and 2 no votes. The motion passed by a majority vote.

Was I ever glad to get rid of those two ordinances! I thought they couldn't get more controversial than that, but unfortunately they did. We would have several ordinances later on that would be just as controversial, or maybe even more so.

More ordinances came up for second and third readings with all voting in favor, except Ordinance 80-66, annexing land just west of the city owned by Kindler and Associates. It passed on third and final reading by 6 yes votes to 1 no vote, passing by a majority.

Ordinance 80-73, dedicating property for a city street, was introduced by Councilman Bills. It was requested to be passed as an emergency, because it was a street already being used, and was named Incline Drive. Motion was made by Councilman Albrecht to pass Ordinance 80-73 on an emergency basis, seconded by Fruits, with 5 yes votes and 1 no vote. Motion passed by a majority.

Councilman Albrecht introduced Resolution 80-46, authorizing the city to sell the old town hall property to Eugene C. Harter, senior partner of Bixland Corporation, for the total purchase price of $87,950. Motion was made for the adoption of Resolution 80-46 and seconded with all voting in favor.

Inducement Resolution 80-45 and Ordinance 80-74, providing the issuance and sale of Industrial Development Revenue Bonds for Esse International, Inc., were both properly introduced with motion made and seconded, with both passing by a majority vote. Ordinance 80-74 went on to pass on second and third readings by a majority vote.

Resolution 80-47 was introduced by Councilman Bills, authorizing the city to purchase property from Dean F. Richins and Alice L. Richins for the purchase of 3.2 acres at a price of $32,000 per acre. Motion was made in favor of the purchase and seconded, with all voting in favor. This was the property that the city used for the Evanston Child Development Center (E.C.D.C.) day care center, because there was such a large demand for child care services. E.C.D.C. was a non-profit organization of the City of Evanston and is still in operation, now located on 3rd Street.

At this time I appointed Michael Pryor to the police department. Motion was made by Fruits to confirm the appointment, seconded by Bills, with all voting in favor.

After a short discussion of other matters we adjourned this meeting at 12:05 a.m. on September 19th.

During our October 9th city council meeting, Mr. Pat O'Hara made a presentation concerning the future of the underpass. He really didn't tell us any more than what we already knew, but he was concerned because his business was near the underpass. Coming through the underpass going north or east, it was located just before you got to the Jolly Roger Restaurant. So he had a right to be concerned and had a right to present any suggestions he might have.

The underpass traffic got worse after the man-camps were built for the construction of the two processing plants that Amoco and Chevron were building. When plant workers got off work, even though most lived at the camps, many would come into town for banking purposes, or to frequent the bars, cafés, and so on. They would often cause the traffic to be backed up on Highway 89 (County Road) back beyond the city limits, causing real problems for those coming from the east on Bear River Drive.

Paydays were the worst because with only two banks, First National and First Wyoming, the bank drive-through windows were so crowded that the cars waiting to cash their pay checks or make a deposit would cause the traffic to back up for blocks. We did have a savings and loan company on the corner of 9th and Main Streets where U.S. Bank is now located, but it didn't have a drive-through, if I remember right.

It would be another three or four years before we would get the overpass completed, causing the city council to take a serious look at the possibility of one-way streets in the downtown area, as well as removing the parking meters. We weren't sure one-way streets would help much, but it could be worth a try. The studies suggested that it would help move the traffic a little faster if we did it right.

During the October meeting I read a letter from Larry Lehman, County Attorney, concerning a response from his Assistant County Attorney, Doug McCalla, who wanted bar owners to be more responsible for the discipline of their own patrons.

I read this letter during the meeting when most liquor dealers were present because the liquor licenses were up for renewal, which happens every year during the first council meeting of October. After a short discussion with the dealers on how they would discipline their patrons, they assured us that they would do whatever was necessary to control any problems. I told them that we were very much aware of their problems, but didn't want to see anyone hurt, including our police officers.

Motions were made separately by the council members to approve all licenses, and seconded with all voting in favor, with the exception of two license holders.

Councilman Fruits made the motion to approve the license for the Bonneville Development Corporation, doing business as the Ramada Inn, seconded by Albrecht, but before the vote Councilman Rice made a motion to amend the main motion for approval putting them on probation; but the amendment died for lack of a second. Voting on the main motion to approve their application was passed with 6 yes votes to 1 no vote. But this did give them the warning that they had to control their patrons better and respect the laws of the Liquor Commission. There had been several problems reported on the Ramada Inn bar, including a shooting. This made the council very concerned and a little hesitant in renewing their license.

The other exception was a motion made by Councilman Megeath, seconded by Fruits, to approve the application of Uinta Investment doing business as Pink Elephant, but again before the vote, Councilman Bills offered an amendment to also have this license put on probation, seconded by Davis, with 5 yes votes and 2 no votes; the motion to amend passed. All voted in favor on the main motion as amended, putting the Pink Elephant on probation. This probation would be effective until the next year when the license came up for renewal. We had also had a lot of police calls on the Pink Elephant over the past several months, but this would give them a good warning.

More ordinances came up for second and third readings with all passing, except Ordinance 80-81, an ordinance changing a Single Family Residential (R-2) zone to Highway Commercial (C-3) zone, failed with 6 no votes.

Ordinances 80-76, 80-78, 80-79, 80-80, 80-82, 80-83 and 80-84 were all properly introduced by the council members, authorizing zone changes, dedicating and describing property as a street, establishing off-street parking regulations, and requiring access to mobile home units from public and private roads. Each ordinance was separately passed by motion on various readings and seconded with all voting in favor. All went on to be passed on second and third readings later, with all voting in favor.

There were five resolutions, all introduced by Councilman Bills, during the meeting: Resolution 80-50, authorizing the city to pay LUAG a sum of $7,000 this fiscal year for services rendered; Resolution 80-51, authorizing the city to pay Western Wyoming Mental Health Centers, Uinta Clinic a sum of $8,000 this fiscal year for services rendered; Resolution 80-52, authorizing the city to pay Uinta Senior Citizens, Inc. a sum of $12,000 this fiscal year for services rendered; Resolution 80-53, authorizing the city to enter into a lease agreement with the Board of County Commissioners of Uinta County to lease space for the Evanston Police Department and Police Judge in the new Public Safety Building and Courthouse annex of Uinta County; and Resolution 80-54, authorizing the city to enter into a memorandum of agreement to the Uinta County Library Foundation for the city to pay a sum of $5,000 this fiscal year for services rendered. All resolutions were adopted by motion and seconded, with all voting in favor.

Also introduced by Councilman Bills was Resolution 80-55:

> A RESOLUTION AUTHORIZING AND DIRECTING THE MAYOR OF THE CITY OF EVANSTON TO ISSUE AND SIGN A PROCLAMATION FOR A HIGHWAY ELECTION FOR THE RELOCATION OF U.S. HIGHWAY 30 AND WYOMING HIGHWAY 89 IN THE CITY OF EVANSTON TO BE HELD IN CONJUNCTION WITH THE GENERAL ELECTION TO BE HELD ON NOVEMBER 4, 1980.

With very little discussion, Councilman Albrecht made the motion to adopt Resolution 80-55, seconded by Bills, with all voting in favor.

Also, applications were prepared on October 23rd by the city and county to request financial assistance from the Wyoming Farm Loan Board for the improvement and creation of new roads within the city of Evanston.

I applied for financial assistance to fund the construction and improvements for routing Wyoming State Highway 150 through to Yellow Creek Road. County Commissioner John Fanos would apply for funds to build Overthrust Road from Interstate 80 to the intersection meeting Yellow Creek Road. Amoco Oil Company would also furnish funding for Overthrust Road and Yellow Creek Road to the East Anschultz Plant.

Councilman Fruits made a motion that after receiving approval of these applications from the Wyoming Farm Loan Board, the first priority should be given to Overthrust Road, seconded by Bills, with all voting in favor.

The purpose of this motion was to get Overthrust Road completed so the city could get the heavy oil field truck traffic off 6th and Lombard Streets. These were the only routes at the time to get to the East Anschultz Gas Plant. The heavy traffic was starting to put a lot of wear and tear on the two streets and the neighbors were getting concerned.

City Engineer Wayne Shepherd reported that the streets in subdivisions Aspen Grove III and Sunset Industrial Park did not meet the proper city specifications and suggested that the subdividers be required to bring them up to standard. Councilman Bills made a motion to accept the city engineer's recommendation to require the streets in the two subdivisions be brought up to meet city specifications, seconded by Albrecht, with 4 yes votes and 1 no vote. The motion passed by a majority.

Because everything moved so fast during these boom times, the city was concerned that all building and construction meet the city's specifications. We knew that if we didn't insist, the city would have to repair a lot of damage in the future at the city's expense, which did happen a few years later with a subdivision that was later annexed. It turned out to be a very expensive situation.

Councilman Megeath submitted a letter of resignation to the city which I read to the council. The letter indicated that he was moving out of Ward 1, the ward that he was representing as a council member. During a short discussion with him, he told the council that he was moving to Ward 2 and therefore had to resign. Councilman Bills then made the motion to accept his resignation with deep regret and wished him well, seconded by Albrecht with all voting in favor.

Following Megeath's resignation I suggested that we appoint Jerrilynn "Jerry" Wall to complete the term in office, which would expire at the end of 1982. I told the council that Wall had shown interest in running and she deserved the opportunity to serve. Therefore,

Councilman Fruits made a motion to appoint Jerry Wall to fill the unexpired term of Councilman Megeath, seconded by Bills, with all voting in favor.

I made the statement at that time, *If I'm not mistaken, I believe Jerry will be the first woman to ever serve on the Evanston City Council.* Nobody questioned me on that.

This meeting finally adjourned, by regular motion at 1:05 a.m. the next morning. It was another long meeting, but very interesting, and we got things taken care of.

For some reason or other, we changed the second city council meeting of October to take place on the 21st rather than the 23rd, which was when it was called for, and the meeting would start at 12:15 p.m. during that day.

Councilman Jimmie Rice, Administrative Assistant Steve Snyder and the newly appointed City Councilmember, Jerry Wall were all excused, leaving only four members of the council and myself in attendance, but a quorum was declared and the meeting was called to order. One of the first orders of business was the introduction of Resolution 80-56 by Councilman Albrecht. This resolution agreed to issue Industrial Development Revenue Bonds to finance a project for Wyoming General Partnership #1. The motion to adopt Resolution 80-56 was made and seconded, with all voting in favor.

Ordinance 80-74 provided for the issuance and sale of Industrial Development Revenue Bonds to Esse International, Inc., for construction of their project. Motion was made to pass Ordinance 80-74 as amended on first reading and seconded, with all voting in favor.

After a short discussion concerning other city business, the meeting adjourned at 1:05 p.m. making it a very short meeting.

During the regular city council meeting held on November 6th, the first order of business was administering the Oath of Office to the newly appointed city council member, Jerrilynn "Jerry" Wall and having her sign the oath. The council members and I then congratulated her and welcomed her as a member of the Evanston City Council.

Councilman Jimmie Rice, representing Ward 2, did not run for re-election, but Arnold Morgan, who was elected as Councilman representing Ward 2 in place of Rice was in attendance. I congratulated him for winning and extended a welcome to him on behalf of the council as Councilman-elect. He wouldn't be sworn in until the first meeting in January, 1981.

The other two council members that were up for re-election this year were Councilmen Albrecht and Bills, with both successful in getting re-elected. They were elected to the council for another four-year term.

This was also a Presidential election year, and Ronald Reagan was elected over President Jimmy Carter. President Carter put the United States in a big recession leaving the entire country very depressed. This was one reason the Evanston area was having such a difficult time; it was the only area in the country that wasn't in a recession, and everyone was coming to our community for jobs.

In January Ronald Reagan would take office as President of the United States, and the entire country was hoping that he could bring the country out of the big mess that Jimmy Carter had left it in.

Ordinance 80-75, approving the Grass Valley Mobile Home Court Subdivision, and Ordinances 80-80, 80-82 and 80-83 came up for third and final readings. With very little discussion they all passed by regular motion and were seconded, with all voting in favor.

Resolution 80-57 was introduced by Councilman Bills, authorizing the city to pay $4,000 to the Evanston Housing Authority to cover expenses of organization and grant applications. Motion was made by Bills to adopt Resolution 80-57, seconded by Wall, with all voting in favor.

Resolution 80-59 was introduced by Councilman Davis, adopting a deferred compensation plan for the employees of the City of Evanston. Motion was made and seconded with all voting in favor. This was a retirement program requiring the employees to apply no less than 10% of their total earnings to the plan, thereby giving them something for when they retired or discontinued working for the city, at which time they could immediately withdraw whatever amount was in their account without further ado. By passing Resolution 80-59, the city council automatically appointed the following to serve as the Committee for the City of Evanston Public Employees

Deferred Compensation Plan: Mayor; City Attorney; City Clerk; City Treasurer. The Administrative Assistant and City Treasurer were appointed as administrators of the plan.

Ordinance 80-85 was introduced by Councilman Bills, providing that the city council would have two regular meetings per month on the first and third Wednesday of each month. We had been having two meetings per month, but they were on Thursdays. This ordinance only changed the day of the meetings. However, there was a motion by Councilman Fruits to table Ordinance 80-85 to a later date, seconded by Albrecht, with 5 yes votes, 1 no vote and one absent, with the motion carried by a majority.

Ordinance 80-86, authorizing the issuance of more Industrial Development Revenue Bonds for a wholesale and retail lumber yard with related facilities, was introduced by Councilman Fruits. This ordinance was pushed by a few builders and contractors because they were tired of having to go to Utah for supplies. However, there was a lumber yard already in Evanston, the Bear River Lumber Company, but I didn't know how well they did with contractors in keeping them supplied and how their prices compared.

The city council thought by passing this ordinance it would help keep money in Evanston. Therefore, motion was made to pass Ordinance 80-86 on first reading and was seconded with all voting in favor. This ordinance went on to pass on second and third readings with all voting in favor.

Ordinance 80-88, regulating the erection, alteration, repair, construction, location and maintenance of awnings, was introduced by Councilman Albrecht. Defined as a fixed or retractable awning, a fixed awning would be a roof type structure supported by a frame or bracketing extending outward from the face of a building and constructed so as to shelter or shade the sidewalk. This ordinance was a request from several downtown merchants for the purpose of extending covers over sidewalks. After introduction and reading of the title, a motion to pass the ordinance on first reading was made and seconded with all voting in favor. The ordinance went on to be passed on second and third readings with all voting in favor.

This was the ordinance that Mr. John Deru was waiting for so that he could construct the overhang covering the sidewalk to give his building the western look. That structure is still in place over the Main Street Deli Restaurant.

A public hearing was held pertaining to unanticipated revenue. This hearing was recorded and the recorded tape would be on file at City Hall.

Following the closing of the hearing, Councilman Albrecht introduced Resolution 80-63 providing for the disbursement of unanticipated revenue funds, totaling $275,178.80. The dispersing of the funds was itemized in the body of the resolution. Motion to adopt Resolution 80-63 was made and seconded, with all voting in favor.

Resolution 80-64 was introduced by Councilman Albrecht, a resolution directing the mayor and city clerk to apply to the Wyoming Farm Loan Board for a mineral royalties grant for water system improvements. Motion to adopt the resolution was made and seconded, with all voting in favor.

Prior to adjourning I spoke of the recent election concerning the routes of the new overpass and Wyoming State Highway 89, which were on the ballot. I stated that the election was overwhelmingly in favor of the route. The news of the election was good, but it would be a few years before it would be constructed.

I also made the announcement that the applications sent in by the city and county for financial assistance for the designated roads had both been approved by the Wyoming Farm Loan Board. I told the council that we could get these projects underway immediately and get that heavy oil field traffic off 6th and Lombard Streets.

With this state assistance we would be able to create a route from Yellow Creek Road to Wyoming Highway 150 without having to go through 6th Street to Front Street. By constructing and improving the roads now known as Southridge Road, Saddle Ridge Road, City View Road and Cheyenne Drive, it improved traffic going to their destinations or homes in the newer subdivisions on the south side of Interstate 80.

Also, I told the council, *Thanks to John Fanos and his commission, in-cluding Commissioners Dan South and Clark Anderson, for their assistance in applying for a grant for the construction of the Overthrust Road. This will be a blessing to those folks living on 6th Street and Lombard.* The county commissioners were all very helpful, but Fanos, who was Chairman of the County Commission, was most instrumental in working closely with the City of Evanston and me in resolving a lot of our problems.

It was noted in a *Uinta County Herald* issue that month that Mountain Fuel Supply Company (presently Questar Gas), which was heavily involved in the exploration of the Overthrust discovery, stated through one of their top officials, *"The Evanston-area residents are living over one of the world's largest oil and gas regions—the Overthrust Belt of southwestern Wyoming and northeastern Utah."*

He continued, *"It is this region and the flurry of exploration being conducted over it that is causing 'boomtown' growth for Evanston and the rest of the area."*

This was something we already knew, but it was always nice to hear it from one of the companies that was directly benefiting from it. Mountain Fuel Supply was also one of the top companies giving Evanston assistance in trying to keep up with the problems caused by the boom.

Prior to adjourning, I read a letter of resignation from Jerry Wall, a member of the Evanston Parks Board. Motion was made by Fruits to accept Wall's resignation, seconded by Bills, with all voting in favor. Wall was resigning from the board because she was now on the city council.

Also, Councilman Bills made a motion to hold only one meeting in December, on the 11th at 7:00 p.m. at City Hall. The motion was seconded with all voting in favor.

During the second city council meeting on November 20th we acted on many more ordinances that were pending for final passage, as well as a few resolutions that were introduced.

Bids for a Deferred Compensation Plan were opened and acknowledged as follows:

Aetna – Sonny Blakeslee of Uinta Title and Insurance Company; New England Mutual Life – Larry Hoffman; Wyoming Benefits,

Inc. – State of Wyoming; Pacific Mutual Life – Larry Hoffman; and Washington National Insurance Company – Dale Christensen. It was suggested that these bids be turned over to the recently appointed Evanston Insurance Committee for their recommendations.

Margaret Russell, representing Upland Industries, the land company of the U.P.R.R., presented a preliminary plat of a Commercial and Industrial Park on their property on Front Street. A lengthy discussion followed, Russell was informed by the city attorney of the steps to be taken to request a subdivision and that zoning could be involved, but no other action was taken at this time.

Ordinance 80-89, authorizing a zone change from Single Family Residential (R-2) zone to Central Business District (C-1) zone, was introduced by Councilman Davis, as requested by Frank Richards, Jr., Grant McFarlane, and Debbie Youngman. There was a lot of opposition in attendance causing a lengthy discussion, but a motion was made to pass Ordinance 80-89 on first reading and was seconded. The motion failed by 1 yes vote and 5 no votes.

Ordinance 80-90, authorizing a zone change from Single Family Residential (R-2) zone to Central Business District (C-1), was introduced by Councilman Bills, as requested by the City of Evanston. The motion to pass Ordinance 80-90 on first reading was made and seconded. The motion failed by a vote of 5 no votes and 1 abstaining.

We had a number of ordinances requesting residential zone changes to business zoning all over town, but most of them failed. It was becoming a big issue, and the council was trying hard to look at each request with an open mind and how it would affect the future. But a lot of folks, for and against, would get upset, and either way the council went, we made enemies. But I guess that came with the job of being a mayor or a council member.

Before adjournment I appointed Joe Loftin to the Parks and Recreation Board to replace Councilmember Jerry Wall. Motion was made by Councilwoman Wall to confirm the appointment of Loftin, seconded by Bills, with all voting in favor.

Finally, Stephen Feingold was recommended by Councilman Bills to be appointed to the Planning and Zoning Commission, but knowing Mr. Feingold, I suspected that the appointment would never be accepted by the council. Mr. Feingold was building a house in the Aspen Groves II Subdivision area and he did not seem to want to comply with any planning and zoning regulations. But out of respect for Councilman Bills and Mr. Feingold, I made the appointment and called for a vote to confirm. Motion was made by Bills to confirm the appointment, and seconded by Davis. The motion failed by 3 no votes to 1 yes vote, 1 abstaining and 1 absent.

This meeting adjourned at 1:05 a.m. by regular motion, another long and lengthy meeting. Sometimes some of us would go up to the Flying J restaurant after these late meetings and sit and talk over a cup of coffee or something to eat just to relax a bit. Being able to visit a little and relax felt good after a long, late meeting.

The November 15th issue of the *Uinta County Herald* headlined with OVERTHRUST ESTIMATE IS BOOSTED. The article went on to say; *James W. Vanderbeek, Vice President and Regional Manager of the Standard Oil Company (Indiana) subsidiary [of Amoco Production Company], predicted Tuesday that the promising Overthrust Belt area along the border between Wyoming and Utah (The Evanston area) may contain as much as 25 percent more oil and gas than forecast just a few months ago.*

Vanderbeek said the area's *"discovered potential reserves"* may total 9.7 trillion cubic feet of natural gas and the equivalent of 914 million 42-gallon barrels of crude oil.

Because of reports such as Vanderbeek made and the fact that the oil companies had been telling us all along that the drilling and the production of the Overthrust was here to stay for at least 25 years, in our planning we knew we should be looking at a population as high as 25,000. This was the main reason we planned our new sewer plant to be able to take care of a population of 30,000 people.

We also were planning our new water system by enlarging the Sulfur Creek Reservoir and enlarging the outlet from Bear River to furnish the city with enough water to take care of a population of 25,000 to 30,000, and get away from the city water wells that were all either petering out or getting contaminated.

However, we had recently drilled three more new water wells and requested a $2,000,000 grant from the Wyoming Farm Loan Board to upgrade our present water plant and portions of our water system.

When election results were announced regarding the new overpass and new route for Highway 89, there was a lot of criticism from a number of people, and not just those who lived on 6th Street. There were Letters to the Editor and letters addressed to me, as mayor, mostly anonymous, telling me that "Ottley's Folly," as some named it, *was a stupid thing to do and that the kind of money spent on the folly could be spent in a better way.* I said to the council, *It's amazing how much criticism you get and how many experts you find your community has when you are making changes and trying to build a better community.* They agreed.

One letter suggested that we needed an off/on ramp from Interstate 80 at the Wyoming State Highway 150 location, but what that person didn't know was that the city had already presented that to the Wyoming Highway Commission and that they had agreed to it, but it couldn't be constructed until funds were available.

The Wyoming Highway Commission and The Wyoming Highway Department, mainly Leno Menghini, superintendent of the department and Dave Nelson, former mayor of Kemmerer and a member of the commission, were most helpful in getting the financial assistance in making Evanston roads better.

At our regular city council meeting of December 11th, the last meeting of 1980, we passed on the third and final reading Ordinance 80-76, to establish off-street parking regulations; Ordinance 80-84, dedicating property as a city street; Ordinance 80-87, allowing mini-warehouses as a permitted use in Light Industrial (L-1) zones, Commercial (C-2, C-3) zones and Heavy Industrial (H-I) zones by a Conditional Use Permit; Ordinance 80-88, regulating the erection of awnings within the city; and Ordinance 80-86, authorizing the issuance and sale of Industrial Development Revenue Bonds for the construction of a wholesale and retail lumberyard. All these ordinances passed on third and final reading by regular motion and were seconded with all voting in favor. Other ordinances were passed on second reading with all voting in favor.

More resolutions were introduced and adopted concerning more Industrial Development Revenue Bonds; entering into agreement with the Wyoming Highway Commission concerning the relocation of Highway 89; and the vacating of a portion of 14th Street between Clark School and Anderson Park. This was to connect the school grounds with the park to keep the school kids safe from traffic on that portion of 14th Street.

Letters of resignation by Elsie Crompton and Gerald (Jerry) Cazin were read and accepted with a thank you to both for their time of service on the Planning and Zoning Commission.

I appointed Conrad Michaelson to the Planning and Zoning Commission to fill the unexpired term of Elsie Crompton, which would expire in January, 1982. Councilman Bills made the motion to confirm the appointment, seconded by Fruits, with all voting in favor. However, the position held by Cazin was not filled during this meeting. It would be done at a later date.

Councilman Fruits made a motion to give all full-time employees a one-time cost-of-living increase for the month of December in the amount of $50.00 per employee, seconded by Bills, with all voting in favor. The idea was to consider the $50.00 as a year-end bonus, which they would receive during the Christmas dinner. It was the council and mayor's way of thanking them for their hard work and cooperation the past year and wishing them a very Merry Christmas.

Councilman Bills made a motion for the mayor, city engineer, city attorney and himself to form a committee to secure an engineering firm to do the work on the Improvement District for Aspen Groves I and II, seconded by Fruits, with all voting in favor.

Councilman Bills made a motion to hold a second meeting in December. It would be held at the Three Knights Restaurant on December 13th. The motion was seconded by Rice, with all voting in favor. This meeting would actually be the annual Christmas Dinner with all city officials, employees and spouses invited. It would be a cash bar but the city would host the dinner.

After a general discussion concerning this past year's achievements, future problems, and next year's appointments, the meeting adjourned at 11:30 p.m.

The *Casper Star-Tribune* came out with two or three articles in their December 30th issue. One headlined, CHEVRON EXTENDS OVERTHRUST FIELD ...stating that the Overthrust Belt, which has produced primarily sulfur-bearing "sour gas" in the past, is but some of the gas from the wells were "sweet gas"—meaning it does not contain sulfur that must be taken out before the gas can be sold.

The *Tribune* continued, ...BUT IT'S DRY HOLE AT THE LO-CAL BANKS. The article went on to say, *"Interest Rates are the biggest problem we've got," Evanston Mayor Dennis Ottley said. "We've got housing, but nobody can qualify. You've got to make $60,000 a year to qualify, but those making that amount or more has [sic.] not been working on that particular job long enough to qualify for bank mortgages."*

*Ottley, a real estate agent himself, stated that the average home in Evanston was about $85,000 for a 1,300 square home. He said, "Despite the high salaries that come with energy development work, the only way some people can afford to buy a house is through help from their companies. The going interest rate for a home is 15% at this time and is going to be increasing in the near future."*

*The Mayor went on to say, "The companies are helping their employees to purchase a home by helping them with down payments, and subsidizing interest rates."*

The Tribune issue also had an article titled, BONDS AID TOWNS DEVELOPING QUICKLY... The article said that the Industrial Development Revenue Bonds helped small towns attract new industry: *The prime example is Evanston, where the local City Council has approved a number of the bond issues recently to help boost the municipal tax base.*

The article went on to read, *Evanston Mayor Dennis Ottley commented on the intent of the industrial bonding law and the way it has worked out. "I think it's just turned around (from what it was intended)," Ottley said. "I don't know who would want to come into a depressed area, (which is what the prime purpose of the bonds were meant for, to increase the economy in depressed areas), but now everyone wants to come here and we have all these requests. This is something we're using better now that we're booming than when we were depressed when the railroad shut down their shop. It's helping us a lot by increasing our tax base with new industry."*

Ottley stated that Evanston had been considering industrial revenue bond requests since early 1979, and said that the council "feels pretty good about them, as taxfree bonds go."

He also said there are other benefits to be gained from the bond issue. He said, "This provides funds for people to do the job right, and it's another means of financing with today's high interest rates."

Well, now 1980, my second full year as mayor, is over. The city officials are well satisfied with what we have gained, but we know that we have a long way to go before we can get the community to where we want it to be, and we know we will be looking at another big year with more big problems.

Oh well; it was once said that "Problems are the price of progress."

TIME, DECEMBER 15, 1980  **Nation**

# Life in "Oil City, U.S.A."

**W**hen Mormon scouts wandered through the Bear River Valley of southwestern Wyoming in the 1840s, they found oil flowing into streams and used it to grease the axles of their wagons. But it was not until 1974, when a deep pool of oil was tapped at Pineview Field outside the small town of Evanston, that the rush began.

Wells now pump oil right out from underneath Main Street, and dozens more dot the surrounding buttes. Cranes lay down sections of pipe across snow and sagebrush that will carry gas from well to processing plants. Helicopters whir overhead. Hundreds of workers live in trailers and tents in fields, along the river banks, or wherever a friendly rancher will let them camp.

An estimated $250 million has been spent on exploration and drilling around Evanston. Amoco and Chevron are spending a total of $700,000 to build two gas processing plants. "We'll be here years from now and still growing," says Garret Eckerdt, an engineer for Chevron. "We haven't even found the edges of the thing yet."

Though road signs outside Evanston still proclaim a population of 4,462, that figure has surely doubled since 1975; it will probably top 15,000 by 1985. Everything in Evanston is booming, partly because many roustabouts make $1,000 or more a week. Business is up 20% at J.C. Penney's, and it would be more than double that if the store had more space. It hopes to move to the new shopping center now being planned, the town's first. Neon lights blink NO VACANCY outside motels charging $35 a night, cash in advance. "Tourists don't stand a chance," says Jennifer Barclay, manager of the Vagabond Motel. Exults Alan Graban, president of the First Wyoming Bank, who has seen his bank's assets double in five years: "This whole thing is simply fantastic. The town has everything going for it."

The boom of progress clogs downtown Evanston

Everything includes a lot of problems. Water and sewage plants are overburdened, so raw sewage is being dumped into the Bear River. Bar brawls, family fights and burglaries have more than doubled the crime rate in the past year. Says Sheriff Leonard Hysell: "We're desperate for detectives." With school enrollment up 20% from 1979, most of the $1 million in funds voluntarily contributed by Amoco and Chevron are long gone, mostly for buses and classrooms. Roads torn up by the big rigs need constant repairing, and traffic jams a quarter of a mile long clog downtown streets. "We are suddenly loaded down with a lot of big city problems," says City Manager Steve Snyder. Adds Mayor Dennis Ottley: "It's driving us all crazy."

Housing is probably the town's most urgent need. An aging, one-story house costs $80,000; there are so few places to rent that a resident who offered to lease his chicken coop for $85 a month promptly found a tenant. The town's 2,500 trailer spaces are filled, and the waiting list runs into the hundreds. Doug Melton, 26, moved from California several months ago and works as an oilfield laborer, but he and his brother David live in a tepee seven miles out of town. Says Melton: "No way am I going to lay out $1,000 a month for a motel room."

"Not a lot of us love to be here, but this is where the action is," says Bob Blaylock, 25, a roughneck who makes $1,300 a week installing oil-rigging equipment. "This is Oil City, U.S.A., and you can put up with a lot."

"Problems . . . you've got problems? I was drilling in South America one time . . . you should have seen those slums."

*How some people may have imagined Evanston's future because of the oil and gas boom.*

Cartoon courtesy of the Salt Lake City Deseret News – 1980 or 1981.

# CHAPTER 15

**1**981....The first city council meeting for 1981 was held on January 8th, and the first order of business was to administer the Oath of Office, conducted by City Clerk Don Welling, to the newly elected city council members: David E. Bills and Russell "Bub" Albrecht, who both were successfully re-elected; and the newly elected councilman, Arnold Morgan of Ward 2. They all took the oath and signed it as required.

Every time the city clerk administered the Oath of Office I always thought to myself that *once they take that oath they are promising to not only uphold the Constitution of the United States and the State of Wyoming, but they are also making a commitment to do the right thing for the citizens of the City of Evanston.* I always took the oath very serious, and that we were all elected to work for the best interest of the city, not for any particular person or group. The citizens of Evanston elected us to lead and not to dictate or bully our way to get things done.

Employees were a little different; other than the police department, they did not take the oath, but they were hired and expected to work for the community in the best interest of the folks. Their job was to see that things were taken care of, subject to the budget, and to treat every citizen with the highest esteem.

Many times, when one of the employees got into a disagreement with a citizen, I would tell them, right or wrong, to be as pleasant as possible with the person. There were many times that an employee would have a dispute or a disagreement with a citizen, and sometimes that employee would get pretty nasty with the person. When that happened, it would get back to me through a phone call or a visit, and I would try to calm the person down by just saying that I would get to the bottom of the problem and get back to them....And I did.

I would often tell an employee that had a dispute or a disagreement with one of the citizens, *Right or wrong, you should at least listen to them, but there is no need to argue with them.* I would go on to say, *Those people out there are taxpaying folks and they are the ones paying your wages, and we all owe it to them to show our respect and listen to what they have to say. You don't have to agree with them, but you shouldn't get nasty with them either. Just tell them that you will look into the problem, or if you are wrong, just apologize and tell them that you will do whatever it takes to correct the situation. But don't treat them like they are second-class citizens because if it weren't for them, you wouldn't even have a job. Remember we are all nothing but public servants to them; whether you like that phrase or not it is a fact, and you should be willing to understand that.* I said the same thing during the work sessions when Evanston's top employees and the council members were all present.

During any one month we would get dozens of letters addressed to me or just to the city in general complaining about something or other. There were complaints about dogs running wild, the city not keeping the roads up and plowed soon enough, police being too mean or just unfair, complaints about parking and traffic flow—the list went on and on, but we always tried to follow up with all complaints, no matter how ridiculous they may have appeared. Most folks, once we talked to them, would understand our position and go away satisfied. But in these trying times it was tough to try to keep everyone happy, so there was no use even trying. And we weren't elected to keep everyone happy anyway, we were elected to keep the town in good shape and serve the citizens the best we could, keeping in mind the citizens' best interests. And that's what I hoped we were all working towards.

At this time I made the following appointments: City Attorney, Dennis W. Lancaster; Police Justice, Stephan Aaron; Chief of Police, Dennis Harvey; City Engineer, Wayne Shepherd; City Treasurer, Phyllis J. Martin; City Inspector, William George; Administrative Assistant, Steve Snyder; City Clerk, Don Welling; Fire Chief, Jon Lunsford; and Assistant Fire Chief, Ken Bloomfield.

Months before I appointed Jon Lunsford as the fire chief, I was approached several times by different members of the fire department asking me to please <u>do</u> <u>not</u> re-appoint Jerry Cazin as the fire chief. These were not only volunteer members of the department that I talked with, but many requests came from the top officials of the fire department. Lunsford, Bloomfield, Potter and several others told me that if I made Cazin chief again that I could lose a good share of the department. They told me that he would not work with the department, that he was still pretty old-fashioned and wouldn't listen or agree to changes, or even try to keep up with the changes. They said that he just ignored the problems we were having with the boom. From the way they all talked, it was either all his way or no way. The members were getting sick and tired of the way he was running the department and some were threatening to quit.

I got a lot of flak by not re-appointing Jerry Cazin as the fire chief, but weeks earlier I called the chief in to talk to me at my office. I told him that I would get to the point, and I said to him right off, *Jerry, I won't be able to re-appoint you as the fire chief.* Maybe I was being a little too blunt, but he already knew why I called him in, but when I said that his head dropped like a ton of bricks, everything went quiet, and after a short moment he raised his head and asked, *Why?* I told him the truth of what I had been told. He then said with tears in his eyes, *Well, I wish you would reconsider, but I'm not going to sit here and beg for the job.* I then said to him, *There's no doubt that you deserve the position, but after talking to the department I feel like it's time for a change and for a younger person to take over.* After a few minutes he settled down and we talked a few minutes about some of the problems the department was having, and then he left with his head hanging like he was trying to hide the tears.

If someone asked me, *What was the toughest decision you ever had to make while you were mayor?* I guess this year's decision of a fire chief would have to be right at the top. But, it surely wasn't the only tough decision—there were many.

After I made the appointments, Councilman Bills made a motion to sever the position of fire chief from the list. It died from lack of a second, but then Bills reworded the motion. His motion then was to confirm all appointments, *except the fire chief,* seconded by Davis, with all voting in favor.

I thought to myself, *Uh-oh, here we go, I'm going to be in big trouble now trying to explain my position on this matter.* But I explained it the best I could, and told the council what members of the department had told me. Apparently, they had told the same thing to some of the city council members.

Then Councilman Albrecht made the motion to confirm the appointment of Jon Lunsford as Evanston's Fire Chief, seconded by Fruits. During the discussion, *Councilman Bills made the following statement and asked for it to be included in the minutes: The current fire chief is the same man he was two years ago. I feel that he has been a dedicated, effective public servant with over 50 years of service to Evanston. His forced replacement at this time is, in my opinion, an affront to a competent, hard-working fireman. The Mayor's proposed replacement is a good man, but he should not be confirmed at this time. Jerry Cazin should be re-appointed Fire Chief. I recommend that the Council reject this appointment. Therefore, I call for a roll call vote on this confirmation.*

Roll call vote was called for with these results: Wall, yes; Fruits, yes; Davis, no; Bills, no, Morgan, yes; and Albrecht, yes. Motion passed by 4 yes votes to 2 no votes. By law I couldn't vote on my own appointments. Jon Lunsford was now our new fire chief.

This past December was the month that the National League of Cities had their annual convention and Russell "Bub" Albrecht and his wife Diane, and my wife Sandy and I were planning on going to the convention, which was being held in Atlanta, Georgia. None of us had ever been to a national convention of the cities before and we thought that this would be a good year for us to attend. We felt that we might even learn something about running a city by going.

So I had Steve Snyder send our registrations in and get us reservations at the headquarters motel, which was called the Omni Convention Center. But when he found out that the Omni was full he tried to get us reservations at a motel close to the Omni. He wasn't having much luck, so I told him to get us set up at a nice motel and that we would just catch a cab at the airport and go to the motel. Snyder had got us reservations at a motel called the White House Motel. I guess with a name like that he probably thought it would be a nice place to stay.

Well, when we flew in to Atlanta we grabbed a cab and told the driver to take us to the White House Motel. We told him that we were from Wyoming and that we were there to attend the National League of Cities convention. He told us that the White House Motel was quite a ways from the Omni where the convention was being held, and we told him that we couldn't get rooms there or anywhere close because they were all filled up. The way the cab driver was talking, the White House didn't sound like a very nice place to stay, but he took us there anyway.

When we got to the White House Motel, we noticed that it didn't look like a very good area. It was located on the other side of town from the Omni, but we figured we would just take a cab to get to the convention and that everything would be okay.

When we entered the motel and noticed that all the people, including the employees, were all Black folks, that didn't bother us. Being from Wyoming, you never saw much prejudice so we didn't give it that much thought, but what we did notice was the place was not looking too clean. We checked in at the desk to check in and got our keys, and went to our rooms only to find them quite filthy. Sandy didn't want to stay there, but I told her that it was getting late and we had no other choice at this time. So we went into our room while Bub and Diane went to their room, which was just down the hall from us.

The place was so dirty that although we thought we could stay there for the night, Sandy would not let me get under the blankets. She told me to just lie on top of the bed, so I did and fell asleep.

I woke up a little while later to find Sandy sitting on the floor against the wall trying to kill cockroaches with one of my boots. She was so pissed off that I think she would have used that boot on me if I had said anything. Anyway, she said she couldn't stay there another minute. I told her I didn't know exactly what to do, but then there was a knock at the door. Bub was at the door upset, and said we were getting the hell out of there. He said the guy next to him was about to die and that they had called an ambulance for him, and he wasn't going to stay there another minute.

Everybody was upset, including me. Diane was pregnant and very upset, and Sandy was really pissed off. So we all agreed to check out of that motel and take a cab to the Omni Center and see what we could get there. By this time it was really late, early in the morning, and we didn't expect we could get a room there. But we didn't know what else to do, so we had the cab driver take us to the Omni.

When we arrived there, we checked in with the clerk and asked her if there might possibly be a vacancy, but there was none. We told the clerk our problem and she told us to go sit in the lobby and wait until later to see what comes up. Sandy and Diane both went to talk to the clerk about finding us a room. After we all went to the lobby Bub and I fell asleep because we had a meeting to go to first thing in the morning, but our wives didn't get much sleep waiting for the clerk to take care of us. Sandy and I felt bad about Diane because she was pregnant, and Bub was trying hard to keep her settled down.

Sandy and Diane woke Bub and me up because they knew we had a meeting first thing that morning. We woke up and went to the men's room to freshen up a little before going to the meeting, but we got there on time and attended the meeting.

When we got out of the meeting our wives told us that the clerk had gotten us rooms. Apparently some folks had checked out and they said we could have the rooms but they were not cleaned up yet. Sandy said that they had the keys and we could still go to the rooms to rest until the housekeepers could get them cleaned. The rooms were on one of the upper floors where you had to use the elevator to get to them.

The Omni had an outside elevator, which was much closer to our rooms, and it also had an inside elevator. Bub would not ride the outside elevator because he could see the ground below him and outside the elevator. For some reason that bothered him, some kind of phobia I suppose, so he always used the inside elevator. However, we were all feeling much better now that we had nice, decent, clean rooms, and we were at the headquarters convention center. After we got back home, we sent flowers to the clerk at the Omni because they had been so nice and helpful.

Not too long after we got to our rooms and settled down, I got a telephone call from Evanston. It was Councilman Bills calling to let me know that he and Davis were not going to stand by and allow me to appoint someone other than Jerry Cazin as the fire chief. He said, *You better get back to Evanston because Ron and I are going to get to the bottom of this whole thing about Cazin.*

I said to him, *Dave, there is no way that we are coming back now that we have been registered and have gotten all settled in at the hotel.*

*Well, me and Ron (Davis) are going to the firemen's meeting tonight and find out just exactly what's going on,* he said.

That's when I said to him, *Dave, please leave it alone, and when we get back we can all sit down and talk about it, but there is no way we are leaving this convention now.*

He said, *Well, Ron and I are still going to the meeting.*

*Just do what you think is best, but be careful you don't make an ass of yourselves,* I said.

~❦~

When we got back to Evanston, Steve Snyder really caught hell for getting us reservations at a filthy motel located in an undesirable neighborhood a long way away from the convention center. Sandy and Diane really gave him a bad time, and did for a long time after getting back, most of it all in fun.

One of the first things I did, when I got back from Atlanta, was get hold of Dave Bills and ask him just what happened at the firemen's meeting. He didn't say much, but later talking to Jon Lunsford and others, I heard that someone in the department told both Bills and Davis to *just butt out and let the mayor do his job.* I guess that was why Bills didn't want to say much about it, but he tried his damndest to override my appointment when I got back and we had our first January meeting.

⁓

During the January meeting, I also made my appointments to the Airport Board, the Planning and Zoning Commission, the Parks and Recreation Board, the Joint Powers Board; and the Evanston Housing Authority Board. All appointments to the different boards and commission were confirmed by the council by motion and seconded with all voting in favor.

Then I made the following city council assignments: Albrecht, Fruits and I would oversee public safety (police and fire); Albrecht and Davis, public utilities (water and sewer); Wall and Fruits, Parks and Recreation; Bills and Morgan, streets and alleys; Davis, cemetery; Fruits and Davis, solid waste and sanitary landfill; Morgan and Bills, planning and zoning; Fruits and Wall, airport; Wall and me, budget and finance; Albrecht, Wall and me, personnel; Bills and Wall, Lincoln Uinta Association of Government (LUAG); Bills and me, Wyoming Association of Municipalities (W.A.M.); I would oversee City Hall and the appointed officials; Albrecht would oversee city shop; and Albrecht and I would oversee the housing authority. These assignments were all accepted without comment.

Councilman Albrecht made a motion to approve a 6 percent cost-of-living increase for all full-time employees until the end of the budget year (June 30, 1981), but to be effective as of January 1, 1981, seconded by Bills, with all voting in favor.

This would be a six-month raise over and above the 15 percent the employees received in the fiscal year budget of 1980-1981. By doing this, the city council was trying to catch up with the high inflation of the cost of living that had occurred over the past decade.

Also, Councilman Fruits made a motion to approve the merit raises recommended by the Personnel Board, seconded by Albrecht, with all voting in favor. The Board recommended a couple of employees to receive the merit raise at that time.

The merit system was a program set up to encourage certain types of suggestions such as new or different ideas for adding income through the solution of a city problem; substantially reducing costs through raw material savings, waste elimination, or savings in labor; or improving working conditions, increasing efficiency, or reducing job hazards.

The suggestion accepted by the Board as a benefit to the city and/ or employees would award the employee with a $50.00 one-time bonus. Early in September, a committee would present the three best suggestions to the council and award them with a monetary payment ranging from $100.00 to $500.00.

I was very grateful to the city employees and always thought that they should be well cared for because they were the backbone of the community and the ones who kept the city running. Although the city employees had, at various times in the past and future, threatened to bring in the union, I thought by treating them with the respect they deserved, and trying to give them decent wages and benefits, they would stop thinking union. And, through my 12 years as mayor, they never did threaten to go union. During Gene Martin's administration, they did make an effort to go union, until I got elected again for my second term. The police and fire department already belonged to a state organization that you could consider a union.

During the January 8th meeting we granted the four unlimited days to the liquor dealers per their request, and acted on several ordinances that were pending for second and third readings, including the passing of Ordinance 80-88, allowing Mr. John Deru to construct his project of an awning hanging across the  sidewalk that he had requested months ago.

I reported on the Insurance Committee's findings concerning the Deferred Comprehensive Plan, and that the committee recommended the plan available from the State of Wyoming through Wyoming Benefits.

Councilman Fruits made the motion to accept the Committee's recommendation for the Wyoming Benefits Deferred Comprehensive Plan, seconded by Davis. With 6 yes votes and 1 no vote (Bills), the motion passed by a majority.

A public hearing was held concerning vacating a portion of 14th Street between Clark Elementary School and Anderson Park, with the recorded tape being on file at City Hall.

Following the public hearing, Councilwoman Wall introduced Ordinance 81-2 to permit the street to be vacated. Motion was made to pass the ordinance on first reading and was seconded with all voting in favor. This ordinance also went on to pass on second and third readings with all voting in favor.

Ordinance 81-2 made it safer for school children to play from the school yard to the park without having to worry about car traffic. At this time Clark School was located next to the park, a different location than it is in at the present.

Resolution 81-3 was introduced by Councilman Albrecht. It authorized the city to enter into a cooperative agreement with the Evanston Housing Authority and forward the agreement to the U.S. Department of Housing and Urban Development to obtain funds for senior and low-income housing. Motion was made to adopt this resolution and was seconded with all voting in favor.

Senior and low-income housing was a must for Evanston, and the sooner the better. It was a shame that it took so much time to complete a project that was so badly needed. There was so much paperwork, and nothing was ever easy when you were dealing with the U.S. government.

It was once said by someone, *"I was taught that the way of progress was neither swift nor easy."* In my experience, I have found that to be very true.

Nominations for the president of the council came up. This was something we had to do after each election, every two years. The following nominations were made: David Bills was nominated by

Davis, seconded by Morgan; Ron Davis was nominated by Bills, seconded by Fruits; and Russell "Bub" Albrecht was nominated by Fruits, seconded by Bills. Motion was made by Fruits to cease nominations and call for the question, seconded by Wall with all voting in favor.

Voting was made by secret ballot with Police Chief Dennis Harvey gathering the ballots, which Harvey and Steve Snyder counted. Snyder announced that Councilman Albrecht was elected to be Council President.

A special plaque was presented to Police Chief Harvey from the Wyoming Public Safety Commission with commendations for <u>no pedestrian deaths</u> in the City of Evanston for over two years.

Councilman Bills made a motion to make the alleys one-way between Front and Center Streets and from 9th to 11th Streets (Harrison Drive). The alley between Front and Main is to travel westerly, and the alley between Main and Center travel is to travel easterly. Second was made by Fruits with all voting in favor.

Allen Kennedy, Superintendent of Public Works, and Chief Harvey were directed to start this project immediately, and have one-way signs installed at all ends of the alleys, and stop signs installed at the exit of each alley.

Councilman Albrecht made a motion to move the second meeting in January to the 29th and have it publicly announced by the local newspaper and notice put on the bulletin boards, which was seconded by Bills with all voting in favor.

Meeting was adjourned by regular motion at 12:50 a.m. of the next morning.

We often talked about starting our meetings at 5:00 p.m. instead of 7:00 p.m., but I told the council that we were not elected to satisfy ourselves, we were here to do what's right for the public. Most of us felt that if we started the meetings at 5:00 and not 7:00, those attending would be coming to the council right from work, and wouldn't have an opportunity to go home and relax for a while, change clothes or have dinner before the meeting. That was the main reason we didn't meet earlier, but we did talk about it quite often.

On January 29th the city council had their second meeting of the month, at which time Step 1 of the Waste Water Facility Plan was presented. A slide presentation prepared by Rocky Mountain Engineering concerning the new Evanston City Sewer System was shown and discussed.

After discussion, Councilman Albrecht introduced Resolution 81-7, a resolution accepting and adopting the recommendations set forth in the study of Evanston's Sewer System prepared by Rocky Mountain Engineering. Motion was made by Wall to adopt Resolution 81-7, and seconded by Fruits, with all voting in favor.

Councilman Albrecht made a motion to acknowledge and accept the annual audit report from the Alexander Grant Company, seconded by Bills, with all voting in favor.

Dennis Poppinga, Director of Recreation and Parks, introduced Mr. Keith Sorenson of Design West. Sorenson made a presentation about a recreation facility in connection with a Human Resource Center housed on the 40-acre tract of land south of Interstate 80 that the city had purchased. A lengthy discussion followed, but no additional action was taken at that time.

Margaret Russell, representing Upland Industries of the U.P.R.R., was in attendance to present the preliminary plat of the Bear River Industrial Park. Councilman Bills made a motion to accept the plat with the recommendation of adding the Anderson Lumber Company (presently White Mountain) property to the plat, and that a provision to include sidewalks, plus curb and gutter be included in the ordinance. The motion was seconded by Albrecht, with all voting in favor.

There was a question of a 10-foot strip of land on the northwest side of 6th Street that had not been included in any plat. This went way back to when 6th Street was named 1st Street, and it didn't show up until the Wyoming State Highway Department started surveying for the new overpass. The city attorney was directed by motion to have a title search on the entire length of 6th Street concerning the 10-foot strip.

Resolution 81-10 was introduced by Councilman Albrecht, amending the Personnel Manual to add a benefit to the deferred compensation plan for permanent full-time employees, that in addition to the mandatory 10% already deferred by the employees, the City of Evanston would match that with another 10%. This was basically giving the employees another increase in pay, but would go into their compensation plan. The motion for adoption was made by Fruits and seconded by Bills, with all voting in favor.

All full-time employees would not only be receiving a reasonable wage, but they would also be getting some great benefits: a good health plan, a good retirement program, vacation time, and compensation time for any overtime worked. The council and I had a lot of employees thank us for everything we had done for them. They seemed to feel better about their jobs and giving better service to the community.

Councilman Fruits and I made a report on a study from the Airport Board. After some discussion Councilman Morgan made a motion for the city to give the Board their full support and backing in accepting the study and to make necessary applications for grant money, as well as have Steve Snyder request from the Uinta County Commissioners some funding for the airport proposals. The motion was seconded by Albrecht, with all voting in favor.

Prior to adjourning, Councilman Albrecht made a motion for me, as mayor, to locate and commit six living quarters for our new employees, which was seconded by Morgan with all voting in favor.

I guess he made this motion because this was what my private business, Uinta Realty, did, find housing for folks. I told the council if I could locate housing for any new city employee, there would be no charge to the city or the employee.

After some general discussion by the council the meeting adjourned at 12:10 a.m. of January 30th.

On January 26th, Councilman Albrecht and I announced to the *Uinta County Herald* that Evanston's application for a grant from the Farm Loan Board had been approved in the amount of $2,200,000 for Evanston's water system, including additional trunk lines, additional water wells, and filter plant improvements.

The article in the *Herald* read: *Mayor Ottley stated that, "We hope that these proposed improvements will maintain the current good service provided to the residents throughout the city."*

The January 31st issue of the Uinta County Herald headlined, OVERTHRUST INDUSTRIAL ASSOCIATION PLANS FORMATION OF IMPACT ADVISORY COMMITTEE. According to the article, the meeting was held Wednesday on January 28th and all area residents were invited to attend and participate in the planning of the "impact advisory groups" organized by the Overthrust Industrial Association (O.I.A.).

The article reported that several representatives from the oil industry were present, plus Chuck McLean, President of the Denver Research Group of Denver, Colorado. McLean was representing the consulting firm employed by O.I.A.

Also in attendance was Julie Lehman, hired by Western Wyoming College in Rock Springs. O.I.A. had reportedly made a $25,000 grant to the college and the college hired Lehman to coordinate committee community activities.

The article mentioned that in attendance also were, *"Evanston Mayor Dennis Ottley, and Uinta County Commissioners John Fanos and Dan South."*

*"We have to have Evanston be a good place to live,"* stated Martin Zimmerman of Amoco Oil. *"It is something which has just got to occur,"* he added.

OVERTHRUST INDUSTRIAL ASSOCIATION MAGAZINE
Issue #4 – March, 1981

## Mayor Ottley: "Proud of Being Involved"

"Being involved" is not new to Evanston Mayor Dennis Ottley. He has been active in Evanston politics for 15 years, serving three terms as city councilman and three years as Mayor. He also has been involved in other community activities as well. "Actually, my work with the Cub Scouts got me started in civic affairs," he says. He has served as president of the JayCees, Commander of the American Legion Post and Chairman of Cowboy Days.

The Mayor is quick to point out that he is not the only Evanston resident who is active in the community. "The public's participation keeps me from getting discouraged when problems seem overwhelming," he says. He cites the support the Mayor and Council receive from the public and from volunteers who serve on various city boards and commissions. "Although I feel good about the town," he says, "I sometimes get frustrated because improving things takes such a long time. But I love the challenge of keeping the town under control and working with everyone to make it a decent place to live."

Mayor Ottley was born in Salt Lake City, Utah, 49 years ago. He lived in and around Salt Lake for 12 years before moving to Provo with his parents and six brothers and sisters. He came to Evanston as a high school student and later served in the army in Korea

for two years, attaining the rank of Tank Commander.

Mayor Ottley has worked at a variety of occupations during his years in Evanston. He was a roughneck and a derrickman in the oil fields, worked for the railroad and, for 20 years, with his brother owned the Husky Truck Stop, an Evanston restaurant and gas station. In 1974 he started Uinta Realty, where he is owner and broker.

The Mayor says the city and his realty company keep him busy, leaving very little time for hobbies, but he does like boating, golf, bowling, and he used to be a hunter. He is a member of the Church of Jesus Christ of the Latter Day Saints, Third Ward, in Evanston. He and his wife Sandra have four sons.

Mayor Ottley says he is proud of helping to establish a good recreation program while he was a councilman, but he is most proud of "just being involved in trying to make Evanston a better place for everybody to live."

# OIA Membership Reaches 36

Membership in the OIA reached 36 in September, with the addition of InterNorth and three of its eight operating companies: Northern Natural Gas Company, Northern Liquid Fuels Company, and Northern Natural Resources Company. Robert Eide, manager of InterNorth's Denver public affairs office, said that the company changed its OIA affiliation from voting to board membership in January.

InterNorth is a diversified energy company involved in the exploration and production of coal, natural gas, liquid fuels, and petrochemicals, with annual sales in 1981 of over $3 billion. InterNorth employs about 11,000 people, 25 of whom work in the Overthrust area.

Said Eide, "We joined OIA because InterNorth has a history of being involved in energy-impact mitigation. We think joining with other companies in this work is the only way to go."

Other members of the OIA board are: Amoco Production Company, Champlin Petroleum Company, Chevron U.S.A. Inc. and Dowell Division of Dow Chemical.

Voting members are:
Anderson/Myers Drilling Company
Anschutz Corporation
Bethlehem Steel Corporation
Bovaird Supply Company
Brinkerhoff/Signal
Burns Drilling
Cities Service Company
Dresser Industries, Inc.
El Paso Natural Gas Company
Exeter Drilling, Inc.
Exxon Company, U.S.A.
Flint Engineering and Construction
Fluids Control, Inc.
Getty Exploration
Halliburton Company and its Divisions:
  IMCO Services
  Halliburton Services
  Otis Engineering
  Wellex

B. J. Hughes
R. L. Manning
Mapco Pipeline, Inc.
Milchem, Inc.
Mountain Fuel Supply Company
Natural Gas Pipeline Company of
  America
NL Industries' Divisions:
  NL Acme Tool
  NL Atlas Bradford
  NL Baroid
  NL McCullough
  NL Shaffer
  NL Sperry-Sun
  NL Treating Chemicals
  NL Well Service
Noble Drilling Corporation
Northwest Pipeline Corporation
Oil Field/Leed Rental Services
Overthrust Gas Products Venture
Parker Drilling Company
R & A Testing
Schlumberger
Vierson & Cochran
Wilson Supply Company

OVERTHRUST INDUSTRIAL ASSOCIATION MAGAZINE
Issue #4 – March, 1981

## Meet the Board

### David Wight

A native of Great Bend, Kansas, David Wight graduated from Texas Tech University, with a B.S. degree in Petroleum Engineering. He joined Standard Oil of Indiana (Amoco) in 1964 and has held professional and managerial positions in Fort Worth, Denver, Chicago, and Liberal, Kansas. As Western Division Production Manager, he is responsible for the company's activities in the Overthrust Belt. He is the newest member of the OIA Board of Directors, replacing Murray Roney. (See story page 19.)

David belongs to the Society of Petroleum Engineers and the American Petroleum Institute. He is a seven-year member and current member of the board of the Cherry Knolls Civic Association and is active in the South Suburban Park and Recreation District Improvement Committee, south of Denver.

*David Wight*

David, his wife Gay, a Spanish teacher at Arapahoe Community College, and their three children live in Littleton. David's hobbies include running, skiing, racquetball, and coaching and refereeing children ages seven to nine in the Littleton Soccer Association.

Speaking of his membership on the OIA Board of Directors, David said, "I'm looking forward to the involvement in communities in the Overthrust Belt, and to continuing the good working relationship established together over the past two years."

*Owen Murphy*

### Owen Murphy

Owen F. Murphy, president of the OIA, was instrumental in founding the OIA and has served on the board since its beginning in June 1980. "I have found the work with the Overthrust communities very rewarding," says Murphy. "The people of the area have accomplished a great deal in the last year and a half, and I like to think that the OIA can take a little of the credit."

Owen joined the Standard Oil Company of California (Chevron U.S.A. Inc.) in 1947 following his graduation from UCLA where he received a B.A. in Psychology. He served in a wide variety of marketing and public affairs assignments with the company throughout the West prior to his move to Denver in 1977 as Public Affairs Manager of a multi-state area.

Owen, listed in *Who's Who in the West*, is accredited to the Public Relations Society of America. He serves on the executive and operating committees of the Rocky Mountain Oil and Gas Association and has recently been elected President of the Colorado Petroleum Association. He sits on the Board of the Colorado Council on Economic Education and is a trustee of the University of Colorado's Student Leadership Institute. His hobbies include cabinet-making.

Owen's wife, Lynn, is a sculptor who works in wood and stone. They are now living in a highrise Denver condominium and Owen says, "While this is only our second experience in cliff dwelling, we really enjoy the benefits of urban living."

11

Besides announcing the formation of the six *"unique"* advisory

groups, Owen Murphy, Secretary/Treasurer of O.I.A. and representative of Chevron U.S.A. said, *An impact study conducted by O.I.A. will be
released in about three weeks,* and he took a reserved stand against the Industrial Siting Act which is currently being considered in the Wyoming
legislature at this time. The Siting Act would be state legislation that
would force companies causing community impacts to furnish some
assistance to the community; whether it be through funding or otherwise. Murphy is trying to indicate that the O.I.A. program is better,
because it would be a voluntary program between the community and
the companies benefitting from the impact (a partnership).

Murphy went on to say, *To my knowledge no public or private agency
ever has undertaken a community involvement program (O.I.A.) of this scope
or magnitude. We believe the only way to successfully manage the complex
impacts that are occurring in the Overthrust Belt is through this type of joint
industry-community action. We intend these committees or groups to be a
model of Western energy development.*

The article read that according to O.I.A. President Murray Roney
of Amoco Production Company, the goal of the six committees was
*to prioritize the impact related problems facing Overthrust communities and to
develop workable solutions for them.*

It was stated that the committees will be formed in each of the
following issue areas: 1. Housing; 2. Physical services (water, sewer,
roads, etc.); 3. Human services and health; 4. Education; 5. Recreation and 6. The environment.

Membership on the advisory committees was open to any resident,
and a recruitment drive was underway by the City of Evanston,
Uinta County, the Evanston Chamber of Commerce, the Lincoln-
Uinta Association of Governments, and the Evanston League of
Women Voters, the article went on to report.

Murphy said he could approve of the concept of the act, but said
he believed the O.I.A. was *a better solution than the Industrial Siting Act.*
He said his objections to the Industrial Siting Act provisions were
*the size of the planning group and they are not being in the affected area.
The homegrown solution is the best,* he said.

Chuck McLean said that the test of whether the oil industry performed a good public relations job would be *whether Evanston is a good place to live in or not a good place to live in. That is going to be the judge.*

The article stated that the O.I.A. currently had 22 members and claimed to be the largest association of its type in the nation. It said its purposes were: 1. To gather data necessary for local officials and planners to make educated decisions about managing Overthrust growth; 2. To provide technical assistance in growth management to local communities; 3. To assist communities to find the funds necessary to manage growth before the very large tax revenues from oil and gas activities begin flowing; 4. To organize the oil and gas industry, both large and small companies, to solve the underlying problems of rapid growth in the Overthrust Belt.

The *Los Angeles Times* published two stories in their February 17, 1981 issue concerning the boom Evanston was having. Their first story was titled BOOM TOWN: URBAN STRESS IN WYOMING. The story went on to talk about several incidents that had happened in Evanston, caused by the boom, concerning domestic problems.

One of those stories went like this: The first sign of trouble came when two children appeared at a neighbor's mobile home with a frantic note written in red crayon by their mother. It read,

*Penny, would you please call the police? Frank has torn my phone out and beat me up, signed Rosemary.*

Then a .30-06 bullet came crashing into Penny's home and lodged in a wall.

When police finally arrived, they asked Rosemary Houston, 27, *Is everything OK?*

*No, it isn't!* she replied. But the door to her mobile home was slammed in their faces.

Then, after hearing two shots, they entered and found Rosemary Houston critically wounded and her husband dead. They had to pull the couple's 2-year old child out from under Frank Houston's body—he had fallen on the infant after shooting his wife and himself.

That was just one incident the paper reported, but we all agreed that family violence was rising in the Evanston area, the city officials, the city police and the sheriff's department were doing whatever they could to keep things under control.

The second article of the *Times Los Angeles* was headlined BOOM TOWN: GROWTH PROBLEMS, and said that the elderly here, for example, after years of quiet, secure living, have literally been chased off the streets at night by fear of crime and traffic. *We used to have socials two nights a month,* says Ester Benn, Director of the Uinta Senior Citizens Center, *but now people don't want to come out at night. Now we have one thing a year at night—and we make sure there is someone to pick (the elderly) up.*

*Persons like Bruce Waters and Kevin Smith, both born in Evanston 25 years ago, see the promise too. In years past they would have had to leave Evanston to find work: "Evanston was stagnating," Smith says. "There was no work here. I would have had to go someplace else." Now, they are both employed here (in Evanston)—as police investigators. "The problem now," Smith said, "is not people leaving to get jobs, but kids dropping out of school to make money."*

That was just a couple of the stories that the L. A. Times mentioned in their article, but we all agreed that things were looking pretty rough at this time, and we were very much aware of our problems and what needed to be done.

Previously there had been a request from a subdivision developer to have the city accept mortgaged land to assure that all improvements were completed before any lots could be sold. Councilman Bills made the motion to accept their request based on one and a half times the amount of the cost of the improvements, plus the value of the land to be mortgaged based on a recent appraisal. Second was made by Albrecht, with all voting in favor.

During the February meetings, reports and discussion were made by Richard Sather and John Deru, representing the Downtown Improvement Committee. They made another presentation of a traffic pattern proposal and other proposals that they felt would help increase sales in the downtown business areas. No action was taken at this time. I made the statement that the city was looking at three or four proposals on the traffic flow and would soon be making a decision on which would be the most beneficial to the city. I also stated that all studies appear to be very similar.

As usual, we acted on more ordinances that were pending to be passed on second and third readings with all voting in favor, and more resolutions were introduced concerning petitions for more land to be annexed, including land west of Evanston off Wasatch Road, and more requests for Industrial Development Revenue Bonds. The resolutions were adopted by motion and seconded with all voting in favor.

The introduction of the ordinances pertaining to resolutions for annexation and revenue bonds were made by council members, and motions were made to pass on first reading and seconded, with all voting in favor. These ordinances went on to also pass on second and third readings with no problems.

Ordinance 81-7, to amend a section of the revised code of the city to specify what persons may be in attendance during executive sessions, was introduced by Councilman Bills. The ordinance read that during executive session, the council may, by a vote of two-thirds of the members present, exclude from the council chambers all persons except the Mayor and Council Members. Other persons may attend at the request and approval of the governing body. Motion was made for passage on the first reading by Albrecht, seconded by Wall, with all voting in favor. Ordinance 81-7 went on to pass on second and third readings with all voting in favor.

Executive sessions came quite often and most of them concerned items such as lawsuits and claims, personnel problems within the city work force, and complaints from a private citizen or business. However, the city could not, by law, make any decision while in the session. Before any action could be taken on a problem the city council had to make the action during an open meeting. Neither the mayor nor the council had to explain anything or comments made in the executive session, but any action taken, such as a motion, had to be done in the public meeting.

I made several more appointments to various boards and commissions during the meeting and were all confirmed by the council.

There was so much development and construction going on in the city that the council felt that there was too much work for one inspector, so the problem was turned over to the Personnel Board for their suggestions.

The board came back with the suggestion that we make City Inspector William George the Chief Inspector and hire another person to be Assistant Inspector at a lower pay grade. A motion was made and seconded that we accept the recommendation of the Personnel Board, with all voting in favor.

A motion was made by Councilman Fruits to direct the Superintendent of Public Works, Allen Kennedy, to install four-way stop signs at the intersection of 9th and Main Streets, seconded by Davis, with all voting in favor.

Chief Dennis Harvey reported that the department had numerous bar calls from the Whirl Inn Restaurant and Lounge. Chief Harvey was directed by the council and me to write a letter to the owner of the Whirl Inn and demand that they make an effort to clean up their own bar problems, and that the department is already over their heads with other problems.

Councilman Bills made a motion to accept the offer of services from Kaiser and Company as the consulting firm to handle the bonds and such in regard to the Improvement District in Aspen Groves I and II. The motion was seconded by Wall with all voting in favor.

During the meeting, I read a letter from the Uinta County Agricultural Agent concerning the mosquito abatement program and requesting a member from the City of Evanston to serve on the abatement committee. This was a program to spray for mosquitoes early in the spring before the eggs hatched. At this time they were using a truck to spray with. I remember the truck going down the alleys and the kids running behind it, just for the fun of it, I guess. But the program worked and we had a lot less trouble with mosquitoes. Prior to the program folks were getting eaten up by the annoying little bugs, but to my knowledge, no one in Evanston ever became ill from a mosquito bite or from the spray.

I then appointed Councilman Bills as the city representative to the mosquito abatement committee. The appointment was moved and seconded, with all voting in favor.

Resolution 81-18 was introduced by Councilman Fruits, authorizing the city to enter into an agreement with Boettcher and Company to act as financial consultants and underwriters for the Evanston Human Resources Center Project and the Evanston Community Recreation Center Project. The resolution was adopted by a motion made by Wall, and seconded by Morgan with all voting in favor.

Ordinance 81-13 was introduced by Councilman Fruits to amend Ordinance 80-27. The change was that subdividers convey 5% of the land to the city for public purposes, or pay 11% in lieu of the land based on an appraisal of the raw land value. In the event of payment in land value, the payment must be retained in a separate account and used only for the acquisition or development of parks, playgrounds, school sites or educational facilities or other similar public purposes. Motion was made by Councilwoman Wall to pass Resolution 81-13 on first reading, and seconded by Morgan with all voting in favor.

Ordinance 81-13 drew a lot of interest from the developers, and some controversy, especially concerning paying 11% of the raw land value in lieu of dedicating land. However, the ordinance went on the next two meetings, passing on second and third readings with all voting in favor.

Resolution 81-13, adopting the master plan of the Evanston Airport that was prepared by B.R.W. Noblitt, was introduced by Councilman Fruits. Motion was made by Councilman Morgan to adopt Resolution 81-13, and seconded by Davis with all voting in favor.

Garry Ellingford gave a presentation and a proposal to purchase the Old Evanston dump grounds. The dump grounds were adjacent to the property already owned by the Ellingfords, and it would fit in with their future plans for the frontage. But City Attorney Lancaster reminded the council that Mr. Don Rutner still had a lease on the property, and informed Mr. Ellingford that until we terminate that lease we could do nothing. Therefore, Councilman Bills made a motion to direct the city attorney to enter into negotiations with Mr. Rutner terminate his lease of the old dumps, which was seconded by Fruits with all voting in favor.

After a report from the departments and a general discussion concerning street cleaning, a new city shop, four-way stop signs, trucks parking in alleys, water wells and trailers on school grounds , I reminded and encouraged everyone to support the Blood Bank held at City Hall on February 24th.

~~~

Several months after I was elected Mayor of Evanston I had a phone call from Mr. Mike Pexton of California. Pexton was one of the heirs of the Pexton property located on both sides of Yellow Creek Road south of Cheyenne Drive. He told me that he had heard about the oil boom Evanston was having and that he had heard that there was a real need for housing. I had never met Mike Pexton, so I had no idea who the person was I was talking to. The call did surprise me, however, he was very pleasant to talk to and appeared to be very interested in Evanston.

He explained to me that his family owned over 1,000 acres adjacent to the city limits and exactly where it was located. I told him about the situation in Evanston and said to him, *Yes, the town is in need of housing, especially affordable housing.* He then asked, *Would this be a good time for us to come to Evanston and start developing our property into a housing project?* I told him that there would never be a better time.

He thanked me for the information and for my honest reply.

~~~

During one of our March meetings of 1981, Councilman Morgan introduced Ordinance 81-21, authorizing and establishing zones for Single Family Residential (R-1 & 2), and Multiple Family Residential (R-4) at the request of Yellow Creek Ranch Company, Inc.—the first step presented to the city council by Mr. Pexton and company in getting started with his development.

The motion to pass on first reading was made by Albrecht, seconded by Wall, with all voting in favor. This ordinance went on to pass on second and third readings as well with no objections.

Yellow Creek Ranch Company, Inc. was a development company that Mr. Mike Pexton and others had formed to start developing the property that he had mentioned to me the previous year over the phone. This would be the first opportunity for me to meet Mr. Pexton. He got his organization going and developed one of the largest subdivisions in town involving residential and commercial, as well as the new Evanston High School.

Following that action there was a resolution adopted to annex certain parts of the Yellow Creek Ranch Company's property. The resolution was adopted by regular motion and seconded, with all voting in favor. An ordinance was also introduced for the annexation of the same property being passed on first reading and later passed on second and third readings, with all voting in favor.

When the Yellow Creek Ranch Company started developing, Mr. Bob Morrison and Mr. Rayo Barker of the Wyoming Credit and Finance Companies got involved as partners in the corporation and started up another real estate agency titled Main Realty. There were now three real estate agencies in Evanston, including Main Realty, Hoback Ranch, Inc. and Uinta Realty.

Main Realty and Hoback Ranch, Inc. listed and sold properties in their own developments, and little elsewhere, so they weren't much competition to my agency of Uinta Realty. However, it was not very long before other agencies came to Evanston: Century 21, Preferred Realty (Coldwell Banker), ERA Real Estate, and some other independent agencies. At this time, because of the boom, they all seemed to be doing all right, including Uinta Realty.

The *Uinta County Herald* issue published on March 4th headlined A FORTY ACRE DREAM COME TRUE (talking about the 40 acre parcel that the City of Evanston had recently purchased from Doyle Child's Holback Realty). The article went on to read: *The 40-acre dream south of Evanston will provide for a home for human services now scattered or forgotten in the county. Also a recreation center complete with two*

*gymnasiums, an indoor pool, a wrestling room and a dozen racquetball courts.
Plus a 10-plus unit home for senior citizens.*

*Such a collection of facilities appears on its way in Evanston, and will be
located on the 40-acre plot of land that the city had recently purchased from
Hoback Ranches, Inc. As time will show, there will be more than anticipated
developed on the 40 acre plot than has been recently declared.*

The article went on to say that *Mayor Dennis Ottley says the collection of complexes will be a source of pride for the community and notes the
location may well be the center of town in five years.*

❧

During the March meetings Resolution 81-19 came up to be acted on with Councilman Albrecht introducing it. It was a resolution
providing for the disbursement of unanticipated revenue funds in the
amount of $500,000. The funds were from a Mineral Royalty Grant
from Wyoming Farm Loan Board for improvements in our water system. A motion was made for adoption by Morgan, seconded by Wall
with all voting in favor.

If I remember right, these funds were added to the water reserve
funds and used to help fund the enlargement of the Sulphur Creek
Reservoir, which was scheduled to be completed in a few years. The
reservoir is presently owned by the ranchers in the area, but by enlarging it three times the size it would give the City of Evanston two
thirds ownership and more water rights, and it would allow the city
to discontinue the use of the city water wells still being used. Some of
those wells were starting to become contaminated.

At this time the city was having difficulty getting the grant approved on the proposed Aspen Groves Improvement District. The
engineering firm that was selected for the improvement district was
Uinta Engineering and Surveying, Inc. Mr. John Proffit, representing
the firm, asked where the engineering stood in case the improvement
district should fail.

After a short discussion, Councilman Albrecht made the motion
for the City of Evanston to pay for the engineering to a maximum
of $20,000 in the event the Improvement District failed and a grant

could not be obtained, pursuant to a contract being entered into. The motion was seconded by Morgan, with all voting in favor.

However, the grant was finally approved and the improvement district project went on as planned and the engineering was taken care of as usual.

According to City Clerk Welling, the city was having problems getting deeds and other documents from developers of new annexed properties concerning the dedicated streets. After some discussion Councilman Davis made a motion to have City Attorney Lancaster obtain quit claim deeds for all streets in recently annexed areas that hadn't been deeded to the city yet, seconded by Albrecht, with all voting in favor.

During the March meetings we passed on more ordinances, as usual, some just introduced, and we adopted several resolutions concerning annexations, zoning, subdivisions (the first subdivision in the Twin Ridge area of Yellow Creek Ranches), dedication of land or cash for public land use, and more requests for Industrial Development Revenue Bonds. Also, we adopted several more resolutions. All were voted on by the council and passed, with all being a unanimous vote.

I read a letter from Utah State University thanking and giving commendations to Steve Snyder and Kevin Smith for their knowledge and help in discussing the impact of the oil and gas boom, and its related services to the City of Evanston.

With all the worldwide publicity Evanston was getting concerning the boom, Utah State University invited Snyder and Smith to give a seminar about the problems that Evanston was having because of the boom, and how well we were handling it. They explained to the group how we had organized the Overthrust Industrial Association (O.I.A.), and that the association was having regular meetings to come up with a mitigation plan to help with our problems. It was finally decided that all parking meters would be removed and the two-hour parking ordinance would be highly enforced. The motion was made by Councilwoman Wall to advertise in the paper and post in obvious locations notices that as of June 1st all parking meters would be removed. The motion was seconded by Bills with all voting in favor.

During the March meetings a motion was made by Councilwoman Wall to accept the recommendation of the Wyoming Highway Department to have the new overpass run directly off 6th Street. The motion was seconded by Albrecht, with all voting in favor. It would still be a few years before it was completed, but those folks in opposition to the project were still referring to it as "Ottley's Folly", but I got used to it. Someone told me long ago that if I was going into city politics that I had better learn to be thick-skinned, especially as mayor. I did learn, and I learned real fast.

Also, Councilman Albrecht made a motion requesting Upland Industry, of the U.P.R.R., to donate some property for an on/off ramp at the proposed Wyoming State Hospital interchange, which was seconded by Bills with all voting in favor. This was another very controversial issue.

At the end of each meeting I would call for reports from the department heads and have discussions on various subjects such as fire protection, private water lines, sprinkling requirements in high-rise buildings, city codes, parking problems, leases, subdivision ordinance changes, inspection fees, annexations, parks, one-way streets, and so on.

Both March meetings went into the early morning of the next day before adjourning, but we got a lot accomplished.

The first newsletter titled "Community Issues" put out by the Overthrust Industrial Association was in March. The headlines read: A TIME FOR STUDY...A TIME FOR ACTION. The first article concerned the "Mitigation Plan," and started out with questions like: *Where is the O.I.A.? Was it just a smokescreen?* Those questions had been raised by some local residents in the few weeks since the last community advisory committee meeting.

The article went on to say: *The O.I.A. is alive and well and working on a comprehensive mitigation plan. On March 30th the O.I.A. Board of Directors established a mitigation team composed of Owen Murphy (Chevron), George Ross (Amoco) and Chuck McLean (Denver Research Group).*

*This team has been working steadily since April 6th when it first met with the Uinta County Commissioners and the Evanston City Council to discuss the specifics of a mitigation plan.*

The article continued: *When asked the duration of the mitigation, Owen Murphy, O.I.A. President explained, "We hope the O.I.A. will be out of the mitigation business as quickly as possible, but our plan is considering a 20-month period. Beyond that time we believe capacities of local organizations will be sufficient to manage growth issues."*

The newsletter went on to talk about the "Socio-Economic Study," the "Community Advisory Committees," "Mitigation Plans," and so on. It spoke of the housing problems, schools, planning and zoning, transportation, recreation, community social services, and health and hospital problems.

During all these meetings that were held concerning the mitigation plans for Evanston I don't believe there was one problem or need that was left out. I was very confident that by organizing the O.I.A., and the O.I.A. contracting with the Denver Research Group, we were in the process of taking care of all of the community needs. We had over 250 local citizens showing an interest and taking part by serving on various committees. This was what I would call a community coming together in a time of crisis.

During our April meetings we again passed on second and third readings on several ordinances pending for passage with all voting in favor, but Councilman Davis introduced Ordinance 81-29, referring to the issuance of permit fees for oil and gas lines, drilling of oil and gas wells; providing standards and regulations for the production of oil and gas; requiring surety bonds; providing for inspection of oil and gas operations; and setting standards and regulations for the protection of public health, safety and general welfare. This ordinance would only pertain to those oil and gas wells and lines within the limits of the City of Evanston. Motion was made by Councilman Albrecht to pass on first reading of Ordinance 81-29, seconded by Bills with all voting in favor and went on to pass on second and third readings with all voting in favor.

The T.J.G., Inc. (Ellingford Corporation) proposal came up again to clean up the old city dump, represented by Garry Ellingford. Apparently Don Rutner had not terminated his lease with the city yet for the use of the dumps, but was in the process of seriously considering it. Therefore, the city couldn't really do anything at this time in considering the Ellingford proposal.

But Councilman Albrecht made a motion anyway for the city to cooperate with T.J.G., Inc. in the policing and the cleaning up of the old city dump upon presentation of a plat by T.J.G. showing the proposed use of the adjacent area owned by the Ellingfords, subject to the terms of the present lease, which was seconded by Bills with all voting in favor.

Mayor Dennis Ottley standing with right hand on downtown parking meter indicating that parking meters will all be removed soon by order of the Evanston City Council 1981.

Mr. Richard Sather, representing the Downtown Improvement Committee, requested crosswalks in areas where pedestrians were finding it difficult to cross the main traffic artery, and voiced his opinion and some of the other downtown merchants' opinions as being opposed to removing the parking meters.

Following Mr. Sather's request a lengthy discussion took place. I told them that we were very much aware of the pedestrian problem in the downtown area and we also didn't want to see anyone hurt or possibly killed while using the crosswalks. I said, *We appreciate the committee's concern and would listen to any solutions that you may have, but remember, Front Street is the responsibility of the highway department, and we have to work with them also on any ideas we may come up with.* I went on to say *that the department is also very much aware of the problem, and they too are trying to come up with some solutions.*

*As for the parking meters,* I said, *the city council has already made a motion to remove them by June 1st, and we will be acting on an ordinance tonight concerning them.* Continuing, I said, *We have been under the impression that your main goal as a committee was to beautify the downtown area with trees, flowers and such. But the council thought by leaving the meters in place it would take away from what you were trying to do. The meters won't look good with the landscaping you have in mind, and besides that, they are all in need of being repaired or replaced. By taking the meters out we plan to up the enforcement of the two-hour parking ordinance.*

I also told the group that when the meters were put in years ago, the proceeds were pledged to fund the town's recreation program, but that pledge got mislaid somewhere through the years. I told them that, since 1967 when I was first on the council, the funds have just been put in the general account and used for whatever came up.

We told the downtown committee that we would be having the city parking officer enforce the law by chalking tires, and walking around the downtown area quite often. The officer would not only enforce the downtown parking, but would also try to help pedestrians at the crosswalks when possible.

Following the discussion, Ordinance 81-30 was introduced by Councilwoman Wall, to repeal Section 10-64 through 10-77 relating to metered parking within the city. The motion was made by Albrecht and seconded by Wall, with the motion failing by 1 yes vote to 4 no votes, and 2 absent. With Ordinance 81-30 failing, the parking meters would remain in use for the time being. Apparently some of the council members had changed their minds.

Resolution 81-29 was introduced by Councilman Albrecht, authorizing the city to enter into an agreement with Architectural Design West, Inc. for services connected with the Human Service Center and Evanston Community Recreation Center projects. Motion was made by Albrecht for adoption of Resolution 81-29, seconded by Davis with all voting in favor.

Resolution 81-27 was introduced by Councilman Albrecht, authorizing the city to enter into an agreement with Willard Owens Associates, Inc., to provide to the city geological and engineering services for location, preparation of plans and specifications for a water well supply system, and supervision of construction and testing of two wells. Motion was made by Wall for the adoption of Resolution 81-27, seconded by Davis with all in favor.

The third reading of Ordinance 81-24 authorized Twin Ridge Subdivisions No. 1 and No. 2 to be accepted as part of the City of Evanston. These subdivisions were the first phase of the Yellow Creek Ranch Company's project, and in dedicating and including it on the plat, the developer had named the park "Ottley Park," which I was very much opposed to.

They named all the streets after governors of Wyoming. I guess I should have been honored to be included right in the middle of all of the governors' names, but it bothered me to think that the only reason the developers may have done that was to get on my better side. However, I could have been wrong, but I was very much against the name and tried to get it changed.

The council did not agree with me and didn't make any changes. The name stayed Ottley Park when Councilman Albrecht made the motion to pass Ordinance 81-24 on third and final reading, seconded by Morgan with 6 yes votes and 1 abstaining (me). Motion passed by the 6 votes, but I did abstain, because I was embarrassed about the park.

General Foreman of Public Works, Allen Kennedy, read a letter from an Evanston citizen complimenting the solid waste (garbage) crew for doing such an outstanding job. Verdon Moore, Foreman of Solid Waste, was not present, but I told Verd about the letter and congratulated him on the job they were doing.

4/8/81  UCH

Ronald Davis, city councilman over sanitation; Allen Kennedy, general foreman; and Jim Bateman, landfill supervisor, stand beside the new landfill compactor which the city put into use April 1st at a cost of $102,876.00. According to Kennedy, the new compactor will add at least seven or eight years to the life of the landfill. He says the operator can do in one hour the work that required four hours with the old equipment.

The new machine is five tons heavier and has special features designed especially for trash compaction. The impact in the area has greatly increased the demands upon the city's landfill.

*Uinta County Herald*, April 8, 1981.

Verd was one of those long-time employees that loved Evanston and had always worked to keep the community clean and a decent place to live. During my years as a member of the city council and as mayor, I often still think of all those past employees that the city had working. Most of them were there because of their dedication to the community, because the pay sure wasn't much. They were probably the lowest paid employees in the state before they got their most recent wage increases. They never had any benefits to speak of other than vacation time, but now they had health insurance, a good retirement program and more since the boom.

One employee I think of often is Allen Kennedy. That guy knew the city better than anyone I ever knew. Hell, he could tell you where every water and sewer hookup was, he could tell you locations of all underground lines. Allen knew the City of Evanston inside and out, and everyone looked to him when they needed information concerning the community. Also, Buff Bruce, former Street Foreman, knew the city very well. Buff was a good man and kept the streets in great shape. These guys were all very dedicated to their jobs.

I announced, prior to adjourning the first meeting in April, that there would be an O.I.A. meeting on April 6th at 3:00 p.m. and that there would be a special city council meeting on April 23rd at 7:00 p.m.

If we were to include our work sessions we were probably meeting four or five times a month on average. But to get things done, it proved to be necessary, and with the O.I.A.'s help we were accomplishing a lot.

During the second regular meeting in April, Councilman Morgan introduced Resolution 81-35 authorizing the city to enter into a contract with Early Bird Contractors, Inc., for all landscape work and the construction of the Evanston baseball fields. The motion to adopt was made by Wall and seconded by Fruits, with all voting in favor.

Resolution 81-36 authorizing the city to purchase a tract of land from Gweneth M. Johnson for the purchase price of $65,000 was then introduced by Councilman Fruits. Motion for adoption was made by Albrecht, seconded by Bills, with all voting in favor.

<hr>

Earlier, during the first meeting in April, I read a letter from Phyllis Martin stating that she was immediately resigning as City Treasurer. She was leaving Evanston to take care of her mother in Nebraska and wasn't sure how long she would be gone. Therefore, motion was made to accept her resignation and seconded, with all voting in favor. But first the mayor and council thanked her for her dedicated service and the hard work she had given to the city in the past, and wished her well in the future.

At this time I recommended Linnea Miller Overy to replace Phyllis Martin as City Treasurer and appointed of Mrs. Overy to the position. A little discussion followed before Councilman Morgan made the motion to confirm the appointment of Overy as City

Treasurer, seconded by Albrecht, with all council members voting in favor. I had to abstain because, as Mayor, I couldn't vote on my own appointments.

Since Mrs. Overy was new, I suggested that Steve Snyder, Administrative Assistant, be appointed as Budget Officer for the next fiscal year. A motion was made by Morgan to confirm the appointment of Mr. Snyder as the budget officer for the next fiscal year, seconded by Bills, with all voting in favor.

⁂

Also during the second meeting regular meeting in April, Councilman Fruits made a motion that on a trial basis, starting on June 1, 1981 through the Labor Day weekend, we plug up all parking meters downtown and give free parking, but enforce the two-hour parking ordinance. The motion was seconded by Wall, with all voting in favor.

City Clerk Don Welling was directed to see that the Special City Council meeting to be held on April 23rd at 7:00 p.m. be properly advertised. The meeting adjourned at 1:18 a.m. of the next morning.

The special meeting of April 23rd was called to have a public hearing concerning the request for a full retail liquor license by the Back Forty Restaurant. The hearing was recorded and the recorded tape would be on file at City Hall.

The 1980 census had been recently completed for the City of Evanston showing an enough increase in population to give the city the right to issue two more full liquor licenses and make them available to the public. One of these licenses was recently applied for by a new restaurant, bar and lounge called The Back Forty located in the east part of the city on Bear River Drive.

This public hearing was held for the purpose on why this license should or should not be issued. There were very few in attendance and no one was there to object. Therefore, after closing the hearing, Councilman Albrecht made a motion to approve the application of the Back Forty Restaurant and issue them the retail liquor license, seconded by Wall.

However, Councilman Bills, after some advice from City Attorney Lancaster, made a motion to amend the main motion to issue the retail liquor license to the Back Forty Restaurant, by making the issuance of said license subject to Resolution 81-38, which hadn't been acted on or adopted at this time. Motion to amend was seconded by Morgan, with all voting in favor.

The vote on the main motion as amended was also passed with all voting in favor.

At this time, The City of Evanston only had one inactive license left that could be applied for after issuing the second-to-last license to the Back Forty. With the boom going on we might need even more licenses because of the overcrowded bars and the numerous bar problems we were having, but it would be another year or so before the State of Wyoming would issue more licenses to the towns and cities based on the 1980 census.

Resolution 81-38 "setting forth and declaring the City of Evanston liquor license policy; general requirements; individual requirements for retail, restaurant, special club, resort liquor licenses and special permits" had not been acted on before the issuance of the Back Forty license. Therefore, following the action taken on the issuance of The Back Forty license, Resolution 81-38 was introduced by Councilman Fruits.

After the reading of the entire resolution by City Attorney Lancaster, Councilman Morgan made a motion to adopt Resolution 81-38, seconded by Davis.

After a lengthy discussion, Councilwoman Wall made an amendment to the main motion to delete Section 2, Paragraph (h), which read; "Any application for a new retail, restaurant license, or resort license, or any application for transfer of any existing retail, restaurant or resort license shall have a minimum of two thousand (2,000) square feet of public floor space in the proposed establishment." The motion to amend was seconded by Albrecht, with a vote of 4 yes votes and 3 no.

The main motion as amended also passed by a majority. This was one of the cases of where I, as Mayor, had to break the tie vote, but that was okay because I would have voted anyway.

Prior to adjourning, Councilman Fruits made a motion for the mayor to send a telegram to the Wyoming Wildlife Federation (W.W.F.) stating that the city was against any lawsuit being filed against Amoco and Chevron, and the resulting socioeconomic problems that may occur if said lawsuit is filed. Plus the fact that Evanston was in support of the sour gas treatment plants of Amoco and Chevron that were now being planned to be constructed in Uinta County. The motion was seconded by Morgan with all voting in favor.

Previously, the W.W.F. had requested that the Evanston City Council go on record as opposing the construction projects, but we didn't.

During the regular council meetings in May more ongoing ordinances were introduced, passed and acted on the various readings with all voting in favor. These ordinances pertained to oil and gas regulations and specifications; Industrial Revenue Bonds; zoning and zone changes; annexations; attempt to elude police; the increase of the annual fee for liquor licenses; and the approval of more subdivisions. All were voted on unanimously.

Ordinance 81-43, providing for an increase in liquor license fees, was on first reading. The ordinance stated that the fee for full liquor licenses would be raised in 1981 from $1,000 to $1,500, and would increase to $2,000 in 1982, and then would be raised to $3,000 in 1983. Motion for passage was unanimous with all voting in favor.

Resolution 81-41 was introduced by Councilman Morgan, authorizing the city to enter into a contract with Eckhoff, Watson and Preator, Engineers, for engineering work related to the preparation of application documents and supporting materials for the Step 2 and Step 3 design and construction grants relating to the wastewater treatment facilities of the City of Evanston. Motion was made by Wall to adopt Resolution 81-41, seconded by Fruits, with all voting in favor.

Resolution 81-42 was introduced by Councilman Morgan, for the City of Evanston to enter into a joint powers agreement with the County of Uinta to create the City of Evanston–Uinta County Human Resource Center Joint Powers Board for the purpose of exercising the express powers authorized by the Wyoming Joint Powers Act.

This resolution pertained to the new Human Service Center that was to be constructed on the 40-acre parcel of land that the City of Evanston had purchased and would be located just across from the new Recreation Center. Motion was made by Councilwoman Wall to adopt Resolution 81-42, seconded by Fruits, with all voting in favor.

Councilman Fruits then introduced Resolution 81-43, establishing one-way traffic in an easterly direction on Center Street from its intersection with Sixth Street to its intersection with 11th Street (Harrison Drive), and in a westerly direction on Main Street from its intersection with 6th Street to its intersection with 11th Street. The change to one-way streets would begin on June 1, 1981. Councilman Morgan made a motion to adopt Resolution 81-43, seconded by Wall. The motion passed by a majority with 4 yes votes, 2 no votes and 1 absent. Bills and Davis were the two dissenting votes opposing the one-way streets.

The one-way streets caused a lot of controversy. Some of the merchants were upset with it, but others approved. One merchant told me that we were going the wrong way, because we were not following the plan the committee came up with. I told him we were going with the plan that the state and other studies showed. Then I asked him what difference does it really make, and that was when he said, we should be going clockwise and not counter-clockwise. I just looked at him and couldn't believe what he said.

I added that whichever direction the traffic went, there would still be angle parking on both sides of the one-way streets. I told the group that the proposal for the direction of one-way traffic followed the recommendation received from the Wyoming State Traffic Engineer, as well as what other agencies that had made the study suggested.

Then I read a letter from Mr. Dale, Wyoming State Traffic Engineer stating, *"We have studied the area and collected field measurements and data. The basic feeling is that a one-way couplet utilizing Main Street as a westerly flow and Center Street as an easterly flow would improve the operational safety and efficiency of traffic movements in the downtown area."*

There would be no stop signs on the one-way streets, but each of the streets intersecting the one-way traffic would have stop signs. Mr. Dale also mentioned this was only on a temporary basis, until the overpass is completed, and stop signs placed in barrels with sand to hold them down would be something to think about.

The one-way traffic proposal also fit another proposal which would route truck traffic coming from the underpass and heading out Wyoming Highway 150 to a Center Street detour extending from 9th to 6th Streets.

Truck traffic heading towards the west end of the Interstate 80 exchange, and towards the underpass at 9th Street, would be routed on Front Street and 11th Street.

We were also working on the elderly housing project and during the meeting Councilwoman Wall made a motion for the city to enter into a long-term lease agreement with Senior Citizens, Inc., seconded by Fruits, with all voting in favor.

City Attorney Lancaster reported a pending lawsuit against the City of Evanston over mineral rights and suggested we go into executive session. Motion was made by Fruits to go into executive session, seconded by Morgan with 5 aye votes, 1 no vote and 1 absent. I believe the dissenting vote was because of the time; it was almost midnight when we went into the session.

The suit, filed in Wyoming Third District Court in Evanston, asked the court to make a judgment declaring the oil, gas, and mineral rights of Evanston streets and alleys for the parties concerned. Those named as defendants were the City of Evanston, Cities Service Company, Amoco Production Company, Mesa Petroleum Company, and Burton Hawks, Inc.

Burton Hawks claimed to have the primary right to recover oil and gas under city streets and alleys in Evanston as the city's gas lessee.

Plaintiffs for the case were Sarah and George Robinson, and Evaline and Kilburn Porter.

In filing the action, the plaintiffs said they were acting *"for themselves and as representatives of a class consisting of all owners of subdivided streets and alleys within the City of Evanston."* They were being represented by Attorney Charles Phillips.

After the executive session Councilman Bills made a motion to direct City Attorney Lancaster to take the necessary action to defend the city's rights, seconded by Fruits, with all voting in favor.

Because of the conflicting dates of the upcoming Wyoming Association of Municipalities (W.A.M.) convention, Councilman Fruits made the motion that our regular meeting of June 4th be postponed to June 11th, and that City Clerk Don Welling advertise the meeting change, seconded by Bills, with all voting in favor.

Amoco and Chevron had purchased, as a partnership, a 62-acre parcel of land south of Evanston, now known as Southridge Park. They purchased the land from a group of investors from Phoenix,

Arizona to develop a subdivision for their workers. In talking to Martin Zimmerman of Amoco and Jim West of Chevron, they both told me that they had to get housing for their employees and help them in financing a home. They indicated that this was because of the high interest rates and the tough qualification requirements the banks demanded. They said the housing assistance would make it possible for their employees to bring their families to Evanston and live a normal life.

During a special city council meeting dated May 14th, the Amoco/Chevron partnership presented the plat of the Southridge Park Subdivision. The plat was a little different from what the council had been used to. Their plat indicated drainage easements which we had never seen on a plat before. Apparently some areas in the country demanded drainage easements along with all other easements shown on a plat, but Evanston had never requested that. We didn't feel it was necessary to have those easements shown, but the council went ahead and accepted the plat as presented and an ordinance was drawn up.

Councilman Morgan introduced Ordinance 81-46 approving and authorizing the Southridge Park Subdivision within the City of Evanston. The ordinance was then read by the city attorney. Following some discussion, Councilman Fruits made the motion to pass Ordinance 81-46 on first reading, seconded by Albrecht, with all voting in favor. This ordinance went on to pass on second and third readings with all voting in favor.

Other business was Resolution 81-45 approving the Step 1 Wastewater Facility Plan for the City of Evanston. This was one more step in getting the new sewer plant underway. Motion was made for adoption and seconded with all voting in favor.

During the meeting, Councilman Bills made a motion to terminate the current lease agreement with Time D.C. Trucking Company as of January 1, 1982, which was seconded by Wall, with all voting in favor. Time D.C. had leased one acre of the property where the new City Hall is now located. Their lease was up on January 1, 1982, but at this time they were still there, behind City Hall. They knew they would have to move out soon because the city was going to need the space to add additional temporary modular-type buildings until we could get a new shop and a new police building.

More new subdivision ordinances were introduced and approved, including Crestview Meadows Subdivision, the Evanston Rail Center Subdivision and the Aspen Grove, Phase III Subdivision. All of them went on to be approved on final reading by regular motions and seconds with all voting in favor.

Mr. Martin Zimmerman of Amoco Production was in attendance to make a presentation on hydrogen sulfate ($H_2S$) and to answer any questions we might have. His presentation was very thorough and very informative, and we all thanked him for his time.

Motions were made and approved to appoint Lance Voss to the Planning and Zoning Board; to accept the Personnel Board's recommendation on Grades and Steps; to hire Sterling MacKay on a part-time basis for three months; to promote Allen "Oop" Hansen to a Grade 12 Step 1; and to confirm the mayor's appointment of Russell Dean to the police department.

A motion was made by Councilwoman Wall to include in the Personnel Manual an annual summer picnic event for the employees along with the annual Christmas party, seconded by Bills, with all voting in favor.

The *Uinta County Herald* issue of June 24th headlined: SEWAGE GOING INTO RIVER AT EVANSTON. The article stated that, according to city officials, the City of Evanston had been dumping raw sewage into the Bear River for the past 10 days. The amount of sewage the town produced had outstripped the sewage treatment plant's capacity.

Evanston City Engineer Wayne Shepherd said, *It's not as serious right now as it could be, but the condition is going to worsen until we can build a new plant.* He continued, *We're hoping the Overthrust Industrial Association (O.I.A.) will bail us out.*

The new 30,000 population sewage treatment plant is one of the projects that O.I.A. is considering in the package along with the Human Service Facility, the Recreation Center, the new fire hall and police station, as well as elderly housing and a safe house for abused spouses and children. We expected this entire package of new facilities to be complete by 1982, at which time we would be able to start construction.

The same issue of the *Uinta County Herald* had an article titled, ONE-WAY TRAFFIC TO BEGIN MONDAY. The article stated that the proposed system of one-way traffic in the downtown area would become effective Monday, June 29th.

The one-way traffic plan fit nicely with the present routing of trucks coming through the underpass to go southeast on Wyoming State Highway 150. Truck traffic heading to the western Interchange I-80 would turn right at the underpass when entering Front Street to 11th Street (Harrison Drive), up the hill to the west interchange.

According to all reports from various sources the new one-way traffic system would help in controlling the traffic in the downtown area, at least until the new overpass was complete. The timing for the completion of the overpass was sometime in 1983 or 1984. The sooner the better!

During our June meetings we passed several ordinances on the second and third readings that had been passed on first reading. These were all passed by at least a majority vote.

Ordinance 81-64 was introduced by Councilman Albrecht, changing the time of the city's regular meetings to begin at 4:00 p.m. Motion was made by Albrecht to suspend the rules making the ordinance become law on first reading, seconded by Fruits with 6 yes votes and 1 no vote. Motion passed by the majority.

Then a motion was made by Morgan to pass Ordinance 81-64 on an emergency basis, seconded by Albrecht with 6 yes and 1 no vote. I was the dissenting vote, but I was wrong because it turned out to be very helpful in getting our business over with at a reasonable time, like 9 or 10 p.m., and not 12 midnight or 1:00 a.m. the next morning.

Amoco Production Company had made an appeal to the Board of Adjustments of the city council that had been turned down by the Evanston Planning and Zoning Commission. The appeal was to allow Amoco to drill three oil wells within the jurisdiction of the City of Evanston. These wells would be drilled from outside of the city limits, but would be directionally drilled to where they would touch down under the city. Most oil wells drilled in the city or within the jurisdiction of the city were drilled by directional drilling.

During the hearing a letter was read from the Wyoming Oil and Gas Inspector recommending issuance of the permits that had been requested by Amoco. Therefore, after the hearing was closed, Councilman Fruits made a motion to grant in favor of the appeals of Amoco, seconded by Morgan, with all voting in favor.

The second meeting of June started at 4:00 p.m., as was made law by ordinance the previous meeting. However, with the long-standing agenda, about midway through the meeting, Councilman Fruits made a motion for a 15-minute recess, seconded by Morgan with all voting in favor. After reconvening, Attorney Tim Beppler introduced Diane Mills from the Dunmar Best Western Motel, who made a presentation, and told of their plans to build a lounge and a more complete facility in order to activate their liquor license, as well as adding more parking area.

The problem of determining a limit on how steep the road grades should be was brought up by City Engineer Wayne Shepherd. Some of the subdivisions were in pretty hilly areas, causing some of the streets to have a steep grade, and Shepherd recommended staying within a maximum limit of a 10% grade. Motion was made by Albrecht to go along with the engineer's recommendation, seconded by Morgan, with all voting in favor.

During the meetings there were ordinances introduced, annexing over 1,000 acres into the boundaries of the city, more subdivisions, more zone changes, more requests for Industrial Revenue Bonds, more building regulations and permit fees, as well as regulating the minimum size apartments must be. These ordinances all were passed on all three readings and became law.

The appointed Budget Officer, Steve Snyder, and City Treasurer, Linnea Miller Overy, presented a tentative budget for the fiscal year of 1981-1982. The general budget proposed was in excess of 8.3 million dollars with the reserve budget just under 14 million dollars.

The reserve budget consisted of 6.4 million dollars pledged to water, sewer, recreation and airport by grants and other funding, while $760,000 was pledged for land acquisition and the remainder of more than 6 million was a reserve cushion to be used in future if and when needed. The motion by Councilman Bills was made to approve and accept the proposed budget, seconded by Wall, with all voting in favor. The date for a public hearing on the budget for the fiscal year of 1981-1982 would be set at a later date.

A public hearing was held on two liquor license applications: the Hillcrest Motel and Safeway Stores. A motion was made to continue both hearings until the July 16th meeting, and was seconded with all voting in favor.

During the period when Evanston was booming, dealers holding liquor licenses that wanted to get out of the business were selling their licenses for an enormous amount of money if the city council approved the transfer. The licenses actually belonged to the city, but there was a question whether or not the city had the right to stop a dealer from selling their license to a reputable person or company. Apparently, it was the feeling of the city council that the dealer did have the right to sell as long as they had paid their annual fee in the amount of $1,500, and the license was valid at the time of the sale.

Liquor dealers, dealers that were retiring or just getting out of the business, were able to sell their license between $100,000 and $200,000. This was because the city was out of their quota of licenses that was set by state law, and did not receive any additional licenses until after the 1980 census was complete, which was in early 1981.

One incident we had concerning a liquor license sale was when Harold Burns, owner of the B-Bar-B Bar and Lounge, had the opportunity to sell his license to Safeway Stores for $300,000. The transfer was turned down, and I felt bad about it because Burns and I had been very good friends for a long time, and he was building a new restaurant and needed the money from the sale of the liquor license to complete the job.

But it had been the unwritten policy of the city that there would be no liquor licenses issued to grocery stores, because it would cause unfair competition. The city always felt that if one grocery store was allowed to sell liquor then other grocery establishments should be able to do the same. That would be only fair to all grocery stores, but it would be unfair competition to the bars and lounges that was in business for that purpose only. Right or wrong this had been the policy of the city from the beginning as far as I knew.

If the state legislature would change the law and delete the requirement limiting the number of liquor licenses that towns and cities could have based on their population and let a community have as many licenses it needed based on competition, then any grocery store or any type of business would have the right to apply for a liquor license if approved by the town or city. But I don't suppose it will ever be changed.

I have always thought that Wyoming liquor laws were very unfair, especially when a person or company could hold on to a license, not actively selling to the public, by just buying a few thousand dollars' worth of liquor each year from the Wyoming Liquor Commission. This caused liquor licenses to be worth thousands and thousands of dollars, when in reality the license doesn't even really belong to the dealer; it belongs to the city, town or county. The dealer is merely leasing it on a year to year basis.

Resolution 81-57 was introduced by Councilman Albrecht, creating the Evanston Airport Joint Powers Board to exercise the express powers authorized by the Wyoming Joint Powers Act, and more specifically to obtain financing and to operate, reconstruct and relocate the Evanston Airport for the use and benefit of the residents of Uinta County. Motion was made by Albrecht for the adoption of Resolution 81-57, seconded by Fruits, with all voting in favor.

Mr. R.O. Berg from Cities Services Oil Company presented to the City of Evanston a check in the amount of $25,000 to be used at the discretion of the city for the development of water wells. We all expressed our thanks and appreciation to Mr. Berg for the generous donation.

I announced that there would be an Overthrust Industrial Association (O.I.A.) meeting at City Hall on June 22nd.

After reports from city officials, the meeting that started at 4:00 p.m. adjourned by 9:00 p.m. Quite a difference!

It appeared that the 4 o'clock meetings were going to work out well for everyone. Anyone wishing to be on the agenda just needed to call City Hall and give the city the time they wished to be added that would suit them the best. City Clerk Don Welling always tried very hard to get folks placed on the agenda at a time as close as possible to the time they had requested. It wasn't always easy, and most of the time it was almost impossible, but Welling tried hard to get them on at a reasonable time. At least the regular city council meetings were adjourning at reasonable hours.

Not too long after the Overthrust Industrial Association (O.I.A.) contracted with the Denver Research Group as the consultants to help with the Evanston and Uinta County mitigation plan the two organizations decided to have a little get-acquainted party in Denver. I guess, with their offices being in Denver, they thought it would be a good time to visit and show city and county officials more of their work on the plan.

They invited any official and their spouse from the City of Evanston and Uinta County to Denver at the O.I.A.'s expense. They paid all travel and motel expenses, and they had a big dinner party for us after the meeting.

My wife Sandy and I decided to go, and Steve Snyder, Evanston's Administrative Assistant was going. County Commission Chairman John Fanos and his wife Barbara also decided to attend.

Chuck McLain, President and Owner of the Denver Research Group made reservations at one of Denver's most elite downtown hotels for us. It was really a nice place to stay, and probably very expensive. The Fanoses and Snyder left for Denver a day ahead of Sandy and me, why I don't recall, but when we got there Fanos and Snyder had a little surprise for us. We checked in and went to our room to get all settled and relaxed when the hotel delivered a large hors d'oeuvre tray of shrimp, caviar, and so on. It even included champagne. Sandy and I thought, *Boy, this is really great that the O.I.A. would do this for us. It must have cost them at least a couple hundred dollars.* Then Sandy said, *We had better call the Fanoses and Snyder, and let them know we are here. And we better tell them about the tray, and ask them to come to our room, because we will never be able to eat all of that food.*

So we called them and they came over, I didn't notice at first, but John and Steve were kind of grinning when they got to our room. Barbara wasn't smiling a bit, but we really didn't think much of it. We just figured that they were having a good time and Barbara was just going along. But later, when we checked out we were handed a bill by the desk clerk for almost $200.00. I asked the clerk, *What the hell is that for?* He told me that it was for the large hors d'oeuvre tray and the champagne we ordered. Fanos and Snyder had already left, because they were on a different flight. But I looked at Sandy and said, *Those Bastards,* and then I kind of grinned, and gave the clerk my personal credit card to pay for it.

It was all just a big joke after we got back to Evanston and got together again. We all just got a big laugh out of it. I told Snyder that my day was coming, but it never did. I was never much on playing practical jokes on people, but sometimes it can be fun if nobody gets hurt too badly.

While we were in Denver, O.I.A. had set the meeting up at Chuck McLain's house, where he lived and where his business was. McLain had purchased an old Victorian house with three stories. He completely remodeled it, not only to live in, but also for his business, the Denver Research Group. The entire house was done very beautifully, and he did a great job.

He requested the meeting be there because he wanted all of us to meet his staff and get an idea of what his business was all about. He also wanted us to see what he had done in remodeling an old Victorian home. His entire layout was very impressive, at least to me and Sandy. After the meeting, McLain gave a big "get-acquainted" party, which turned out to be a lot of fun and very interesting, then we left because it was getting late. We had to catch our flight back to Evanston the next morning.

The July meetings weren't much different from previous meetings. As usual, a number of ordinances that pertained to new subdivisions, rezoning, annexing, building codes, and so on, were acted on the second and third readings. All these ordinances were passed by regular motion by at least a majority.

Ordinance 81-68 relating to the use of solar energy as a property right was passed on final reading giving folks the right to solar access and the right to use solar energy.

Ordinance 81-75 to adopt various national codes such as building, electrical, fire, plumbing and the uniform mechanical code was also passed on final reading.

Some new resolutions and new ordinances were introduced during the July meetings, such as Resolution 81-61, introduced by Councilman Morgan, agreeing to a site acquisition and development for low-income housing with Farmer's Home Administration. It was passed by motion for adoption, and seconded with all voting in favor.

A public hearing was advertised for July for a limited retail liquor license application by the Eagles Lodge, but the application was not valid. Therefore, the representative from the Eagles was told by City Attorney Lancaster what to do to make the application valid. The hearing was postponed until they could come up with a valid application. Their license was pulled the previous year because of legal violations.

The bids on landfill excavation of 33,000 cubic yards of dirt were opened as follows: H.K. Contractors – $26,400.00; Hatch Construction – $37,950.00; Brett Ellingford – $63,360.00; and D & E Construction – $32.999.67. Councilwoman Wall made the motion to award the contract to the low bidder, H.K. Contractors, seconded by Fruits, with all voting in favor.

Resolution 81-64 to enter into an agreement with the Wyoming State Highway Department for work on the Overthrust Road was introduced by Councilman Albrecht. Motion to adopt was also made by Albrecht, seconded by Fruits, with all voting in favor.

Ordinance 81-78, an ordinance requested by Amoco Production Company to zone some vacant property located in the northwest corner of Section 19 just outside of the city limits but within the city's half mile jurisdiction as Agricultural General Zone. This ordinance passed with 6 yes votes and 1 no vote. The dissenting vote was Councilman Bills, who seemed to vote quite often against any issue that came up concerning the oil industry. Why? I never knew.

The Wyoming Wildlife Federation's petition to sue Amoco Production Company and Chevron U.S.A., Inc. was granted, and would be held in the state court in Cheyenne. The lawsuit was over W.W.F.'s opposition to the construction of the proposed sour gas treatment plants located in Whitney Canyon and Ryckman Creek.

Councilman Bills approached me one day and requested that I go to Cheyenne to be a witness in defense of the W.W.F. against the oil companies. I told him that at the city council's request we had already sent a telegram stating that the City of Evanston was opposed to the W.W.F. suing the companies. I said that the vote was unanimous, which included his vote. I told him that Fruits had made a motion in April that was seconded with every member of the council voting in favor of it.

I finally told him that I wouldn't make a good witness for either side because I don't even know what the lawsuit is all about. I told him that those treatment plants were out in the county, and that if anyone went, it probably should be the county commissioners, not the city. I said to him, *The city had already made their decision that we were not in favor of what the Wyoming Wildlife Federation is doing. Don't you understand that?* Nothing more said. Hell, I could never figure out where he was coming from.

More ordinances were introduced during the meetings such as not parking a vehicle within 20 feet of a fire hydrant, issuance of more Industrial Development Revenue Bonds, annexations, and zone changes. All of these ordinances went on to pass on all three readings with all voting in favor.

Councilman Fruits made a motion to investigate a program that would encourage tree planting in the city, seconded by Bills, with all voting in favor. A program was applied for and we came up with the idea of using the program to also plant trees in the downtown area.

Councilman Albrecht made a motion to authorize the city engineer to purchase the necessary equipment to upgrade the wastewater disposal plant, seconded by Morgan, with all voting in favor.

Councilman Bills made a motion to have the road from Grass Valley I aligned with the road from Grass Valley II. The motion was seconded by Wall but failed with 1 yes vote and 6 no votes. The council couldn't agree with Councilman Bills on this, because the developer had already had the roads aligned on the preliminary plat that had been previously approved. There was no sense in even acting on this particular issue.

I read a letter from Kevin Smith stating that he was resigning from the police department. Councilman Fruits made the motion to accept his letter of resignation and thank him for his service, seconded by Davis, with all voting in favor.

Kevin had been a big help to the city and the police department. He had taken part in the mitigation planning set up by the Denver Research Group, the consulting firm contracted by O.I.A.

Fire Chief Jon Lunsford stated that there had been 25% more fire incidents in 1981 than in 1980, and he pointed out the need for a new truck. It was the consensus of the council that we should call for bids for a new truck and the chief was instructed to proceed.

I then made two appointments to the Evanston Police Department, Eric Dunning and Kelly Studer. Councilman Fruits made the motion to confirm the appointments, seconded by Morgan, with all voting in favor.

Councilman Albrecht made a motion to pay Don Rutner $5,000 for the termination of his lease with the city on the old dumps, seconded by Morgan, with all voting in favor. Don Rutner owned a junkyard on Bear River Drive at the time and leased the old city dump ground for the right to obtain all the old vehicles and other junk in the vicinity of the dumps. He paid the city so much from the sale of the junk, and was gathering a lot of heavy junk from the dumps that he had paid the city for. Now the city was looking to clean the area up and get the property back on the tax rolls. When we put the property up for sale, Rutner still had a lot of time left on his lease.

TJG, Inc. (Ellingford) had already indicated an interest in purchasing the property, mainly because it was adjacent to the property they already owned, and the city was trying to settle a deal with Rutner to let the city out of the lease. A deal was eventually made, and TJG, Inc. ended up owning the property.

During the meeting Councilman Fruits made a motion for the city to charge a building permit to Uinta County for a new ambulance building and then donate the amount of the permit to the Uinta County Ambulance Service. The motion was seconded by Bills, with all voting in favor.

Budget Officer Steve Snyder announced that there would be a special meeting held for a public hearing on the budget for fiscal year 1981-1982 and other business at City Hall on July 21st at 7:00 p.m.

At the beginning of the special meeting, the budget hearing for the fiscal year of 1981-1982 was opened for comments and questions. As usual, the public attendance was small, but there were a few people at the hearing that had requested funds from the city, plus a few folks that had questions and were interested in how the tax dollars were spent.

After the hearing was closed, Councilman Albrecht introduced Resolution 81-69, naming appropriations for the fiscal year ending June 30, 1982, and that the expenditures of each officer, department or spending agency, be limited to the amount appropriated.

Motion was made by Councilman Morgan to adopt Resolution 81-69, seconded by Bills, with all voting in favor.

The total general fund budget for 1981-1982 was approved for approximately 7 million dollars, plus a reserve fund of approximately 16 million dollars. The reserve fund included 14 million dollars in grants, plus special assessments, and over 1 million dollars in the water fund. It was the largest budget the City of Evanston had ever had, but it would get much bigger in the future.

Other business that came up during the special meeting was action on several outstanding ordinances. They were all passed on second and third readings with no objections, except that Ordinances 81-80 and 81-81 were tabled on the third and final reading, by motion, until the regular city council meeting of August 6th.

The ordinances that were tabled pertained to the Red Mountain Mesa VI Subdivision, and the Fair Meadow Park Subdivision. Apparently, there were some questions pending on the roads, but no one was in attendance that could answer the questions; therefore the two ordinances were tabled.

Bid openings on two 4-wheel drive vehicles were presented by Allen Kennedy, Superintendent of Public Works. The low bids of $11,255 and $11,285 were accepted by motion unanimously.

Safeway Stores' application for a liquor license was brought up with Councilman Morgan making the motion for approval, seconded by Albrecht. After a considerable amount of discussion, a roll call vote was requested with Morgan voting yes and the other 5 council members and me voting no. The motion failed by 6 no votes and 1 yes.

Prior to adjournment, I appointed some special committees to take care of a few areas of concern: Human Service Committee – Jerry Wall, Arnie Morgan and me; Utility Committee – Bub Albrecht, Roy Fruits and Ron Davis; Occupation License Committee – Jerry Wall, Arnie Morgan and David Bills.

Also, I instructed Wayne Shepherd, City Engineer, to proceed with subdividing the 40 acres the city is now calling the Haw Patch Subdivision.

Our August meetings were much of the same old agenda, with dozens of ordinances and a few resolutions to take care of. One of the first orders of business was a motion made by Councilman Bills to approve the transfer of ownership of the Southridge Park Subdivision from Marco International to Amoco Realty. The motion was seconded by Albrecht, with all voting in favor.

Marco International was the company that Amoco and Chevron purchased the property from and Amoco Realty would be the agency handling the sales and assisting in the financing for the two oil companies' employees.

Ordinance 81-94, introduced by Councilman Fruits, was an ordinance zoning an entire parcel of 160 acres as a Planned Unit Development Zone (P.U.D.) requested by Powdos Partnership. This was a partnership of six local people; Proffit, Ottley, Wall, Davis,

Ottley and Schueltz who had originally purchased the property for a major horseracing facility, but the way financing was at the time, the partnership decided to forget the racetrack and go with the developing a P.U.D. During the development of the property, the partnership donated 10 acres of the property to the Uinta County Memorial Hospital Board for a badly needed new hospital. The rest of the property had been developed for affordable housing and some commercial use that has included mostly medical offices and clinics.

Following the introduction of Ordinance 81-94, Councilwoman Wall and I both declared a conflict of interest, because we both held ownership in the Powdos Partnership. We removed ourselves from the room while discussion and voting was going on. Motions were made and seconded on all three readings over the next few meetings with all voting in favor.

This was the first P.U.D. zoning applied for and approved by the council for that type of development, but more came later in other areas. It got to be a pretty popular way of zoning, because it was platted to zone various areas of a large development in a way that was acceptable to the city officials and future plans.

Ordinance 81-96 was introduced by Councilman Bills to create a revised code of the city providing for the underground placement of all utility lines. This ordinance demanded that all utility lines go underground, an ordinance badly needed but late in coming. This included all power and telephone lines, along with all other utilities. This ordinance went on to pass on all three readings with a unanimous vote.

Ordinance 81-99 was introduced by Councilman Albrecht, creating a new section of the code of the city to provide that the manufacturing, transportation and hazardous materials permitted in Light and Heavy Industrial Zones be subject to a Conditional Use Permit. We had reports and complaints of hazardous materials being stored in various areas of the city. Therefore, we thought it best to designate areas where that type of material could be stored. This ordinance also went on to pass on all three readings unanimously.

Amoco Realty requested right-of-way for a road going from Wyoming State Highway 150 to their Southridge Park Subdivision, which the city granted by resolution. They had to purchase property from the Broken Circle Cattle Company to complete the right-of-way. Amoco and Chevron then built the road, now called Southridge Road, from Highway 150 past the new Aspen Elementary School grounds to their new subdivision.

Resolution 81-74 was introduced by Councilman Fruits, declaring a property owned by the Union Pacific Land Resources Corporation (Upland Industries) to be utilized for a water well, pumping plant and appurtenant facilities. Motion was made by Albrecht for adoption, seconded by Wall, and passing by a majority of 5 yes votes, 1 no and 1 absent.

Resolution 81-75 was introduced by Albrecht and Resolution 81-76 was introduced by Fruits. Both came on the floor to be voted on. Resolution 81-75 pertained to entering into an agreement with Alexander Grant and Company to perform a feasibility study concerning the need of the city for a computer; Resolution 81-76 authorized the city to apply to the Wyoming Farm Loan Board for a Federal Government Royalty Impact Assistance Account Grant in the amount of $3,756,832 for construction of wastewater treatment facilities. Both resolutions were moved for adoption and seconded, with all voting in favor.

During the meeting Councilman Fruits made a motion to enact alternate watering days, using odd and even house numbers. Motion was made by Wall, passing unanimously.

I read a petition from a group of citizens requesting that the agenda for city council meetings be published in the local newspaper prior to the meetings so the public would have notice of what was coming up. Motion was made by Councilman Bills to direct Steve Snyder, Administrative Assistant, to have the agenda for all meetings published in the *Uinta County Herald* prior to the meetings. The motion was seconded by Wall, with all voting in favor.

Resolution 81-80 was introduced by Councilman Bills, directing the city to apply to the Wyoming Farm Loan Board for a Coal Severance Tax Grant in the amount of $305,000 for the construction and asphalt paving of a frontage road, Cheyenne Drive, from Yellow

Creek Road to the new Overthrust Road. Motion was made by Bills, seconded by Wall with all voting in favor.

The Evanston Police Department had started getting complaints from people receiving annoying, obscene and threatening telephone calls. Because of this, Ordinance 81-105 was introduced by Councilman Albrecht prohibiting such calls. Motions were made and seconded to pass this ordinance on all three readings with all voting in favor.

Resolution 81-81 was introduced by Councilman Albrecht, another resolution directing the city to apply for another grant from the Wyoming Farm Loan Board in an amount not to exceed $4,000,000 for the new wastewater treatment facility. Unlike Resolution 81-75, this grant was requested as a Coal Tax Grant, while the 81-75 request was from the Federal Government Royalty Impact Assistance Account.

Motion was made by Bills to adopt Resolution 81-81, seconded by Albrecht, and passing by a unanimous vote.

The engineer's estimate of the facility was 8.4 million dollars, and both grant applications were later approved. The State of Wyoming knew that we were dumping raw sewage into the river and getting a lot of flak from the various government agencies from Wyoming, Idaho and Utah. The problem was getting worse all the time, no matter how often we repaired and serviced the old plant. Every time we worked on it, it would work great for a while, but with the rate of increase in population the flow of raw sewage into the river continued to be a real problem. But there was nothing we could do about it until we got the money to construct a new plant. This was also part of the mitigation plans that O.I.A. was helping us with. We were getting a lot of assistance getting things done, but sometimes it just didn't happen quite soon enough. Things were getting very hectic and troublesome, but we were all working hard and being very patient, and hoping that some agency didn't come along and start penalizing or suing the City of Evanston.

The Human Service Committee made their recommendation for the following expenditures: Mental Health – no funding;

LUAG – $3,500; Library – $7,000; Senior Citizens – $12,000; Big Brothers – $5,000; and SWARA, (Southwestern Wyoming Alcohol Rehabilitation Association) – $10,000. Motion was made by Albrecht to allow these expenditures to be paid, seconded by Wall. All voted in favor.

We were getting many street vendors coming into the community to sell products for short periods of time. They would come in and set up, mostly on the east and west ends of town, leasing a small space from someone and selling whatever product they had. Sometimes they didn't even lease space they just set up on the fairground property or some vacant area. Making sure they had purchased a business license just like every other business in Evanston had to do was another problem for the police, in addition to removing them from public grounds unless they had permission to be there. Although most of them weren't around very long, they were still required to pay for the annual license.

All things were starting to really come together as far as the O.I.A. mitigation plan was concerned. It was announced by Owen Murphy, president of the association that the "direct grant portion" of the program would end in 1983 when the impacted community would have sufficient tax revenues from oil and gas facilities to meet the program's cost.

Governor Ed Herschler and Secretary of State Thyra Thompson were big supporters in helping Evanston obtain grants and other funds from the State of Wyoming. All state officials appeared to be supportive of our needs.

When a group of us went to Cheyenne for a meeting with Thyra Thompson to get her support the Human Service Facility she was very accommodating. Those present at the meeting from Evanston were County Commissioner John Fanos, Citizen Denice Wheeler, City Administrative Assistant Steve Snyder, me, and a few others that I don't recall. We met with Thompson to talk about financial assistance from the state for the Human Service Center. Denice Wheeler did a good share of the talking about the needs. She did a great job. She deserves a lot of credit because she was the most impressive

person of our group at the meeting, and probably one of the most instrumental persons in making the Human Service Project successful.

In July the *Deseret News* of Salt Lake City came out with an article headlined: PLAN FOR GROWTH, EVANSTON MAYOR
WARNS. The article went on to read: *Mayor Dennis J Ottley has a mes-
sage for Utah cities and communities expecting an impact from energy development:
Start planning years in advance; establish meaningful communication between
officials on all levels of government, the local citizenry and businessmen; and get
backing from the governor and Legislature. "It is simply too late to begin planning
after the impact has hit," Ottley, who was a city councilman in Evanston for 12
years before he became mayor two-and-a-half years ago, told the* Deseret News.

The article went on: *Evanston has been paying the price for not being
prepared since 1975 when an unexpected number of new people flocked to the
city to handle the early stages of the Overthrust belt oil and gas boom. All
sorts of socioeconomic problems immediately developed and the crisis has gained
momentum each year.*

The article continued: *Ottley, who tags himself an optimistic person,
thinks the city is gaining on—and eventually will overcome—the dilemma.
"But we could have eliminated or cushioned our problems with vigorous planning four or five years in advance," Ottley said.*

The article went on: *Ottley isn't taking his fellow councilmen or himself
to task for this lack of planning. After all, the Overthrust boom hit virtually
overnight after more than 500 dry holes had been drilled which left most everyone—including the industry oil geniuses—dubious.*

*"I'm saying that if you are reasonably certain there is going to be an
impacted area from energy development, be prepared," said Ottley, a quiet,
soft-spoken but firm and sincere man.*

*Ottley is not constantly shedding tears because the oil industry folks created
a bunch of headaches.*

*"Gosh no," he said. "In the late 1960s and early 1970s, after the Union
Pacific Railroad pulled out, this town was about ready to dry up and blow
away. We went around begging industry to come here and keep our town alive.
They just laughed at us."*

*For those expecting to get caught up in the boom-town syndrome, Ottley
singles out this warning: "No matter how well your economy seems always*

*work on trying to keep up a well off economy, even if it is flourishing, because the economy of any community can change without much notice. Plus always plan on the problems in the human service areas, especially domestic police problems which are among the problems to be one of the king-size headaches."*

*Along that line, the city has pushed for, and successfully developed, a healthy recreation program—facilities to keep young people active and happy. "That is a must for an impacted area," said Ottley.*

The article went on talking about the problems we have had and how we have gone about solving them. It talked about how the O.I.A. came forth, and how the state highway and other state and federal agencies helped. And as I said, I thought everything was going to turn out for the best, but we were just a few years late getting started.

The September council meetings were pretty much the same old thing with several ordinances being passed on second and third readings, plus a few new ordinances and resolutions concerning rezoning, annexations, new subdivisions, and so on were introduced, but early in the meeting the liquor license for the F.O.E. Eagles came on the floor for discussion. Following a lengthy discussion and after representatives of the Eagles Club assured the city that they would make every effort to abide by the law, Councilman Albrecht made the motion to approve the application of F.O.E. Eagles for a limited retail liquor license, seconded by Fruits. A roll call vote was requested with the following results: Albrecht – yes; Fruits – yes; Wall – yes; Davis – no; Bills – no. I voted yes and Morgan was absent. The motion was passed by the majority.

John Proffit, Engineer, presented a site plan for Billy's Emporium planned unit development. A motion was made by Albrecht to approve the plan, seconded by Fruits, with all voting in favor.

Billy's Emporium was an establishment that was built by two brothers that came to Evanston with the oil boom and figured it would be a wonderful establishment for Evanston, because they were planning on being here with the oil companies for a long, long time (what a surprise). The Emporium was a large entertainment center with a long liquor bar (they claimed it was the longest bar in Wyoming), and a stage where they would have famous entertainers come and perform. It also had a large dance hall and lounge. It probably was the largest entertainment center in the state. They got their plat and a full liquor license approved. They promised to have the facility opened by winter.

They did get it opened on time and they had a big opening night, which packed the place with old and new locals. The entertainer for the opening night was Hank Thompson, one of America's most noted country/western performers. Every weekend they would have some famous western personality: such as Hank Williams, Jr., Mel Tillis and others. It was an enormous and beautiful establishment and everyone seemed to think it was great to have a place like that in Evanston. It was located on the new Overthrust Road in the building that is now the Evanston Alliance Church.

After things started changing in 1983 and the boom appeared to be over, Billy's Emporium went broke and the brothers left town just like a lot of the oil and gas affiliated companies did, leaving their homes and businesses to be foreclosed on by the mortgage holders. A lot of folks got hurt financially, and my wife Sandy and I were among those folks.

During the September meetings, Ordinance 81-117 was brought up and introduced by Albrecht to allow medical, dental and health clinic offices and office buildings and opticians' and optometrists' shops in Residential zones (R-2, R-3 and R-4), subject to obtaining a Conditional Use Permit if said property is located contiguous to a Commercial zone (C-1 or C-3). Motion was made by Councilwoman Wall to pass Ordinance 81-117 on first reading, seconded by Albrecht. A roll-call vote resulted in the following: Wall – yes; Fruits – yes; Albrecht – yes; me – yes; Davis – no; Bills – no; Morgan was absent. This ordinance went on to pass on second and third readings by a majority vote.

The city council passed a resolution allowing Duke's Dumpsters (now Waste Management) the right to collect solid waste (garbage) for commercial and industrial areas only. This would allow all the business and industrial companies in Evanston the choice to stay with the city's program or go with Duke's. Duke's would have to pay the city for the use of the landfill.

Passing the resolution took a big load (pardon the pun) off of the city's solid waste department. There was no way, with Evanston's growth, that the city could have handled the increase in garbage collection caused by the boom, especially since the garbage crews would have to handle all the large sizes of containers by hand. Hopefully the city would have the funds to change our waste collection system soon; it was in the plans.

Former Mayor Bob Burns had recently sold Western T.V. Service to Lloyd F. Char, changing the name to Overthrust Cable Vision, Inc. Mr. Char made his presentation and requested a transfer of the franchise. The city attorney was directed look in to the process of the transfer.

All liquor licenses came up for renewal during one of the September meetings, as they all expired on October 1st each year and had to be renewed. All licenses were approved except the Whirl Inn, which had been on probation for the past year. City Attorney Lancaster was requested to check on the regulations and restrictions that may be placed on the Whirl Inn license before we approved their application.

Liquor licenses were going crazy with all the transfers and interest in buying them. Evanston still had one license available, but the way things were going, it wouldn't be much longer before it was gone. But the city council wasn't in a hurry to dispose of it unless something really nice came up.

I gave a report to the council on a Bear Lake Regional Commission meeting that I had attended with the governors of Wyoming, Utah, Idaho and Montana to discuss impact, water, etc. I told the council that I had a lot of questions thrown at me concerning impact, and they also mentioned our problem of dumping raw sewage into the Bear River. I explained to them that we were doing everything we could to correct the situation.

I also told the council that I mentioned to the group that we had commitments from the state for the funding and were working on funds to purchase the site we had located for the new sewer treatment plant. They all seemed to be satisfied with my explanation. Utah and Idaho were concerned because the Bear River also flows in their states and some of their communities also get their culinary water from the river.

The *Uinta County Herald* issue of September 8th had an article titled, WHITTAKER SAYS CITY WATER SUPPLY TESTS UP TO STATE PURITY STANDARDS. The article read: *Responding to recent rumors that parasites infesting the Evanston water supply have caused a number of hospitalizations since early last week, Water Filtration Plant Operator Butch Whittaker said Monday that state bacteriological reports on last week's city water samples have given the local water supply a clean bill of health. Whittaker said test results from Wyoming Department of Health and Social Services Division of Health and Medical Services reveal that city water is safe and contains no concentrations of bacteria harmful to health.*

*Whittaker added, "Our water is absolutely up to standard and even a little better than standard as far as E.P.A. and D.E.Q. are concerned at state and federal levels."*

The article went on to say, *Memorial Hospital Administrative Assistant Bob Shannon said that the Evanston hospital has admitted, treated and released one person for a parasitic gastric infection, but the patient was not an Evanston resident and had been using a private water supply outside the city limits. Shannon said, "The patient, treated last week, was an isolated case and the only confirmed parasitic infection treated recently at the hospital."*

The article went on, but Evanston had always been noted for its clean water. When testing the water, which was quite often, the water department and the state took samples from different areas of the city so that the samples would include water not only from the treatment plant, but also from the wells in the city.

Resolution 81-96, to enter into an agreement with EWP/Construction Services, Inc. for the design of the new Sewage Treatment Plant, was adopted, and Resolution 81-97 was also adopted to have the city engineer prepare a final application to the Farmer's Home Administration for a grant to purchase the site for the new wastewater treatment plant and to direct the mayor to sign the application. Both of these resolutions were adopted by regular motion, and seconded with all voting in favor.

During the October meetings we had more of the usual passing of various ordinances and resolutions, but one of the first orders of business was the opening of bids for new equipment, repairs and up-grading of the old wastewater treatment plant. Motion was made to accept the low bids in the total amount of $242,429, if the city engineer found that all specifications were met. The motion was seconded with all voting in favor.

By accepting the above bid, we thought that we would be able to put enough repairs into the plant to keep it going for another year or two without dumping raw sewage into the Bear River. However, with the fast growth and increase in sewage, it would probably need more repairs sooner than we expected. At this time Evanston was getting pretty desperate for the new sewer treatment plant.

After putting the Whirl Inn liquor license on probation for the past year, Councilwoman Wall made a motion, seconded by Fruits, during the October 8th meeting, to approve their re-application for a liquor license. A lengthy discussion followed, and after a considerable amount of public input, most against issuance of the license, Councilman Albrecht made an amendment to the motion that the Whirl Inn be allowed to dispense liquor from the main liquor store and drive-in window only. The motion to amend was seconded by Bills, with 4 yes votes and 3 no votes. The main motion by Wall to approve the application with the amended stipulations, also with a 4 to 3 vote, motion passed  by a majority. A roll call wasn't called for, but Councilmembers Wall, Fruits, Albrecht and I voted yes, while Morgan, Bills and Davis voted no.

A year ago, when the Whirl Inn, Inc. liquor license came up for renewal, it was put on probation for the year because of the overwhelming amount of complaints from the neighborhood. There was a large attendance of citizens at that meeting in opposition to the approval of the license. Although the Whirl Inn was located on the main highway through town, there were a number of residential homes located so close that the neighbors had problems with noisy drunks, fights and other commotions coming from patrons leaving the establishment.

At this October 8th meeting there were also a number of folks who lived near the Whirl Inn who were still very much against the issuance of the license, and when the council passed the motion to allow the business to continue by selling only from the street level package liquor store and drive-in window, it still made a lot of folks upset.

The *Uinta County Herald* came out with an article headed, COUN-CIL MULLS WHIRL INN LICENSE RENEWAL. It stated that *A neighbor, Sue Regneir, told the council, "I think it's about time somebody had the nerve to stand up and say 'We don't want that in our community.'" Then she added, "They (local liquor dealers) want that kind of clientele because those people (speaking of oil people) have the bucks in their pockets.... We are prostituting ourselves for money, every one of us."* It was always tough to put someone out of business just because business was so over-whelming, but the proprietor had a responsibility to make sure their business was operated properly by law. So the majority of the council was trying to be as fair to the liquor dealer and the residential folks as they could without hurting the establishment's business. However, there had been so many police calls and problems, inside and outside of the Whirl Inn. The number of patrons they allowed in the bar and lounge, with a dance floor, was way beyond the permitted number of patrons that the fire department allowed. The department placed a sign in each establishment showing the number of customers that were allowed at any one time, based on square footage, for the safety of everyone. This was a state required fire code.

Again, this is why the state should not dictate how many licenses a community can have based on population. In my personal opinion, I think they should let competition take care of it, because the way it is, a person or business can just sit on a license for a long time if they have a mind to and maybe they can eventually sell that license for big bucks.

Following the action taken on the Whirl Inn, Inc. liquor license, discussion of the Ramada Inn license came up. Although the Rama-da was nowhere near any residential property, we were having the same kind of problems at their establishment. They had their license approved earlier, but after hearing Chief Dennis Harvey's report on police activities, Councilman Bills made a motion to rescind the previous motion relating to the granting of the Ramada Inn liquor license, seconded by Davis. After a lengthy discussion and questions and answers (pro and con) involving owners Jim Hansen and Frank Nelson, and Chief Harvey and others, I called for the vote. The vote was 1 yes and 6 no votes. The motion failed by a majority, with Bills casting the only favorable vote, the Ramada Inn got their license renewed.

Construction activity was getting so out of hand that the council had passed many ordinances requiring developers and contractors to come up with complete plans before any permits or subdivisions were approved. Any construction or remodeling of any building required complete plans to submit them to the city inspector (previously called the building inspector) for approval, prior to starting any construction. Also, there was the requirement that builders apply for Conditional Use Permits from the Planning and Zoning Commission for certain construction. This also took a lot of time and caused a lot of delay in getting things done.

Also, there were many motions made and passed allowing extensions of subdividers additional time for submitting their plats to be recorded. The times were also tough for developers and contractors as well as the council, mainly because there was so much competition, and it seemed like things were moving so fast.

Ordinance 81-133 was recommended by the city attorney and introduced by Councilman Morgan to provide that all ordinances be authored by a city council member or the mayor. The author's name shall be a part of and published in the minutes with the ordinance, and to set forth the procedure for passage of ordinances. The motion was made by Bills to pass Ordinance 81-133 on first reading, seconded by Morgan, with all voting in favor. Ordinance 81-133 went on to pass on second and third readings with no opposition.

Apparently some outsiders had the impression that an ordinance could be authored and introduced by just anyone; therefore the city attorney suggested that we pass the ordinance. He stated that if anyone outside the council wants an ordinance or resolution introduced, they must get a member of the city council or the mayor to author it. It would be February of 1982 before Ordinance 81-133 became law.

Ordinance 81-134, to provide for an updating of the officers appointed by the mayor for a bi-annual term instead of every year was introduced by Councilman Albrecht. Motion was made by Albrecht to pass, and seconded by Bills, with all voting in favor. This ordinance went on to pass on second and third readings with all voting in favor.

Resolution 81-106 was a resolution concerning an amendment to form the City of Evanston–Uinta County Human Resource Center Joint Powers Agreement. A motion was made to adopt and was seconded with all voting in favor.

Councilman Bills made a motion to direct the city attorney to proceed with re-codification and reprinting the Evanston code book, seconded by Morgan, with 4 yes votes and 1 no vote. The motion passed by a majority. It was great to get the re-codification of all our ordinances project completed. It was the first time this had been done, as far as I know, since Evanston was incorporated.

The November meetings weren't much different, just more pending ordinances to be introduced and acted on, and additional resolutions were introduced, but in other business, more police officers and members of the Planning and Zoning Commission submitted their letters of resignation. Replacements had been made and confirmed by the council.

Resolution 81-113 was introduced by Councilman Davis, authorizing the city to apply to the U.S. Bureau of Land Management (BLM) for an airport site. Most of the land west of Evanston where the airport is now located is BLM land; therefore it was necessary to adopt the resolution to present to the government agency in order to obtain the land. Motion was made by Albrecht to adopt Resolution 81-113, seconded by Fruits. All voted in favor.

A motion was made to put the old city dumps up for sale and was seconded with 5 yes votes and 1 no vote. The motion passed by a majority. The city did end up selling the property to TJG, Inc. (Ellingford). They came up with the best bid and they also cleaned the dumps up and covered the area, making it look nice.

We had already passed an ordinance that all residential homes and businesses (new and old) would be required to have water meters. This was part of the water project with O.I.A. and the state. In order to get state and federal funds to upgrade our water system and enlarge the Sulphur Creek Reservoir, we were required to install water meters on all main buildings and secondary buildings if they were on separate water hookups.

During this November meeting, Councilman Albrecht made a motion authorizing the city to purchase 4,000 water meters from the Waterworks Equipment Company, contingent on the city receiving a grant for the meters, seconded by Fruits, with all voting in favor.

A lot of the local citizens that had been living in Evanston prior to the oil and gas boom were pretty upset and very much against having water meters. They were used to paying a flat fee for water and sewer, and now they were afraid that their water rates would automatically go up. Also, a number of water users hadn't been paying anything, for some reason or other, and they sure didn't want meters. They never received water bills because they had never notified City Hall that they were hooking into the city water system. New folks that had moved to Evanston in recent years weren't bothered by it at all, because where they previously had lived they probably had meters and were used to them.

This was one of the programs that really hurt me in the next year's mayoral election. County Commissioner Fanos said to me, *Denny, you know by doing this you are committing political suicide.* I responded, *John it's something that has to be done. I know that a lot of people are going to be upset about it, but I didn't run for mayor to keep everyone happy. I ran because I hoped to be able to make a difference in making Evanston a decent place to live. It's inevitable,* I added, *that water meters would come someday if we want to improve our water system, and receive grant monies from the state or feds. You knew that they would demand meters to be installed if they were funding the water project.* He agreed with me, but he was right, it was political suicide. *I'll just have to wait and see,* I said.

But one day after the city started charging for water based on the water meter readings, my wife Sandy ran into Lu Shee (Lucy) Yee, an elderly Chinese woman who owned a restaurant on Front Street, a Chinese food restaurant, with her husband Butch Yee (now deceased), called the Ranch Café (at present it is Bon Rico Restaurant). Sandy happened to run into Lucy as she was about to cross 10th Street at Main Street, heading towards City Drug. Sandy had worked for Butch and Lucy at the Ranch Café for years and they had become very good friends. This particular day when Sandy met Lucy on the corner, she asked Lucy, *Where are you going and can I help you across the street?* The street was icy and slick, and Lucy was on her way to pay her water bill at the City Hall. Lucy answered, *Yes, please,* and then Lucy flashed a bill, half pissed off, in front of Sandy's face and said, *I'm going down to pay my water bill, because your "son-e-bitchie" man put in water meters.* Sandy kind of chuckled at Lucy but helped her all the way to City Hall so she could pay her bill, then walked with her and helped on the slick streets all the way back to the Ranch Café.

Lucy always appeared to be ornery and pissed off at something or other, but that was just Lucy and everyone that knew her just accepted her ways. She was actually quite a nice person. Sandy and I had always got along with her and Butch, and they both appeared to still like us. Butch was always quite friendly and never said much to anyone. We continued to be close friends with them until they both passed on. They were some of the old Chinese folks left over from the early mining days in Almy.

After Butch died, Sandy took Lucy shopping in Salt Lake City several times, and when they would go into a store, Sandy would always tell the clerk to watch Lucy because she was a little sticky fingered. Sandy and the clerk both would keep track of what Lucy put in her shopping bag. Lucy always ended up paying for everything that she was trying to hide, thanks to Sandy.

The water meters made little difference in anyone's water bill, but did raise most of them a slightly, but once the older citizens of Evanston got used to them and eventually accepted them there were no more complaints; but that wasn't until after the election.

We hired a planner by the name of Harold Young. We paid his moving expenses in the amount of $350.00, to move him to Evanston. He was hired because he appeared to have the right credentials. We put him on a yearly contract and hoped he would be what we needed to start the planning process for the future of the community, and that he would have a lot of good advice for zoning.

Councilman Albrecht made a motion that the city council hold an executive session to discuss pending litigation between the City of Evanston and Whirl Inn, Inc., seconded by Bills, with all voting in favor.

Whirl Inn, Inc. had filed a lawsuit against the City of Evanston in District Court concerning our not re-approving the application for the full liquor license without the restrictions. On November 21st the court, by a 6 person jury, made the decision that the Whirl Inn would be allowed to continue its operation without restrictions, they notified the City of Evanston.

On November 23rd, the *Casper Star-Tribune* came out with an article titled, WHIRL INN ALLOWED TO CONTINUE ITS OPERATION. The article went on to say, *The Whirl Inn, Inc. will be allowed to continue its operation which includes a liquor store and drive-up window, the Hide-Out Lounge and a discotheque.* The article went on: *The decision on the Whirl Inn liquor license was reached about 4:00 p.m. Saturday in a jury trial brought by the Whirl Inn against the City of Evanston.*

*District Judge John Troughton rendered the court's decision after the jury brought in their answers to three questions:*

Would the welfare of the people residing in the vicinity of the Whirl Inn be adversely and seriously affected by continued operation of the disco and lounge? The jury answered no.

Would the desires of the residents of the City of Evanston be met or satisfied by the continued operation of the disco and lounge? The jury answered yes.

Is the license area of the liquor store and drive-up window so small as to be usable only for sales for off-premises consumption? The jury said yes.

The article continued: *Troughton recognized the City Council had issued the limited liquor license because they believed the operation of the disco and lounge would adversely and seriously affect the residents living in the area. But, Troughton said, this action was not upheld in the trial so the council has acted "arbitrarily and capriciously" and their decision "lacked discretion."*

*To J. D. Kindler of Whirl Inn, Inc., Troughton said, "The court recognizes there are problems in this operation." He said the Whirl Inn "had inherited the problems over the years" and admonished the Whirl Inn to do something about them.*

In closing remarks, the article continued: *for Evanston, City Attorney Dennis Lancaster stressed the "the burden of proof" was on the Whirl Inn. According to Lancaster, the city acted in good faith after receiving input from the citizens of the city. He said the rights of the Whirl Inn included "no right to infringe on the rights of other people."*

# Uinta County Herald

Wednesday, October 14, 1981     Evanston, Wyoming 82930     Volume 47, Number 75     Price, 20c Per Copy

## Whirl Inn liquor
# License renewed with limitations

In a 4-3 vote the Evanston City Council voted Thursday to renew with limitations a liquor license for the Whirl Inn.

The Council amended the Whirl Inn license to include only the downstairs package liquor store and drive-in window while discontinuing liquor sales in the Hideout Lounge and Whirl Inn Disco.

A crowd of more than 100 local residents and business people were on hand at City Hall to participate in discussion of the issue.

Council members Jerry Wall, Roy Fruits, Russ Albrecht and Mayor Dennis Ottley voted in favor of the amended license with Arnie Morgan, David Bills and Ronald Davis casting dissenting votes.

A number of residents who live near the Whirl Inn were at the meeting to speak against the license being granted.

"I can't sleep on Friday nights. At 2 a.m. they start coming out and I have to listen to screeching tires, people screaming four letter words and all kinds of noise," said resident Pete Nelson, who lives near the Whirl Inn.

"All of a sudden it (Evanston) isn't ours anymore. They came in and made us all millionaires and now we owe them," Nelson added.

On hand to speak in favor of the license being granted was J.D. Kindler, owner of the Whirl Inn.

"We don't have enough bars in Evanston. If you shut down the Whirl Inn it will just overcrowd the other bars in town," said Kindler.

"Then the young people will just have more neighborhood parties, which are the worst kind for the police. We control people at the Whirl Inn better than anywhere in town," he said.

Councilwoman Jerry Wall spoke in favor of the Whirl Inn license being renewed.

"I don't think closing the Whirl Inn will solve the problem," said Wall. "I've been there, the problems are parking and overcrowding, so if you close it you're just causing more problems elsewhere," she said.

Councilman David Bills spoke against the Council renewing the amended license.

"I object to crippling a business," said Bills. "I say let's either work with them or close it. I recommend we not renew the license."

After the motion passed Bills stated that he didn't think the Council's action would solve the problem. "No, I don't think we have solved it, but, considering the alternative I feel what we did is better than the alternative."

Councilwoman Wall, who spoke in favor of the license being renewed, stated after the motion that the action would have an adverse effect on the Whirl Inn.

"It will hurt his business," she said. "And all it will do is cause more problems at the other establishments who will have the overflow.

"I represent the new people in town, too," said Wall. "They are also taxpayers and should be represented as well as people who have lived here longer."

Councilman Albrecht, who voted in favor of the amended license renewal, stated early in the meeting that he felt the license being issued in the first place was a mistake.

"The mistake was made years ago by a previous council. It should not have been issued in the first place," said Albrecht. "I can't go on any longer on this. I'm tired of getting calls. I get them every night."

Whirl Inn owner Kindler expressed to the council that their action was premature.

"There are two other new places opening up in town and with our purchase of the Chuck Wagon parking area the problems we are facing should be alleviated," said Kindler.

Jae Dee Kindler defends his right to a renewal of his liquor license at the Whirl Inn during Thursday's city council meeting.

Not too long after the trial the city council received a very blunt, but quite pleasant letter from a group called "Evanston Concerned Citizens" signed by Rick Sather. In this letter they thanked the city council for their concern and the support given them. They also listed 10 items referring to Judge Troughton's comments stated at the trial, and were very concerned that J. D. Kindler's remarks concerning purchasing the Chuck Wagon property next door and constructing another fast food establishment. They felt that this would just create more traffic and less parking.

On December 8th, City Attorney Dennis Lancaster wrote a letter to District Court Judge John Troughton, filing for the City of Evanston, Defendant in the civil case, its objections to the form of the Order as proposed by Plaintiff's attorneys received by Lancaster's office on December 3rd. In the letter Lancaster wrote, *"Since in all likelihood the City will be appealing this matter to the Supreme Court, I would like to be notified immediately upon entry of the Judgment and Order so that we can perfect our appeal."*

Then he explained some of the city's objections to the trial. The objections concerned the wording of the Orders, such as the restrictions placed on the Whirl Inn; that during the probationary period the problems continued and had never been corrected; the issuance of the license being restricted; the followings of the state law; and the fact that one of the selected jury members was indeed a relative through marriage.

Lancaster ended his letter by stating that he was aware that the trial was made up of just an advisory jury, and the Court was not bound by their determination, but he was very concerned with the disclosure.

A copy of this letter was given to each council member and me to read over and determine whether or not we should appeal to the State of Wyoming Supreme Court. At our next meeting in December, the council made a motion to go into executive session to discuss the matter.

During the month of December, we only had one regular meeting scheduled for the 10th of the month. The annual Christmas Dinner for the employees was held on December 5th at The Three Knights restaurant at 6:30 p.m. It turned out to be a fun evening.

On December 10th, our only regular meeting of the month, there was a lot of unfinished business to take care of and some new business, as usual. Early in the meeting, Mr. Bob Dean of Time D.C. Trucking Company made a request for an extension of their lease with the city until May 31, 1982. Their lease was actually due to expire at the end of 1981, but they needed more time to get set up elsewhere. The request was to extend their lease until May 31, 1982. The request was granted by motion with all voting in favor.

Mr. Rick Sather and several other concerned citizens were in attendance at the meeting. Sather, representing the Concerned Citizen's Committee, was there to make a presentation to the council concerning the previous court case between the Whirl Inn and the city. He spoke of the concerns he had mentioned in the previously received letter from the committee. Sather stated that he lived in the area of the Whirl Inn and was quite disappointed at the decision of the court, along with many other citizens of Evanston. Following his presentation a lengthy discussion was held, but no action was taken on any of the subjects mentioned by the committee at that time.

During the meeting Mr. Cal Schmidt, representing Mountain Bell (now known as Century Link) requested to dig a hole in Yellow Creek Road to install new cables (for telephone lines). There was a lengthy discussion held, and late that evening Councilman Fruits made a motion to allow Mountain Bell's request to dig a hole in Yellow Creek Road, seconded by Wall. The motion failed with 7 no votes.

During the discussion on the Mountain Bell matter some derogatory remarks were made by the council members as reported in the "Perspective" column of the December 16th issue of the *Uinta County Herald*:

The editorial titled PERSPECTIVES by David Fierro read: *Cally Schmidt of Mountain Bell was doing his job. There he stood in front of the Evanston City Council asking the city for permission to tear a 10' x 10' hole in the recently constructed Yellow Creek Road.*

*"We originally wanted to dig three holes but we've decided to just dig one hole," said Schmidt.*

*The members of the council reacted like he had asked if he could construct a monument to Moammer Khadafy (Emperor of Libya) in the town square.*

*"You want to do what?" bellowed David Bills. "We just spent a lot of money to construct that road and now you want to come along and tear it up," said City Engineer Wayne Shepherd.*

*Schmidt went on to explain that the phone company needed to get the cables under the street to recover some bad lines. "The job would probably close the inbound lane for two, maybe three days," said Schmidt. "I am concerned if we get bad weather though, because if we get icy conditions there could be a dangerous situation with the pit being open for two days," Schmidt added.*

*Schmidt explained that the lines Mountain Bell wanted to work on would eventually serve Yellow Creek, Honeywood Cove and Chapparal Estates. "Right now the people out there are getting their service from over the mountain," he said.*

*"What would you do if we refuse this request?" asked Jerry Wall with a mischievous grin on her face.*

*"I guess we'd have to come back in and lay new cable. And from a cost effective standpoint the company wouldn't want to do that," said Schmidt.*

*"Can't this wait until spring?" asked Roy Fruits.*

*"I guess it could," said Schmidt.*

Then Mayor Ottley (the article went on) *spoke up and said that it sounded like the council needed more time to consider the matter and asked that the matter be delayed until the city engineer and the council could find out more about the issue.*

*"I don't think the council is prepared to decide on this matter tonight, Mr. Schmidt," said Mayor Ottley.*

*"It doesn't sound like the council is ready to decide on this tonight, Mayor," said Schmidt.*

*The council then decided to hold off on making a decision until the city engineer could look further into the matter.*

*"Make sure you leave your name, address and phone number so we can contact you, Mr. Schmidt," said Roy Fruits.*

*"And leave a phone number that works,"* joked David Bills.

*"Now aren't you glad you came here tonight?" Ottley asked Schmidt.*

*Schmidt just smiled and muttered something under his breath.*

*Sometimes government in action is fun to watch.*

# Perspectives

## by David Fierro

*10/14/81 uch*

Cally Schmidt of Mountain Bell was doing his job. There he stood in front of the Evanston City Council asking the city for permission to tear a 10x10 hole in the recently constructed new Yellow Creek road.

"We originally wanted to dig three holes but we've decided to just dig the one hole," said Schmidt.

The members of the Council reacted like he had asked if he could construct a monument to Moammer Khadafy in the town square.

"You want to do what?" bellowed David Bills.

"We just spent a lot of money to construct that road and now you want to come along and tear it up," said City Engineer Wayne Sheperd.

Schmidt went on to explain that the phone company needed to get the cables under the street to recover some bad lines.

"It should give us another 6 to 7 percent improvements. This is a recovery job. We are trying to get back to the point where we are meeting the standards we need to meet," he said.

"The job would probably close the inbound lane for two, maybe three days," said Schmidt. "I am concerned if we get bad weather though, because if we get icy conditions there could be a dangerous situation with the pit being open for two days," Schmidt added.

Schmidt explained that the lines Mountain Bell wanted to work on would eventually serve Yellow Creek, Honeywood Cove and Chapparal Estates. "Right now the people out there are getting their service from over the mountain," he said.

"What would you do if we refuse this request?" asked Jerry Wall with a mischievous grin on her face.

"I guess we'd have to come back in and lay new cable. And from a cost effective standpoint the company wouldn't want to do that," said Schmidt.

"Why is the cable under the road, anyway?" asked one of the Council members.

"Well, originally it was in the bar pit, but then when the new road was put in the cable was left in the same place and the road went over it," Schmidt added.

"It isn't that we need the lines now, but if we have any more failures we won't have a backup. This repair job will give us 26 additional backup lines," he said.

"Can't this wait until spring?" asked Roy Fruits.

"I guess it could," said Schmidt.

Then Mayor Ottley spoke up and said that it sounded like the Council needed more time to consider the matter and asked that the matter be delayed until the City Engineer and the Council could find out more about the issue.

"I don't think the Council is prepared to decide on this matter tonight, Mr. Schmidt," said Mayor Ottley.

"It doesn't sound like the Council is ready to decide on this tonight, Mayor," said Schmidt.

The Council then decided to hold off on making a decision until the City Engineer could look further into the matter.

"Make sure you leave your name, address and phone number so we can contact you, Mr. Schmidt," said Roy Fruits.

"And leave a phone number that works," joked David Bills.

"Now aren't you glad you came here tonight?" Ottley asked Schmidt.

He just smiled and muttered something under his breath.

Sometimes government in action is fun to watch.

*Uinta County Herald*, April 8, 1981.

The article ended with Mr. David Fierro's last remark.

Maybe the council was a little rough with Mr. Schmidt, but Schmidt wasn't exactly pleasant either. He came off being quite surly, as if we had no other choice than to just say yes and allow him to dig up the road. But, as usual, the press didn't say anything about that. Editorials always like to make government look silly without telling both sides of an issue.

I believe the primary purpose of denying Mountain Bell's request was because of the time of year. I know that was a big concern of mine. December is not a good time to start digging holes in the ground and working on something underground, especially holes that large. I felt bad about not letting the telephone company have their way, but as far as I was concerned, next spring would be a better time anyway.

This past November, the city council had decided to hire an assistant engineer. The work load was getting pretty heavy for Shepherd because of so much going on with subdivisions, annexation, and so on. During this December meeting, City Engineer Shepherd introduced James Golding as his recently hired Assistant City Engineer. The council accepted the new employee without question.

Councilman Bills made a motion to change the personnel manual for mileage to be paid at the same rate as the State of Wyoming pays, seconded by Wall, with all voting in favor.

Councilman Morgan made a motion for a one-month cost of living bonus to all full time employees based on grade level and number of years worked times five, seconded by Davis, with all voting in favor.

After reading City Attorney Lancaster's letter to District Judge John Troughton and after hearing from the Concerned Citizens Committee, the council made a motion to go into an executive session concerning the lawsuit that had turned out in Whirl Inn's favor.

Coming out of the executive session, Councilman Bills made a motion for the City of Evanston to appeal the decision of the District Court to the Wyoming Supreme Court, seconded by Davis with 5 yes votes and 2 no votes. I was one of the dissenting votes, but I don't recall who the other was. My concern was the cost, because court would probably be held in Cheyenne, and we would have to hire other attorneys to represent us in the case and they don't come cheap. I also didn't think it would change the decision of the District Court.

The National League of Cities met for the 1981 Congress of Cities in December with Councilman Albrecht and me, Councilwoman Wall and her husband Cloey, and Councilman Fruits and his wife Bobbi attending. The convention was held in Detroit, Michigan, but due to our late registrations, Steve Snyder, Administrative Assistant could only get us reservations in Windsor, Ontario, Canada, across the channel between Lake Erie and Lake Huron. We had to commute through the toll tunnel from Windsor to Detroit to get to the convention center. It was quite an experience, much different from Atlanta, GA., but we did have a good time and I think most of us learned a few things about running a city and what was happening in other communities in the country.

After getting back to Evanston, and during our first regular city council meeting of the year on January 7, 1982, we gave our report to the city council on what we had learned and gained by attending the National League of Cities convention. We reported that Councilman Russel "Bub" Albrecht had been appointed as a member of the Housing and Economic Board of the N. L. of C., and I had been appointed to the National Energy Board of the N. L. of C.

❧

Towards the end of 1981 our sporting goods store, "Lockeroom Etc. ," wasn't doing too well and seemed to be doing worse every day. The wholesale suppliers that we purchased our inventory from gave us a line of credit so we would have time to sell our inventory before having to pay for it, but that started getting out of hand because the business just didn't seem to be able to keep up. When we ordered merchandise it was always a pretty large order, and we always seemed to be close to our limit before making payments, but we had always been good for it until business got going sour.

Two reasons we were going under were, first, a good share of local folks would not trade with us because I was mayor. It appeared that I was stepping on too many toes and a lot of locals were upset because of my decisions, but the decisions were not mine alone; they were also the council's decision as well. However, they pointed to me as the power behind those decisions. I voted on an issue based on what I thought was best for Evanston. The second reason was because we were carrying way too much credit on the books. It appeared that we were too loose offering credit to the locals, including new folks moving into town, but everyone seemed to be making big money and we figured that there wouldn't be a problem with most folks paying, but we were wrong. When we closed the store, we still had thousands of dollars on the books that we never received.

We had already ordered our merchandise for the holiday season, thinking and hoping that the season would help pull us out of the hole we had gotten ourselves into. But business was getting so bad that we weren't bringing in enough to even pay the help. We let all our help go and tried to handle the business with just our family. We had a very large stock of inventory, but the business just wasn't there.

Dave, my son, was managing the store and was trying to do a good job. Even though Evanston was right at its peak of the boom, for some reason or other, Evanston just wasn't buying from us. At that time we were the only sports store in town, but it seemed like everybody was going to Wasatch Front to do all their sporting goods shopping, and we were slowly going under. It didn't appear there was any chance that it would get better. Business was so bad that we started thinking about closing up completely, but the store was so far in debt to our suppliers that we were hoping there was some way to catch up.

At the time we were located where Gasamat (Smoker Friendly) is presently and were leasing from Dave Moon. We had a ten-year lease with him with the stipulation that we could renew; that is why we spent so much money remodeling the store. It was a very costly venture and at first the store was doing a great business. However, after the store started going under, Moon was good enough to let us out of the lease without any kind of penalty. We were very grateful to him for being so good about the lease, because he could have held us to the lease and then I don't know what we would have done.

We thought that it would be best to keep the store opened through the holiday season of Christmas and New Year's, but right after the season was over we decided to liquidate the inventory.

My son Dave went to work for Elaine Blakeslee Michaelis, owner of Uinta Title and Insurance Company, with Sonny Blakeslee, Elaine's son, as an insurance agent. My wife Sandy, my daughter-in-law Tammy and my daughter-in-law to be, Lindy Harvey, took over the store to help liquidate it. Right after the holiday we moved all inventory to the old town hall building that Uinta Realty, Inc. was leasing for liquidation.

Most of the stock was sold for about ten cents on the dollar, and some was given away, and if I remember right, Stevens and Brown in Sugarhouse, Utah bought some of it at a very cheap price. But we knew there was no way to save the store, so we just accepted our lumps and went under knowing we would be highly in debt and knowing that we would have to depend on the real estate agency to get it paid off.

⚬⚬⚬

The new owner, Gene Harter, Senior Partner in Bixland Corporation, and his partners had finished with the remodeling of the old town hall sometime mid-year in 1981. Mr. Harter, whom I had never met, approached my oldest son Randy, who was assisting me in operating Uinta Realty. Harter asked Randy if there was a possibility of Uinta Realty being interested in managing the entire building and leasing it out for him for a fee based on a percentage, or of Uinta Realty leasing the entire building and then subleasing the spaces out for themselves.

After Randy talked to me about it, we decided that we would go with the latter, because there was a large demand at that time for leased office and retail store space. Harter agreed to a long-term lease at $6,000 per month, which didn't seem bad at the time. We were able to get most of the building leased out and it looked like we had made a pretty good decision.

The reason I had never met Mr. Harter before was because he lived in Lafayette, California and was never present at the council meetings when we acted on the bids. He just had his partners represent the Bixland Corporation at the time of the bid openings and at the meetings when the bids were awarded.

Because Uinta Realty, Inc. had such a good lease on the building, we thought we would go ahead, at Uinta Realty's expense, and have Young Electric Sign Company put up the "OLD TOWN HALL" name sign and the marquee on the building, as well as install the clock in the bell tower. This all cost an enormous amount of money.

Ever since I moved to Evanston I had always wondered why there was no clock or some kind of bell in the tower. All there was covering each open space, meant for a clock or something similar on the four sides of the tower, was a piece of plywood. Therefore, I thought it would be a good public relations move for Uinta Realty, Inc. to put clocks where the openings were. It wasn't!

All the time we were leasing the building the clock was working well, with the bell ringing once on the half-hour and the number of times on the hour. We thought it was pretty neat having it up there. It was kept in good order because Phil Mensing, who was running the projector at the Strand Theater, was also taking care of the old town hall clock and had for years. He really enjoyed it and treated it like it was his own. Phil was a good citizen and was always helping folks around town with various mechanical problems that they may have had. He was very mechanically inclined.

~~~

However, getting back to "Lockeroom Etc.", we moved our merchandise into the largest and best space in the old town hall right after a furniture store called "Triad" went broke. While we were there we liquidated all inventory from the store and then decided to move Uinta Realty, Inc. into the space. It was a great location, and we were able to take on more agents, making our agency the largest real estate firm in Evanston. This was the same space that the old fire hall and later the local museum were in, prior to the city selling the building to Bixland.

1981 had been a very busy year for Evanston. The boom and fast growth was being handled as good as expected by the city and time was becoming very essential. We had a lot going on and a lot to look forward to, but, being as 1982 would be election year for the mayor'sposition, I had a tough decision to make, and I wasn't looking forward to that.

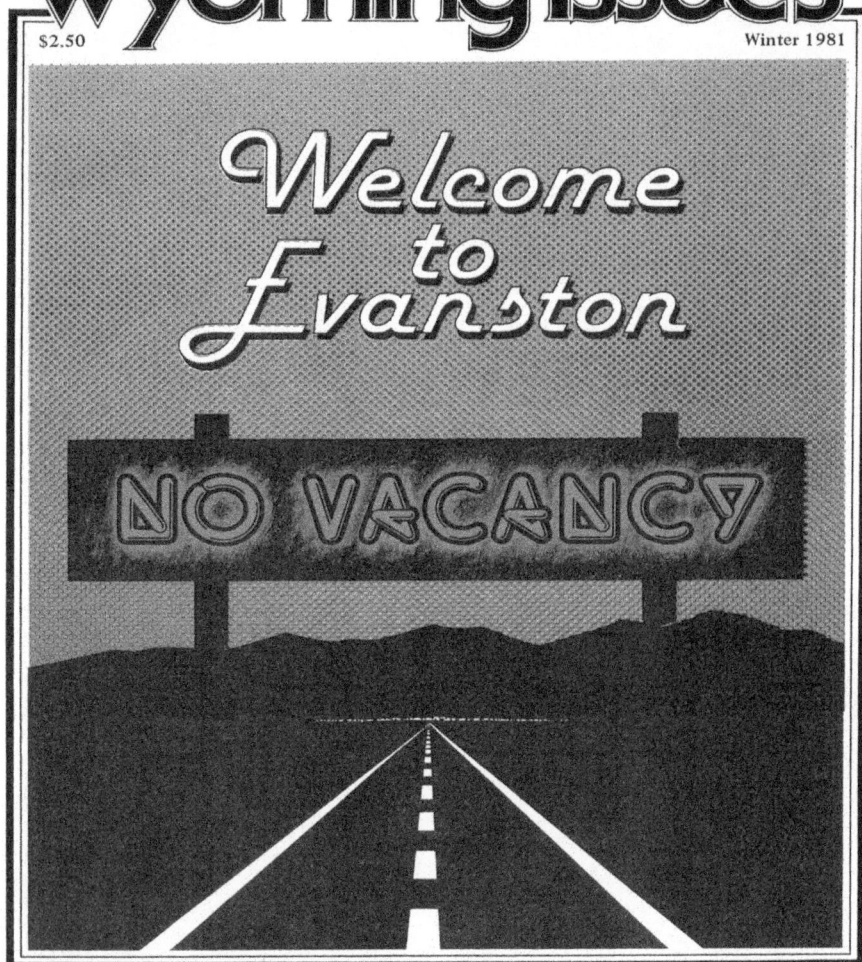

# CHAPTER 16

1982....The year I'll never forget. The Overthrust Industrial Association (O.I.A.), through their consulting firm Denver Research Group, had Evanston's mitigation plan almost complete. After dozens of meetings with city and county officials, and many citizen groups, things were finally coming together. The plans seemed to cover all needs that the mitigation plan had included. There was still some question on some of the funding, but commitments had been made by various government agencies for grants and loans, plus the financial assistance from O.I.A. Things were looking good, but everyone still had a lot of work to do before any construction could get started.

The first regular meeting was on January 7, 1982 with all members of the council present except Councilman Albrecht. He was excused for a doctor's appointment which took him out of town. All appointed officials were present, and a large group of concerned citizens.

After taking roll call, approving minutes and the financial statement including the payment of bills, I gave my year-end report thanking all the city employees, my staff of appointed officials, members of the city council, all committee members, and the O.I.A. and Denver Research Group for all their help and assistance in all the projects and programs that we had accomplished with success during 1981.

I also mentioned some of the difficult decisions we had to make, the unfinished business we had undertaken, and where we were at concerning the Whirl Inn lawsuit. I ended my report by saying that I was very pleased with all those who took part in making 1981 a success, and that I felt good about what we had accomplished, although we still had a long way to go to reach our goals.

Following my report I made the following appointments to several boards and commissions: Gaylon Thornock, 5-year term with the Airport Board; Jake Williams, Conrad Michaelson, Jerry Revelli and Doug McCalla each to a 3-year term on the Planning and Zoning Commission; Kevin Smith, Ron Atkinson and Dan Wheeler each to a 3-year term on the Parks and Recreation Board; Marie Hicks to a 5-year term and Rick Lavery to a 4-year term on the Housing Authority; and Don Welling and me to a 1-year term on the Evanston Joint Powers Board. Councilman Davis made a motion to confirm the appointments, seconded by Morgan, with all voting in favor.

Some of the unfinished business we acted on included several ordinances that came up for second and third readings, which were all passed by a majority vote. We also acted on a few new ordinances and resolutions and held hearings on a few appeals concerning decisions made by the Evanston Planning and Zoning Commission; and the Evanston Liquor Dealers put in their request for the four unlimited special days where they could stay open as late as they wanted, as permitted by state statute.

During this meeting I read a letter from the City of Gillette thanking the City of Evanston for sending them a copy of our new Itinerant Merchant ordinance and our Drug Paraphernalia ordinance.

Councilman Morgan made a motion for the City of Evanston to proceed on acquisition of land site, and right-of-ways and easements for the location selected for the new sewage treatment plant. The motion was seconded by Bills. All voted in favor.

The ordinance passed in December of 1981 requiring that all new ordinances would require an author/sponsor prior to being introduced went into effect in February. The name of the author/sponsor would be required to be stated in the minutes along with the name of the person introducing the ordinance. Therefore, all new ordinances that came on the floor beginning February 1, 1982 must name the author in the minutes, but that person would have to be a member of the city council or the mayor.

However, if someone outside the council wanted to have an ordinance introduced and brought on the floor for discussion they would be required to request a member of the city council or the mayor to agree to sponsor it for them, and in the future that happened quite frequently.

City Planner Harold Young reported that the city/county master plan was expected to be formulated within the next few months, with a totally new master plan scheduled for some time in the fall of this year.

The Uinta County Commissioners were in the process of enlarging the Uinta County Courthouse, and building a new library with a large parking lot. During the second regular meeting in January, I read a letter from the commissioners requesting the city to vacate 8th Street between Main and Center Streets. Motion was made by Councilman Fruits for the mayor to talk to the city attorney about vacating that portion of 8th Street, and to get the necessary paperwork started for a resolution. The motion was seconded by Wall, with all voting in favor.

Other business that came up during the January meeting included a motion by Councilman Bills for the mayor to enter into an agreement with the Wyoming Farm Loan Board for a multi-application for 5 projects, seconded by Albrecht, with all voting in favor.

This application requested $3,400,000 for the Sewer Treatment Plant; $1,500,000 for the Public Works Building; $800,000 for the Public Safety Building; $1,200,000 for the Human Service Facility; and funding for a new fire hall.

Councilman Fruits made a motion for the mayor to apply for an O. I. A. grant for some road equipment, seconded by Albrecht, with all voting in favor.

I had Steve Snyder prepare the application for me to present to Owen Murphy, President of O.I.A. Later, the request was approved and we were directed by Murphy to start requesting bids for the equipment.

The Evanston City Council received a written report during the meeting from Fire Chief Jon Lunsford. I was very impressed by the report and it appeared that all members of the council were as well. We expressed special commendation to Lunsford for such a thorough and impressive report, and the council requested that the report be shared with the rest of the community by sending copies to various divisions of the city and county. The report stated that the department composed of 43 members. Three members were on full time pay, plus the other 40 members were strictly volunteers with no monetary compensation.

The report also stated that the City of Evanston presently had a class six (6) fire rating, which in past years had been the best rate a city could have that had a volunteer fire department. The report also said that they had 269 calls in the year of 1981, and some of those calls were not only in Uinta County, but also in Rich County, Utah. He stated in his report that all their calls were not necessarily fire calls. Following was a breakdown of the types of calls: Structure fires – 62; Auto-truck fires – 42; Grass-brush fires – 36; Hazardous material spills – 24; Extrications – 16; Ambulance – 43; Public assists – 46.

The report discussed the various activities of the fire department. It was a very busy department and all those involved were well commended for their services.

Most of our meetings were still running quite late. This last January meeting lasted until 11:30 p.m.

Councilman David Bills had announced early in January that he was going to run for the Mayor of Evanston this election year of 1982. Besides the mayor's seat, there would be three council members up for re-election: Councilwoman Wall, Councilman Davis, and Councilman Fruits, and Governor Ed Herschler and all other state officials would be up for re-election.

On January 20th an article came out in the *Uinta County Herald* titled: PROPERTY TAXES REMAIN LOW IN THE CITY OF EVANSTON. The article went on to say that: *It's been at least 15 years since city property tax rates have been raised, according to Steve Snyder, Administrative Assistant to the Mayor.*

The article quoted Snyder: *"We have $19 million in capital improvements scheduled for 1982-1983 and we don't anticipate having to raise the city taxes then, either. We've been assertive about going after grant money rather than loans, and that has helped us keep the cost to the citizens down,"* he said. *"The state has gone out of the way to help us,"* he added.

The article went on: *The current city property tax is 7.1 mills, or $71 per $100,000 valuation. That figure does not include other mill levies such as school districts, county mill levies and special taxing districts which keeps the Evanston total mill levy to 7.1 mills.* The article quoted me as saying, "*We are proud of the fact that we have been able to avoid raising property taxes.*"

*Mayor Dennis Ottley* (the article continued) *is grateful to the state and organizations like the O.I.A.* "*They have been great to work with. In addition to the funding, which is important, we have received some very necessary technical assistance to help us keep pace with the growing needs of the people of Evanston,*" *Ottley said.*

The current mill levy of the City of Evanston was 7.1 mills at that time. However, the maximum mill levy a city can request, by law, was 8.0 mills. Special projects, such as something for public use, or districts such as a fire or recreation district, had to be voted on by the people. Whatever the mill levy voted on for that purpose would be in addition to the current mill levy.

That issue of the local newspaper also announced that September 1, 1982 would be the completion date set for the Amoco natural gas treatment plant at Whitney Canyon.

During the February meetings more unfinished business concerning several pending ordinances were acted on, with all passing by motions on second and third readings. These ordinances consisted of new subdivisions, annexations, revising some codes of the City of Evanston, and requesting zone changes. With very little discussion on any of them they passed without further opposition.

Ordinance 82-3, sponsored by me and introduced by Councilman Morgan, prohibited obscene conduct, distributing obscene material and promoting the same; providing notice of obscene material or action; providing standards for evidence and defenses; and providing penalties for violation.

Motion was made to pass on first reading by Councilman Albrecht, seconded by Davis. But Councilman Bills made the motion to table Ordinance 82-3 until later in the evening, seconded by Morgan, with all voting in favor.

Later, when Ordinance 82-3 was brought back on the floor, a lengthy discussion followed. I explained to the council the ordinance was important because of the obscene material that had been recently distributed within the schools all the complaints we had gotten, not only from the school officials, but also from parents. Many comments were made by the council, pro and con, and from the few citizens that were in attendance.

The *Uinta County Herald* issue of February 10, 1982 had an article with the heading: ANTI-PORNOGRAPHY ORDINANCE PASSES FIRST HEARING THURSDAY. The article stated: *City Attorney Dennis Lancaster drafted the ordinance in response to recent rulings in Sweetwater and Laramie counties that had found the Wyoming state obscenity law to be unconstitutional.*

*Prior to completing the final draft on the proposed new city ordinance, the city attorney's office obtained copies of the Sweetwater and Laramie County judgments in order to produce an Evanston ordinance that would be in compliance with the constitution,* the article went on to read. *"We revised the ordinance we had to put us in compliance with the Supreme Court ruling (Miller vs. California, 1973),"* the article quoted Lancaster saying.

However, following the discussion during the meeting, Councilman Morgan suggested that everyone study the ordinance carefully, and made the motion to pass Ordinance 82-3 on first reading. The motion was seconded by Bills. A roll call vote was called for with Bills, Morgan, Albrecht and me voting in favor of passing the ordinance, and Wall and Fruits voting against, with Davis being absent. The motion passed by a majority and would be brought back on the floor for the second and third readings at later meetings.

At 6:55 p.m., the Evanston City Council received a telephone call concerning a bomb threat. The meeting was immediately vacated until the police and fire officials cleared the threat, after which we reconvened and continued with our business as if nothing had happened.

During the February meetings two resolutions were introduced and adopted designating certain areas and acreage within the 40 acres south of Interstate I-80 that the city had purchased. One resolution deeded 6.008 acres to the City of Evanston-Uinta County Human Resource Center Joint Powers Board, and the transferred 8.311 acres to the Housing Authority of the City of Evanston to be used for the Senior Citizens Center.

Resolution 82-27 to issue Industrial Revenue Bonds to finance the proposed new Evanston Bowling Lanes was introduced by Councilman Albrecht. Motion was made by Councilwoman Wall for adoption, seconded by Albrecht. It passed with 5 yes votes, 1 no vote by Bills, and 1 absent. It looked like Evanston was going to get a nice bowling alley since the last one closed a few years ago, but the project had to go through three readings of an ordinance before it was approved. After the third and final reading of the ordinance was approved the bowling alley was built. It was located in the building that now houses Mountain Regional Services, Inc. The Evanston Lanes, like Billy's Emporium, also went broke when things slowed down.

Councilman Fruits made a motion to approve the application for a restaurant liquor license for Shakey's Pizza Parlor, seconded by Wall. A roll call vote was called for with Wall, Fruits, Albrecht and me voting yes, and Davis and Bills voting no. Motion passed by a majority. Shakey's Pizza Parlor was located where Maverick on Front Street is at the present, and it was the first and only pizza parlor that Evanston had at that time.

Proudly, I declared February 11, 1982 as Red Devil Day as the Evanston High School basketball team had won the State Class A Championship. It was a day of community pride, and the Evanston High School Athletic banquet would be held at Billy's Emporium on March 3, 1982.

I read a letter from Former Fire Chief Jerry Cazin protesting the proposed closing of 8th Street between Main and Center Streets. There would be more letters and complaints coming from folks protesting the closing before the decision became final.

The last meeting in February adjourned at 12:10 a.m. of the next day. I was glad we started our meetings at 4:00 p.m. and not at 7:00 p.m. as we were previously.

During our March meetings, I reported on a trip that Councilman Albrecht and I had made to a National League of Cities conference in Washington, D.C. Both Albrecht and I were on national committees. I was on the National Energy Board and Albrecht was on the Housing and Economic Board.

I reported that both Albrecht and I had the opportunity to meet with Senator Simpson, Senator Wallop, and Congressman Cheney while in D.C. We talked a lot about the problems Evanston and Uinta County had because of the boom, and about the O.I.A.'s function. We also said that whatever help they could give us would certainly be appreciated. They all assured us that we would get their total support and that they knew all about the problems we were having.

Both regular city council meetings in March were very busy with dozens of pending ordinances to take care of on second and third readings, and several ordinances were sponsored, introduced and acted on, and a few new resolutions were introduced and acted on. Both meetings were very busy and lasted until after 11:00 p.m.

Ordinance 82-32 was sponsored by Councilman Albrecht and introduced by Councilman Davis, providing for the salaries of the Mayor and City Council Members. This would give the mayor an annual salary of $12,000, and the Council Members an annual salary of $3,000, to be paid in twelve monthly installments.

Councilman Fruits made the motion to adopt Ordinance 82-32 on first reading, seconded by Albrecht. Roll call vote was called for by Councilman Bills. He opposed the passage of this ordinance because it was an election year and he felt that Administrative Assistant Steve Snyder should take more of the load, *"as if Snyder didn't have enough to do,"* I thought.

Councilman Bills had to realize that no one presently on the council, including the mayor, would be eligible for an increase in pay until they ran again for re-election and won. By law elected officials cannot vote themselves an immediate raise. The three holdover council members would not get the raise until they ran again, and that would be another two years without the increase, but the three newly elected officials would get the raise as well as whoever got in as mayor. But

I don't think Bills even thought of that, unless he knew he was a hold-over member of the council and that he would have to wait until he ran again in 2 more years, and won, before he received any increase.

A roll call vote was called for with me, Albrecht, Wall, Fruits, and Davis all voting in favor, and Bills voting no. Morgan was absent. This ordinance went on to pass on second and third readings by the same majority vote.

Mr. Roger Ranta, Superintendent of Schools for School District No. 1 requested the City of Evanston remove the requirement of a Conditional Use Permit for schools. He also requested the right for the school district to be able to add modular class rooms to their school grounds. No action was taken at this time, but later there was a motion approving the School District's requests.

I read letters of resignation from Debra Allport as Animal Control Officer, and from Robert "Tobe" Tueller because of his retirement. Both resignations were accepted with a lot of appreciation shown to both for their service to the city.

City Attorney Dennis Lancaster brought up the fact that through annexing areas by using roads that are contiguous, which is legal, we have created islands in the city that are not annexed and that we should try to do something about that. He was directed by the council to proceed to contact the property owners to discus voluntary annexation.

Over the next few months Lancaster was quite successful in getting some of these islands annexed. Most of the property owners were happy about it because it gave them city services and made their property much more valuable, but there were still a few areas, such as properties where fireworks stores were located, that had to be looked at.

Fireworks were illegal for use or sale in the City of Evanston. Therefore, before these areas could be annexed, the property owners would need to have Evanston change the ordinance to allow fireworks to be used and sold in the city limits, which did happen a few years later.

Julie Lehman expressed her thanks and appreciation to the Council for being chosen as Citizen of the Year. This was an annual award given to a person who was very active in the community and gave much of their time to make the City of Evanston a better place to live. The person is chosen by the city council and the mayor. Julie Lehman had been very active in the mitigation plans that were drawn up by the Denver Research Group. Julie was also the first Director of the Evanston Housing Authority Board.

During the March meetings of the City of Evanston we formed a Beautification Committee by appointing these people from the various voting wards: Ward 1 – Ruth Reese, 1 year; Dale Henderson, 2 years; and Connie Burns; 3 years; Ward 2 – Blanche Smith, 1 year; Richard Ludwig, 2 years; and Larry Lehman, 3 years; and Ward 3 – Janice Fife, 1 year; Richard Kelley, 2 years; and Mike Pexton, 3 years. Motion was made and seconded to confirm the appointments.

Resolution 82-32 allowing the mayor and council to vacate 8th Street between Main and Center Streets was introduced by Councilman Fruits, but there was an awful lot of opposition to vacating that portion of 8th Street. Therefore, Councilman Bills made the motion to table Resolution 82-32 until the regular meeting scheduled on April 8th. The motion was seconded by Wall with all voting in favor.

On March 10th I received a letter from Owen Murphy, President of the O.I.A. that read:

*Dear Dennis:*

*Yesterday's news conference was a success, I think, because of the generous contribution of time and work by all participants. Thank you for your help in bringing to the attention of the public the capital construction program developed by the Farm Loan Board, Uinta County, Evanston, and the Overthrust Industrial Association. We can all be proud of our part in this outstanding example of government–industry cooperation. Again, thank you for your help.*

*Sincerely,*
*OVERTHRUST INDUSTRIAL ASSOCIATION,*
*Owen F. Murphy, President*

I thought it was a pretty nice letter. I read it to the council and the folks in attendance at the next meeting. It reassured everyone that the O.I.A. and the Denver Research Group were working with the city and county very closely to complete the mitigation plan that would help the area immensely.

The April meetings were pretty much the same, taking care of regular business first, such as approving all previous minutes and the outstanding bills. We also acted on several pending ordinance on second and third readings with all passing by at least a majority, and we took care of new business as usual.

The Pioneer Investment Group (Pioneer Bank) requested that the eastern property line of Front Street be rezoned from Highway Commercial (C-3) to Central Business District (C-1), making it possible to build a new bank building which ended up as the Pioneer Bank, presently Wells Fargo. Mrs. Janice Bodine read a letter from the Downtown Improvement Corporation in favor of the zone change requested by the Pioneer Investment Group.

Following a short discussion, Councilman Morgan sponsored and introduced Ordinance 82-47 rezoning the easterly side of Front Street per the request of Pioneer Investment Group. Motion was made by Albrecht to pass on first reading, seconded by Wall. Motion passed with 4 yes votes, 1 no vote, and 2 absent. Bills made the dissenting vote.

Councilwoman Wall made the motion to take Resolution 82-32 off the table. The resolution was introduced by Councilman Fruits and declared the intention of the mayor and city council to vacate 8th Street between Main Street and Center Street, and the alley running through Block 17 of the original Town of Evanston. The motion was seconded by Morgan with all voting in favor. We voted on the main motion to adopt, previously made by Councilwoman Wall and seconded by Bills, with all voting in favor.

That spring the City of Evanston had a delegation from U.S.S.R. (Russia) visit the area for a few days. Several men came here to study our oil and gas industry, and they wanted to see how we were coping with the impact of the boom. They were very interested and friendly.

We all had the opportunity to visit with them and found out that one or two of them actually spoke English. It was a nice experience.

There was a big dinner held in their honor, welcoming them to Wyoming. The dinner was set up and paid for by the oil companies. County and city officials were all invited, and a number of officials representing the oil industry were present. Several of us, including me, got to speak during the dinner and we all did a lot of visiting afterwards. I really enjoyed visiting with the Russians and was glad to have had the chance to meet people from another nation.

Also, later on we had a delegation from Rio Blanco and Garfield Counties in Colorado. Most of the delegation were from the Rifle and Meeker, Colorado areas, because they were looking at oil out of oil-shale, which they had a lot of, and there was a lot of interest from the oil companies in exploring the possibility at that time.

Dennis Ottley

Деннис Оттли

The above is my name tag (English and Russian) in which I wore during the dinner with the Russian delegates in Evanston the spring of 1982.

The purpose of the group from Colorado visiting Uinta County and Evanston was to learn how we were handling our impact and mitigation plan caused by the boom. We had a meeting with them to discuss our mitigation plans, because they were trying to plan ahead in case of an impact problem. They were considering the possibility of a big boom if the oil-shale proved to be worth producing. But the project never got off the ground.

We had several requests for different projects during our April meetings. One of those requests were for safety purposes, because of kids playing around the Yellow Greek Ditch that was running through the Haw Patch area, some of the people living in the area of Uinta Meadows requested the ditch be piped. After investigating the cost and discussing the problem with the ditch company, the council denied piping the entire ditch. The ditch was used for irrigation purposes for the ranchers in the Yellow Creek area.

John Proffit and other neighbors requested to initiate an improvement district for No Name Street. This request was approved and street improvements were completed.

Cindy LaGrec, a representing the Home Owners in Aspen Grove II Subdivision, requested that the city furnish the curb and gutter for their district, but this was denied. In the initial planning of the improvement district it was left out because, at that time, the homeowners in the subdivision didn't want the curbing and gutter. They claimed they wanted to keep the "country appearance" with just drainage ditches along each side of the streets. When the planning was going on the city requested them to have curb and gutter, but they rejected that idea.

After Mr. Harold Young had been city planner for several months, the Personnel Board gave their report to the city council. Their report suggested that Mr. Young was not doing a satisfactory job and recommended his release. During the discussion I made it clear that I was very much in favor of the recommendation to release him. My reasons were that he didn't seem to appreciate any public input nor would he take any suggestions from anyone, including city officials, concerning the city master plan. He appeared to be hardnosed and didn't seem to care about what others thought. He was also very rude at times with folks applying for a building permit. He just didn't appear to be a person anyone could reason with. And we sure didn't need someone like that.

After hearing the report and after a lengthy discussion, Councilman Morgan made the motion to accept the Board's recommendation and terminate Young's employment and contract, seconded by Fruits. A roll call vote was called for with Wall, Fruits, Davis, Morgan, and me voting in favor. David Bills was the only dissenting vote, and Albrecht was absent.

The vote to release Mr. Young was 5 yes votes and 1 no vote. Motion was approved by a majority, but rather than just fire him the council agreed to accept his letter of resignation by the same majority.

The *Uinta County Herald* came out with an article on April 23, 1982 concerning the city having released Harold Young. The article was titled, CITY PLANNER YOUNG RESIGNED AMID CHARGES HE WAS "RAILROADED."

The article read: *Evanston City Planner Harold Young resigned from his position with the city Tuesday amid charges that he was "railroaded" out of his job by a group of developers and members of the City Council.*

*Councilman David Bills said Thursday that Young was a victim of "an orchestrated effort by a number of developers and members of the Council to get him."*

The article went on to say, *Mayor Dennis Ottley called for Young's resignation last week and was backed up by the city's Personnel Board, which consists of Ottley and Council members Jerry Wall and Russ Albrecht. "He was also fired partly because of his personality, in my opinion. He is a strong person he doesn't have an oily smooth personality. He rubbed some people the wrong way," said Bills.*

*Bills said that all members of the Council have some conflicts of interest but he pointed out that those members of the Council who are developers, Ottley and Wall, have built-in conflicts,* the article went on to say.

*"In real estate and development there are some instant conflicts that are sometimes difficult to work around. To their credit, Mayor Ottley and Jerry Wall have made every attempt to deal with conflicts," said Bills.*

*"I've seen the mayor have to leave a single Council meeting on four different occasions. That is admirable, but I think it cripples him on those four issues. I think some Council members have conflicts that they don't even recognize,"* he added.

Bills also said, *"I am not saying that Mayor Ottley is in the oil companies' pocket, but there are a few questions we need to ask."*

When Sandy, my wife, read the remark by Bills she made a jokingly remark, *Well, if that's true about my husband being in the pockets of the oil companies, where's mine?* She was pretty upset by Bills's remark, and she let him know it, and it wasn't pretty.

The article continued: *Mayor Ottley said that he did not have a conflict of interest problem in the Young case.*

*"I don't feel there was a conflict of interest in my case,"* said Ottley. *"I don't look at the developers as a separate body. They are citizens, too. They are in business in this town. I think everyone who is in some kind of business has conflicts of interest,"* he added.

The article added: *Ottley agreed that there were developers who wanted Young out. "The people who cried to me were developers and other people who were trying to get building permits. They said they got a cold reception from Young. There were also Council members who wanted him out. I don't recall anyone who personally told me that they wanted him to stay." Ottley continued.*

David Fierro of the *Herald* staff always appeared to make government look bad. In his article he forgot to interview other council members besides Bills who all voted to release Harold Young. He didn't interview any developers or citizens that had dealt with Young. Mr. Fierro made the statement that I admitted that the cards may have been stacked against Young (I made no such statement). He stated that he thought the cards may have been marked *(the City of Evanston doesn't play with cards).*

I thought to myself, *I guess Bills is starting his campaign early; hell it's only April and no one else has even announced.* But I will say this much: Although Mr. Bills lost in the primary election he still appeared to be out to get me by campaigning against me right up until the general election in November. I had never been through such an immoral, unethical and underhanded campaign in my life until this election year. I have always felt that a person running for election should either run on his or her record of public service or what they can do for the community to make it better place to live. I have always run on my record and future ideas, never using derogatory tactics or remarks against my opponent(s). I sure wasn't looking forward to this election campaign, although I did want to win.

Sure, I had conflicts, but I handled them as best I could, and the city attorney made sure I was doing things the right way. I would venture to say that 99% of the issues that came up where I had a conflict were voted on by a unanimous vote, and that is the same with other council members who may have had a conflict.

There was no issue that had any heavy protesting where there was a conflict. Mr. Bills was way off base and just trying to start trouble with his lies and innuendos. This is the the beginning of how this became Evanston's first election to be so unethical.

I can only say that during all my elections, other than defending myself, I have always run strictly on my own record, and that's what I will always do. I have no intention of telling the voters stories, true or false, about my opponents. I have always run a clean election, but the dirt didn't stop with Bills. It continued throughout the election and not just on the mayoral race, but also on some of the council members' races.

During the first regular council meeting in May, Councilwoman Jerry Wall read the following statement approved by a majority of the city council:

STATEMENT OF EVANSTON CITY COUNCIL

*On April 15, 1982 the Personnel Board of the City of Evanston met with Mr. Harold Young and his attorney, Mr. Thomas Mealey. The purpose of the meeting was to request Mr. Young's resignation as City Planner.*

*At that meeting Mr. Young asked the Personnel Board not to publicize the reasons leading to this request. He was concerned about finding other employment in the planning field. Against my better judgment, I and other members of the Personnel Board agreed to simply state "personality problems" as the reason.*

On April 19, Mr. Young attended the Planning and Zoning Commission and had some things to say about the Personnel Board. At this same meeting, and in interviews to both the Uinta County Herald and the Casper Star Tribune, Councilman Bills has misrepresented the actions of the Personnel Board and questioned the motives of its members. In view of these attacks on the Board and on myself; therefore, I feel that any agreement made verbally by me on April 15, to Mr. Young is nullified. I am going to state for the record my complaints against Mr. Young's actions as City Planner.

Shortly after Mr. Young assumed his duties as City Planner, he gave an interview to the Uinta County Herald in which he stated the tremendous task in front of him. It's not in question that planning in a boom situation is a tremendous task. However, the implication of the article was that there had never been an effort made here. References were made to the "hodgepodge" of ordinances and policies and to the ineffective use of the Planning and Zoning Commission. The Planning and Zoning Commission, in my opinion, is very effective. The members are dedicated and hard working. They are volunteers and no matter how they vote on any issue, it upsets someone. Planning and Zoning members have a really thankless job and I commend them for their efforts—efforts which were tireless even before Mr. Young arrived.

Some weeks later I picked up the Uinta County Herald to read headlines that proclaimed that Harold Young says we are overbuilt. I have several problems with this. Probably the most basic is the efforts of government to control the marketplace. I think that if there are too many homes, the price will drop and contractors will stop building. Conversely, if there are too few, as we've seen here, prices are not within the grasp of most citizens. The other problem with this article is that this City Council and other governmental groups in this area have been working hard to obtain grants to aid us with the monstrous problems caused with impact. Grants are not easily obtained, especially when your planner is stating that everything is going downhill. This Council has spent the better part of four years trying to get a larger sewer treatment facility approved by the E.P.A. HUD questioned our Housing Director regarding the article. This still leaves the Farm Loan Board to deal with on everything from an improvement district to roads to the recreation center.

The City Council is elected by the people of Evanston. Try to view this as a corporation, which in fact, it is. Every voting citizen of Evanston is a *stockholder. They elect the Council, which functions as the Board of Directors. City employees are just that—employees of the people of Evanston. Now, let's examine Mr. Young's relationship with his employers.*

*First of all, he represented the City Council at a County Planning and Zoning meeting on an issue that the Council did not even know about. The project in question was not in the city limits and Mr. Young opposed it on behalf of the City.*

*When Mr. Young later investigated the project further, after the County had approved it, he decided it was acceptable after all. I do not want anyone to represent me and my view unless I have requested them to do so. I can get into enough trouble all by myself.*

*Secondly, he referred to another City Official as "imbecilic" to a citizen and in the earshot of other staff members.*

*Thirdly, he questioned the city attorney's allowing subdivisions to be subdivided into lots and blocks. He said they were all illegal as this was not allowed in Wyoming. Actually, the statutes states "shall be subdivided in lots and blocks".*

*All of these things are very minor in comparison to Harold Young's treatment of citizens. These are numerous examples:*

*1. Mr. Young told Mike Pexton he could not come to any more planning and zoning meetings and speak. These are open, public meetings by law. No one can be told he cannot attend. Mr. Young was called on this and retracted the statement.*

*2. Blaine Sanders brought in his zoning maps. Mr. Young took a portion of the project papers and threw them across the table with the statement, it would not be considered. He also made fun of the coloring on the maps, turned his back on Mr. Sanders and generally tried to humiliate him.*

*3. When the hearing of the Master Plan was held, Mr. Young had so orchestrated the agenda that anyone who had any problems with the plan was not included. Everyone on the printed agenda was "pro plan" with no criticism. There was only one developer included and he was from out of town and his project happened to fall into an area where the plan was in agreement. Mr. Young would not give any of the local developers a copy of the plan ahead of time, willingly. One even had to call B.R.W. Noblitt in Cheyenne for a copy. We had a copy machine right here in City Hall.*

*4. I feel that all the opposition to Hoback Ranches' PUD was obviously orchestrated. No city employee or official should ever try to orchestrate public opinion to an issue to the detriment of one of Evanston's citizens.*

*5. Along these same lines, Mr. Young tried to make a deal with Mike Pexton, lining him up against the other developers in the Overthrust Road area. Mr. Pexton immediately went to the developers in question, as he felt that it was improper for the planner to play one citizen off against another. I agree completely.*

*6. A downtown business was told there was no ordinance allowing an awning over the sidewalk, which in fact, there is.*

*7. I attended a meeting of the Salvation Army last month and was sitting next to a local minister, who proceeded to lodge a complaint against the attitude and comments of the City Planner when he spoke to the Ministerial Association.*

*8. There were several complaints of Mr. Young's refusal to return calls on projects until the deadline for the Planning and Zoning had passed.*

*Overall, Mr. Young was rude to the general public, who, I remind you again were his employers. Granted, most of these people are engineers and developers, but these are the people a planner deals with every day. The planner does not meet the citizens who come in to buy a dog license. If the planner is justified in treating citizens this way just because they are developers—who are not, by the way, second class citizens—then, I submit to you that any citizen can be treated in a like manner by any city employee. Think of the possibilities—the elderly gentleman who doesn't think his water bill is correct, the young lady who is frightened and calls the police, or the child who comes to City Hall to register for a swimming class. Do you really want this type of behavior not only condoned, but applauded as "just doing his job?" I can only conclude that this is the intent of those who have been using this justification for the situations in the Planning Department.*

*I would also like to tell you about the morning of April 9, 1982. It was Good Friday and the teachers were not in school* [David Bills is a high school teacher]. *At 9:30 in the morning, Councilman Bills called me at my home and said he felt that the entire attack on Duane Thomas the previous evening at City Council meeting had been orchestrated by Mr. Young and that he now felt Mr. Young should be fired. He also said he would back whatever action the Personnel Board took in this matter. We talked at some length. The only conclusion I can reach from Mr. Bills's actions since April 16 is that he saw an opportunity to gain publicity for his mayoral campaign by smearing the Personnel Board and its members, who include Mayor Ottley. He also was given an opportunity at the last City Council meeting to state his feelings. He asked for a roll call vote on the motion to support the Personnel Board action. Mr. Bills's vote was the only dissenting vote on the motion. He did not utter one word regarding all these concerns---NOT ONE WORD. But then, it was late in the meeting and the press had left. I cannot tell you how disappointed I am in Councilman Bills. Until this incident I held him in high esteem.*

*There are two other issues I would like to touch on. The first one is my conflicts of interest. I excused myself for the PUD of Hoback Ranches the last two meetings, as my husband and I own adjacent property. I have talked to no one regarding my feelings on this project. Now, I am giving up my right as a neighboring landowner to say what sort of development I would or would not like to see next door to me. I have not even discussed this with Mr. Thomas. Now, it seems to me that I am hurt more than anyone else in the community by this action.*

POWDOS partners on the land they donated to build Uinta County Memorial Hospital. Left to right, Cloey Wall, Dennis Ottley, Robert Ottley, John Proffit and Robert Schuetz.

# POWDOS donates hospital site

A partnership called POWDOS has donated a 10-acre tract of land at the corner of Yellow Creek Road and Overthrust Drive to be the site of the new Memorial Hospital.

POWDOS is a partnership consisting of Dennis Ottley, Robert Ottley, John Proffit, Cloey Wall and Robert Schuetz who donated the 10-acre tract of land which has been appraised at $500,000.

"This is a very significant gift," said Hospital Administrator Norman Campeau. "We certainly appreciate the generosity of these businessmen," Campeau said, "and in as much as this is National Hospital Week we would like to take this opportunity to announce what they have done toward helping establish a new

hospital in our county."

The donated site has been approved by the Wyoming State Department of Health as an appropriate site for a hospital.

"This is the first major gift to the building fund campaign," Campeau added, "and we sincerely hope it is one of many as we conduct our community phase of fundraising during the next few weeks."

Bids will be let for the hospital construction phase within 60 days, according to fundraising campaign manager Dale Reed. Construction should begin by late this summer with a projected completion date of between summer of 1983 and December of 1983.

*Uinta County Herald*, Wednesday, May 12, 1982.

*My husband is a stockholder in Uinta Engineering & Surveying, Inc. I have nothing to do with the operation of this business. My husband is also a partner in POWDOS. I am not a partner, but it is true that I would benefit from any money generated by POWDOS. POWDOS is presently developing some of its land in order to enable them to donate land to the new hospital. I have excused myself from any proceedings on this development and I have not even seen the plat.*

*Last, but not least, I would like to talk about the Uinta County Herald. This article regarding the "railroading" of the planner was also printed with statements in it about me, without asking my views of the situation. This is the second time in a little over a month that David Fierro has written a front page article about the City Council on Mr. Bills's information alone. The first article stated that the Council had doubled its own salary. Mr. Fierro did not check or he would have discovered that in Wyoming no elected official can vote himself a pay raise. I feel that Mr. Fierro is presenting the people of Evanston with biased, one-sided reporting and the Uinta County Herald is printing it.*

*Thank you.*

This letter was written and read by Councilwoman Jerry Wall during the first regular city council meeting in May. I was totally in agreement and very proud of Jerry for writing it, and all city council members, except Mr. David Bills, were supportive of the letter. The entire statement was true and to the point. Some discussion followed with Councilman Bills responding to Wall's charges by first telling her that the conversation he had with her had been confidential and that he did not appreciate her making the statements public. *Mrs. Wall has basically misrepresented the conversation we had and I do not appreciate it,* Bills said.

*You're not going to attack me and not have me defend myself,* replied Councilwoman Wall.

Harold Young made a few comments during the discussion, but Councilman Morgan, who was absent at the meeting when the Young was asked for his resignation, stated that he totally agreed to the dismissal of Mr. Young and to the statement just made by Councilwoman Wall. There was never any more mention of the issue again. The City of Evanston bought Mr. Young out of his one-year contract until it expired.

I was getting a little concerned, along with the city council, whether or not the City of Evanston was *"overbuilding,"* but the developers and contractors didn't seem to be worried about it. On April 28, 1982 the *Casper Star-Tribune* published an article titled, EVANSTON 'OVERBUILDING' WORRIES LOCAL RESIDENTS. The article went on to read: *Concerns of residential "overbuilding" here have been heightened by a population study that claims the peak has been reached and the boom will soon level off.*

I agreed with the article as far as the boom being at its peak and maybe in a year or so, things could start tapering off, but with Amoco Production Company and Chevron U.S.A., Inc. each building a huge sour gas treatment plant, and with the market of sulfur so much in demand, none of us was getting too worried about the article, but by mid-1983 the boom did seem to start tapering off.

The year of 1982 was just as busy as past years. We were still looking at new subdivisions, annexations, new zones and rezoning, mobile home parks and new apartment complexes, and more requests for Industrial Improvement Revenue Bonds. As busy as it was, it certainly didn't appear that the boom was going to be over anytime in the near future, and it didn't appear that we were overbuilding.

U.S. Senator Malcolm Wallop (R-Wyo.), Chairman of the Finance Subcommittee on Energy and Agriculture Taxation, announced that there would be a hearing in Evanston on April 17th on legislation which would allow boom towns in Wyoming and the West to tap their future tax base to relieve energy impact problems.

*Sitting in the heart of the energy-rich Overthrust Belt, Evanston knows all too well the problems that come with rapid energy-related growth,* Wallop said. *Once a community of 5,000, in three short years it has more than doubled its population.*

*Whenever a rural community like Evanston grows even by 1,000 people,* Wallop continued, *the pressures on the local government are tremendous. On the average, a city must find an additional 100,000 gallons of water per day and a place to store it; install $175,000 worth of sewer treatment facilities; build six miles of streets; add 4.8 elementary and 3.6 high school classrooms; and on and on and on,* Wallop added.

Senator Wallop had asked me to represent the City of Evanston and the Wyoming Association of Municipalities in giving my testimony at the hearing for the purpose of sketching in the general picture of impact and the problems we had in responding. My testimony was quite lengthy but to the point and a few questions were directed at me that I answered as best as I could.

I thanked Senator Wallop for taking the initiative to hold this hearing in Evanston and for his proposal. I said, *We appreciate your concern for the energy-impacted communities and your willingness to come to Evanston and hold your committee meeting in the community where the impact is occurring.*

Future action indicated that we were getting a lot of support from Wyoming Senators, Wallop and Simpson, and Congressman Cheney. This helped Evanston a lot in obtaining federal funding for the water and sewer projects, and other projects such as the airport.

In the first part of May, the City of Evanston started getting federal and state funding for the land acquisition for the airport property. Former Evanston Mayor Bob Burns, Chairman of the Wyoming State Aeronautics Commission, presented me with the first check in the amount of $137,000.

On May 5th I announced that I would be running for re-election for the office of mayor this upcoming election in 1982. I told the *Uinta County Herald* that the reason I waited so long was because I wanted to discuss it with my family and give them some time to think about it. My wife, my sons and their families have all given me their support 100 percent, I told the *Herald*.

But one other reason I was holding back was because we had just liquidated and shut down our sporting goods store, "Lockeroom Etc.," and by doing this it put Sandy and me in debt far over our heads. We thought if the real estate business continued as it had been that we would be okay, but that ended up being a long chance.

I said to the *Herald*, "I want to stay in there and keep going. Some of the projects we have going I want to see completed." Among the major things the mayor would like to see finished are several street projects, especially the rerouting of Wyoming State Highway 89 north, the article continued.

The *Herald* quoted me saying that the folks who lived on County Road have a *"hard time of it"* with all the heavy traffic.

*Ottley would also like to see the underpass redone after the new overpass (Ottley's Folly) is completed,* the *Herald reported. He talked of "looking at lots of other new roads," because of Evanston's severe traffic problems.*

*The mayor said he's been involved in city projects for the last 30 years, three and a half as mayor and 12 years on the city council,* the *Herald* stated. "*I've seen Evanston at its worst and I've seen it at its best,*" Ottley said.

The article went on with Ottley's prediction for Evanston's future: "*...that this fairly fast growth is going to continue for three to five years before it starts leveling off." Then he said, "We're going to have a pretty good little community when it's all said and done.*"

I guess I was being a little optimistic at that time, because the boom started tapering off, but I have always tried to be an optimistic person and look at the bright side of all issues.

But the article went on to quote me as saying that "*to have a well-balanced community you have to listen to everyone's needs, and I think I have done a good job of that so far.*"

During the first regular city council meeting in May, Mr. J. D. Kindler approached the council on the possibility of annexing his property that adjoins the Centennial Valley Subdivision. He proposed transferring his sewer system and his water well to the city, retaining his water storage tank.

Councilman Bills made a motion that the council go on record as being in favor of Mr. Kindler's proposal, seconded by Morgan with all voting in favor. I voted in favor of the motion, but before we actually accepted his proposal there would be a number of issues to consider, mainly about the underground utilities and the condition of the streets. No further action was taken on the matter at this time.

Resolution 82-55 was introduced by Councilman Fruits, to authorize the city to convey property to the Evanston Airport Joint Powers Board to be used for the construction of the new Evanston/Uinta County Airport. Most of the airport property previously belonged to the Bureau of Land Management (BLM).

Councilman Morgan made the motion to adopt Resolution 82-55, seconded by Fruits, with all voting in favor.

Resolutions were introduced and adopted by unanimous vote to apply for a $500,000 grant from the Wyoming Aeronautics Commission for the new airport, and a $400,000 grant from HUD for the senior and low-income housing program.

Former Mayor Bob Burns, a current member of the Wyoming State Aeronautics Commission, presents a $137,000 check for airport land acquisition to Evanston Mayor Dennis Ottley.

# State grant for Evanston airport will help fund land acquisition

by Greg Livovich
of the Herald staff

Plans for Evanston's new airport got a little higher off the ground Monday when the city received a $137,000 land acquisition check from the Wyoming Aeronautics Commission.

John Proffit, a member of the Evanston Airport Board, said the state money will provide 80 percent of funding needed to purchase the 165 acre tract which includes an access road to the facility planned for ridge-top in the Thomas Canyon area about four miles northwest of Evanston.

Proffit said the City of Evanston and Uinta County will provide an additional $35,000 to acquire the acreage while local officials are currently negotiating with the Federal Bureau of Land Management for some additional land to house the proposed $6 - 7 million facility which will replace the present airport in the Bear River Valley north of Evanston.

Wyoming Aeronautics Commission, considering Evanston's rapid growth and oil industry transportation demand, has named the proposed airport the highest priority airport project in Wyoming, Proffit added.

He said that two other grant applications totaling $800,000 are under study by the state board, and the funds, along with an anticipated $100,000 each from Evanston and Uinta County, will be used to begin Phase I site preparation. "We hope to start moving dirt by some time in August," Proffit said.

Site preparation estimates in the 1980 airport master plan total $2.76 million. According to the master plan "cuts of 20 ft. and fills exceeding 30 ft. will be required for

airport on the Bear River Valley floor would have required less ground preparation and site prevailing winds, according to the master plan.

Proffit said the Federal Aviation

During the second regular city council meeting in May, I appointed Conrad Michaelson, Jake Williams, Councilman David Bills, and Councilwoman Jerry Wall to a steering committee to work with B.R.W. Noblitt, Inc. to come up with a land use plan. Motion was made and seconded to confirm the appointments with all voting in favor.

Ordinance 82-59, vacating 8th Street between Center and Main Streets and the alley running through Block 17 of the Original Town of Evanston as requested by the Uinta County Commissioners, was sponsored by Councilwoman Wall and introduced by Councilman Fruits. The commissioner's purpose for this request was to construct an underground parking lot for their employees. The entrance would be off the Center Street and 8th Street intersection, and would be for a two-block expanded county complex, including the public library.

This was a controversial issue. The city received dozens of letters from many outstanding citizens, but a motion made by Councilman Bills to pass Ordinance 82-59 on first reading and seconded by Wall was overcome by a motion made by Councilman Bills to table Ordinance 82-59 until the June 17th meeting. The motion also suggested the county commission hold a public meeting for public input and explanation of their plans, seconded by Fruits, with all voting in favor.

The commissioners called for a public hearing in the next few days and got input from a large group of protesters. One of the concerns that were raised was the already congested traffic that we presently had in the downtown area.

I spoke up and said, *First of all, let me say that the council has indicated that even if the street is vacated it wouldn't be done until the planned 6th Street overpass is completed in the fall of 1983.*

However, I admitted that the closure may potentially cause some inconvenience to downtown motorists who would be forced to drive an additional block to make the loop to Main Street, but I said, *I feel that the advantages gained would be worth the trade-off.*

*I think it will provide more downtown parking for office people and shoppers, which we really need, and also allow the county to have a nice two-block facility,* I said.

I continued, *I'm in favor of keeping the downtown area alive and I think this facility would help that. I want the people to know that we wouldn't close the street without first seriously considering all aspects and possible effects.*

The Safeway grocery store and several rental units were still remaining on the block in question. County Commissioner Dan South said that Uinta County has already made a good faith offer to Safeway. *If they do not accept the offer we do have the option of condemning the property,* South said.

South said that expanding the county facilities at the present site would be the best way to provide for future growth for the county without moving out of the downtown area. *It will give us more flexibility this way. We'd be foolish to not plan that way,* South added.

South also stated that they had offers from developers offering them donated property to build a new complex outside the downtown area, but were rebuffed because the county did not want to leave its present location. Action on Ordinance 82-59 would not be acted on for the first reading until the regular city council meeting of June 17th.

During our second regular city council meeting in the month of May, I sponsored Ordinance 82-57 allowing members of the Evanston Police Department to live within a one mile area outside the corporate limits of the city and Councilman Albrecht introduced it. There were one or two officers that were already living outside the city, but they would be "grandfathered" in. But the reason for the ordinance was that we knew some of the officers wanted what you might call "country living," but we wanted them close enough so they would be able to answer any emergency calls immediately. Motion was made to pass on first reading and seconded, with 5 yes votes and 1 no vote. But Councilman Bills tried to amend the motion by changing the 1 mile to ½ mile, but the amendment failed. This ordinance went on to pass on the second and third readings with all voting in favor.

Resolution 82-63 came up concerning the Wyoming State Highway Department's preliminary engineering on the Wyoming State Highway 150 S and Wyoming State Hospital interchange project.

Motion was made by Councilman Albrecht to adopt Resolution 82-63, seconded by Bills, with all voting in favor.

For the past several years it had been a city requirement that all utilities, including power, telephone, cable television, and so on, be installed underground when new subdivisions went in and/or property was annexed and developed. During this meeting it was mentioned that the City of Evanston would like to see all utilities throughout the city go underground, but the utility companies claimed it would be too expensive and there would probably be a significant increase to our consumers, so we never pushed it.

On June 11, 1982 The *New York Times* came out with an article on the Evanston boom titled, WHEN OIL BOOM FADES IN THE ROCKIES. It went on to say that *the oil rigs in the Overthrust Belt discovery had decreased and that the boom may be over in months to come, but the city council was still feeling good about the growth, because of the increase in production, and the oil and gas officials seemed to think good about it.*

On June 14, 1982 the *Casper Star-Tribune* came out with an issue titled, OFFICIALS OPTIMISTIC OVERTHRUST WILL PICK UP AGAIN. The article quoted *James W. Vanderbeek, Vice President of the Amoco Production Company, as saying, "The Overthrust (Belt) is an once-in-a-lifetime find."*

*But due to the worldwide oil glut, the energy boom in southwest Wyoming, especially around Evanston, has been leveling off, causing many layoffs.*

The article continued: *However, according to Vanderbeek, "For us, there's been no slowing of activity." So far, he said, the finds here total almost one-third the proven reserves of Alaska's remote Prudhoe Bay, which has an estimated 9 billion barrels.*

The article continued: *Over at Chevron Oil Company, Bill Jackson, Production Manager for the Rocky Mountain Division, said his company was running just 12 rigs in the Overthrust area near Evanston, compared with 30 a year ago.* The article quoted Mr. Jackson: *"Let's say we're cautiously retrenching. I expect in three to four months that things will pick up again, but the real boom has peaked. I doubt if we'll ever get back to 30 rigs again."*

After reading articles in The *New York Times* and the *Casper Star-Tribune*, and hearing all kinds of rumors and hearsay, what is a person supposed to think? The city council and I were just trying to keep up and continue with the projects we already had underway.

During the city council meeting on June 10th, Ordinance 82-3, which had been tabled, finally came back up for third and final reading. It was the ordinance that prohibited obscene conduct, distributing obscene material, and promoting the same; providing notice of obscene material or action; providing standards for evidence and defenses; and providing penalties for violation of the ordinance. Councilman Albrecht made the motion to pass Ordinance 82-3 on third and final reading, seconded by Bills, and passed with 4 yes votes, 2 no votes (Wall and Fruits), and 1 absent (Morgan). The motion passed by a majority.

It came to the council's attention that, where some of the new subdivisions were too low for the sewer, the developers were required to install lift stations. Most of the time these lift stations would take care of more than one subdivision, and the city was concerned about the maintenance on these lift stations and who was going to service them. Therefore, an extra fee was charged to the developers for the right to install a lift station.

We were still concerned how long it was going to be before we started dumping raw sewage into the Bear River again, but we were hoping we would be good until the new treatment plant was complete. On June 24th, officials from the City of Evanston, Uinta County, O.I.A. Board members and members of the Evanston Chamber of Commerce were invited to the dedication ceremony of the Trailblazer Pipeline. Some 200 oil and gas industry leaders and government officials from across the nation all gathered at Whitney Canyon to dedicate the $550 million, 800-mile-long Trailblazer Pipeline System, signaling the start of a new chapter in U.S. energy transportation.

At that time the Trailblazer Pipeline extending from Whitney Canyon, north of Evanston, to Beatrice, Nebraska, was one of the largest natural gas pipelines built in this country in the past 30 years. It was 36 inches in diameter and was the first pipeline to transport large volumes of natural gas from the energy-rich Overthrust Belt of northeast Utah and southwest Wyoming to Midwestern and Eastern markets.

The Trailblazer was another reason that the city and county officials thought that the oil and gas boom was going to stay around for years to come.

That summer I had Administrative Assistant Steve Snyder make an appointment for me to talk to Upland Industries, the land company of Union Pacific Corporation. I discussed the possibility of the City of Evanston purchasing the land where the old U.P.R.R. ice ponds were, and that we were hoping to use it for recreation purposes and to extend the walking path past the old Red Bridge, a historic location where many young kids went swimming in the Bear River (sometimes "skinny dipping"), to the County Road bridge.

We wanted to turn the entire area into a recreation complex where folks of all ages could walk or jog, swim and/or fish and, in the winter, do some ice skating or ice fishing.

The folks at Upland Industries said that there was the possibility that the city could purchase the property, but that they would have to bring it up to Upland's Board of Directors for a purchase price.

So during our June meetings Councilman Albrecht introduced Resolution 82-72, a resolution authorizing the city to purchase property in Bear River Park Subdivision from Upland Industries. This resolution gave the mayor the authority to negotiate on behalf of the City of Evanston, and to enter into a contract for the purchase of said property for a price up to the appraised value of the property. The motion was made by Councilman Albrecht to adopt Resolution 82-72, seconded by Bills, with all voting in favor.

Upland Industries sold the Ice Pond Property to the City of Evanston at the appraised price of $185,000, but not until 1988. The actual purchase didn't occur until June of 1988, because the original price that the U.P. Railroad asked for was $680,000, which was way too high. So during Mayor Gene Martin's administration starting in 1983, the issue was more or less dropped.

However, in November of 1987, the city started negotiating with the U.P. once again for the ice pond property, and by July of 1988 the city and railroad finally agreed to a purchase price of $185,000, the appraisal price at that time. The city paid the railroad $9,250 of earnest money to make the deal legal, and then paid another $83,250 at closing, with the balance of $92,500 plus interest due on or before July 31, 1989.

A Bear River Project Board had been formed to start planning and developing the entire area, including the Red Bridge, from Bear River State Park to County Road Bridge. The project was referred to as the "The BEAR Project." It had turned out to be a great project for all ages of the community. I believe that Tim and Katie Beppler were the first to oversee the board at that time.

We discussed the proposed budget, which had to be passed sometime in July after the public hearing. The proposed 1982-83 fiscal year budget exceeded $11,300,000 in the General Fund, and there was a Reserve Fund over $8,800,000 that included funding from various grants, some funds pledged for water, and so on. But there was almost $4,000,000 in cash reserve that was unpledged, carried over from the previous year. Councilman Bills made the motion to approve these figures as a tentative city budget for 1982-83. The motion was seconded, with all voting in favor.

1982 was the first year of the "Overthrust Chili Cookoff," sponsored and conducted by the new oil field service companies. It was held in the middle of the street in front of what now is Quail Tools, 83 Allegiance Drive. Councilman Fruits made a motion for a malt beverage permit to be issued to the sponsors of the Cookoff, and that the area designated in the Evanston Industrial Park would not be covered by the Open Container Ordinance on June 19, 1982, seconded by Wall, with all voting in favor.

As mayor, I was selected by the committee to be the final judge in the Cookoff, though I wasn't sure what I was doing. However, I know I tasted a lot of chili, some good and some pretty bad. I did get through the program and after the first group of judges passed on to me the final three winners, I had to select the winner from the three. I finally selected what I thought was the best chili, and it was put in a Mason's quart fruit jar and was auctioned off at the event. The auctioneer sold the winning jar of chili to the highest bidder, Lonnie Edwards, in the amount of $2,500.00.

The first Chili CookOff in Evanston turned out to be a big, big success and was held every year after that. The next time, I believe, it was held at the Uinta County Fair Grounds, and I was a judge almost every year for several events. Over the years I tasted a lot of "very good" chili, but I also tasted quite a few that weren't "so good" chili. But it was fun.

The *Salt Lake Tribune* issue of June 13, 1982 came out with an article titled, OIL FIRMS BIVOUAC WORKFORCE. The article was referring to Evanston and the man-camps that had been provided by Amoco and Chevron for construction crews working on the sour gas treatment plants several miles north of Evanston.

The article compared them with the old CCC (Civilian Conservation Corps) back in the 1930s during the Great Depression and during World War II. The news issued referred them, at that time, as barracks, but the article talked about man-camps.

This week in June, Governor Ed Herschler notified me that the City of Evanston had been awarded a $400,000 community development block grant by the Department of Economic Planning and Development (DEPD) for the construction of the first phase of a elderly housing project.

Twelve units of a proposed 60 unit elderly housing project would be constructed in the city-owned Haw Patch Subdivision. The elderly housing project would be administered by the Evanston Housing Authority, and the first units would be built on what they now call Ortega Court, named for Art Ortega, who had been on the Board and had just passed away before the project got underway. The street name was a great honor and well deserved for Art, because he worked really hard on getting the elderly housing project off the ground. The total project was estimated at $2,250,000.

Uinta County Herald, 6/23/82

## For elderly housing
# City is awarded $400,000 grant

by David Fierro
of the Herald staff

EVANSTON — Mayor Dennis Ottley was notified this week by Gov. Ed Herschler that the city has been awarded a $400,000 community development block grant by the Department of Economic Planning and Development (DEPD) for the construction of the first phase of an elderly housing project.

Twelve units of a proposed 60 unit elderly housing project will be constructed in the city-owned Haw Patch subdivision. The elderly housing project will be administered by the Evanston Housing Authority.

The grant from DEPD came somewhat as a surprise to city officials who had been either rejected or postponed in four previous requests for funding on the project from federal agencies.

What made the grant approval more surprising was the rapid response from the state agency, according to Ottley. The application was submitted in May and the response came back to the city June 21.

"It was surprising because normally when you deal with state or federal agencies they don't move too swiftly," said Ottley.

The work on the first 12 units is expected to start as soon as the funds arrive in Evanston, according to Housing Authority Director Julie Lehman.

"We intend to start with the project as soon as we possibly can," she said.

The funding for the elderly housing project's first phase marks a milestone in Ottley's term as mayor. "It has been a major priority of mine since I took office," said Ottley.

Architect Jim Engelke of Jackson has been contracted to design the elderly housing project and Lehman was gratified that Engelke's first move was to visit the Senior Citizens Center and obtain input from the senior citizens about the project.

"The senior citizens will definitely have some input into the design of the facility," said Lehman.

Lehman said that the goal of 60 elderly housing units represents the current need in the Evanston area but expansion is not out of the picture.

"The figure of 60 units was obtained by surveying the current senior citizen population and from population estimates. We will meet the need. We have eight acres now and if those eight acres are not sufficient we will consider expansion," Lehman added.

Lehman said that the elderly in Evanston are being faced with the obstacles of increased cost of living, rising utility costs, rising maintenance costs, a higher crime rate and major changes in their traditional neighborhoods and shopping areas.

"We have to realize that we are dealing with people who are generally on a fixed income. We surveyed the seniors in Evanston and found that of 22 people surveyed, a majority of them were renting in places where the rent had tripled and the rest of them were living in fear that their rents would be raised," said Lehman.

"Socio-economic studies show that most elderly residents do not benefit from 'boom town' areas," she added.

Lehman pointed out that it is not the intent of the project to isolate the senior citizens from the rest of the community.

"The intent is to provide affordable housing with access to human resources and transportation to and from the downtown area," said Lehman.

A shuttle system from the elderly housing area to the downtown area is being built into the system, according to Lehman.

Senior citizens have raised some opposition to the location of the project but Lehman said the city was unable to locate the project in the downtown area.

"It is not the philosophy of the
Continued on page 12

Housing Authority Director Julie Lehman and Mayor Dennis Ottley review plans for elderly housing project in Evanston.

*Uinta County Herald,* June 23, 1982.

When the Elderly Housing Program first started, some senior citizens complained about the location. I heard one of them say, *Who the hell would want to live up there on that windy hill?* I'm sure this is one of the projects that hurt me in the upcoming election, but once those first units were completed, it didn't take long before they were completely occupied.

During the June 17th meeting, Councilman Albrecht made a motion to bring Ordinance 82-59, concerning the vacating of 8th Street between Main and Center Streets, off the table, seconded by Bills. It had previously been tabled until this meeting, because there had been a lot of opposition to it.

I opened the floor for more discussion, because County Commissioner Dan South was in attendance and several other citizens for and against the ordinance was also there. After giving the public a reasonable time for discussion, I finally called for a vote on the main motion to pass Ordinance 82-59 on first reading. There were 5 yes votes, 1 no vote (Davis) and 1 absent. The motion passed by a majority.

During this meeting I appointed members to serve on the Evanston/Uinta County Airport Joint Powers Board: Councilmen Roy Fruits and Arnie Morgan and me. This board would include both city and county officials. Councilman Bills made a motion to confirm the appointments, seconded by Fruits, with all voting in favor.

Just before adjournment of the second June meeting, City Clerk Don Welling announced that there would be a joint city council and Downtown Improvement Committee meeting on June 18th to review the plans for the downtown area.

During the first monthly city council meeting on July 8th the Evanston Lanes Bowling Alley announced that construction would be completed and their opening date would be September 15, 1982. Also, Rodeway Inn now known as Motel 6 on Bear River Drive, announced that they would open in about 6 weeks, and Shakeys, now where Maverick on Front Street is, was shooting for October 15, 1982 for their opening date.

Resolution 82-85 authorizing the city to purchase Lot 9, Block 6 of the Original Town of Evanston from Mildred Condos was introduced by Councilman Morgan. Motion was made by Fruits, seconded by Bills, with all voting in favor.

Summer of '82:

# BUILDING TODAY—
# FOR TOMORROW

June 30, 1982

Published by the City of Evanston, Wyoming in Conjunction with The Overthrust Industrial Association.

## What's going on at Haw Patch?

Old timers say that young people used to go to Haw Patch where they would court and spoon, pick haw berries and have picnics. Haw Patch, they say, has been used as a recreation area for fifty years or more.

Haw Patch's future as a recreation area is assured, now, as it becomes the site of Evanston's new Recreation Center. Instead of picking berries and stealing kisses, though, visitors will be able to play basketball, swim and lift weights.

Haw Patch is also the site of three other public projects: a Human Resource Center, which will bring together a variety of human services agencies, and two low-cost housing projects, one for senior citizens and another for persons with moderate incomes. (See map on page 3).

**Project Details:**

**Recreation Center.** The new 53,400 square-foot Recreation Center will house facilities for racketball, jogging, swimming, weight lifting and basketball. A game room for Foos Ball, ping pong and electronic games, multi-purpose rooms for dance, meetings or gymnastics, locker rooms, a snack bar, a steam room, and a whirlpool will also be a part of the Center, all located on nearly seven acres of land.

The Center should be under construction by August of this year, and is expected to be completed by December of 1983. Donations of $1,500,000 from the Overthrust Industrial Association (OIA), $275,000 from Uinta County, and the remainder from the City of Evanston will pay for the Center.

**Human Resource Center.** Wyoming's first center for human service agencies will be built at a cost of $2,225,000 on six acres of land at Haw Patch. The Wyoming Farm Loan Board authorized an 8-1/2 percent loan for $1,700,000 and the OIA made a $550,000 donation for the building. These monies and all aspects of the construction, maintenance and leasing of the Center are supervised by a five-member Joint Powers Board, appointed by the City of Evanston and Uinta County in May, 1981.

The 35,000 square-foot center will have space for state offices of vocational rehabilitation, public assistance, revenue, probation and parole. Professional help for alcohol abuse, sexual assault and family violence also will be located there, as will counseling, family planning and the office of the public health nurse. Construction should begin in July of this year, and the offices should be ready for occupancy by May, 1983.

**Senior Citizen Housing.** A little over eight acres of land will be dedicated to low-cost housing for the elderly. The Evanston Housing Authority, through two federal funding sources, plans to build 32 units for qualifying senior citizens at a total cost of $1,198,000. The OIA has committed $150,000 to a permanent trust fund to be used to supplement the rents of any low-income occupants. The buildings are expected to be available by December, 1983.

**Low Cost/Moderate Income/Multi-Family Housing.** Nearly $2,000,000 in low-cost housing for those with moderate incomes will be built on about five acres of land at Haw Patch. The Evanston Housing Authority will oversee the 28 multi-family units, which the Authority expects to have completed by December, 1983.

How did all these projects come together on an Evanston hillside? It started three years ago when the Mayor and Council, working with Uinta County's Human Resources Confederation, secured a $379,300 grant from the Energy Impact and Development Assistance Program of the Farmers Home Administration in order to buy the land. Land costs for the 40 acres were $226,209 and the remaining money—and more—is being spent by the City on site development. All of the land has been donated by the City to the four projects at Haw Patch.

Without the donations of land and money, and thousands of hours of volunteers' time, Haw Patch probably would remain a brush-covered Wyoming hill, suitable only for berry-picking. With the generosity of the people and the work of their governments, important public facilities will be erected, and new recreational opportunities offered to Uinta County residents, opportunities that go beyond the long-practiced pastimes of picnicking and spooning.

*More City of Evanston Projects on Page 4*

Mayor Dennis Ottley

Model of Evanston Human Resource Center to be built at Haw Patch

Haw Patch south of Interstate 80, site of recreation center, human resource center, and two public housing projects.

# MEETING OUR GOALS

## New County Facilities: An addition to the Courthouse and a new Library

Construction of the $3,500,000 addition to the Uinta County Courthouse will get under way in July and is scheduled for completion in January 1984. The addition will create approximately 48,000 square feet of new office space, plus about 5,200 square feet in the basement for an emergency operations center. The original structure will remain the center of the complex.

Over half of the new floor space, about 26,000 square feet, will be given over to offices and a court room area for the District and County Courts.

A site for the new $1,500,000 Library is located nearby, although plans for the building itself are not firm.

Financing of the additional Courthouse space involves a $1,500,000 no-interest loan and a $500,000 grant from the Wyoming Farm Loan Board, a $500,000 grant from the Overthrust Industrial Association, and $1,000,000 from general County revenues. The current building was constructed in 1874 at a cost of $15,400. Additions were made in 1887 and 1910. It is believed to be the oldest Wyoming Courthouse still in use.

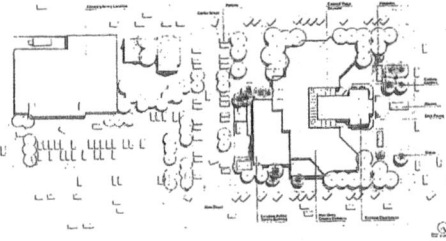

*Bird's-eye view of Courthouse addition and site of new library*

*Existing Uinta County Courthouse*    *Existing Uinta County Library*

*Model of additions to Uinta County Courthouse*

For more information call:

| | |
|---|---|
| City of Evanston | 789-9890 |
| Wyoming Highway Department | 789-3363 |
| Uinta County | 789-9093 |
| Uinta School District #1 | 789-7575 |
| Evanston Housing Authority | 789-6208 |
| Lutheran Hospitals & Homes Society of America | 789-3636 |
| Joint Powers Board (Human Services Center) | 789-3655 |

## Project Construction Schedule

| PROJECT DESCRIPTION | June | July | Aug | Sept | Future | RESPONSIBLE ENTITY |
|---|---|---|---|---|---|---|
| 1. Reconstruction of Front St. (U.S. 30) Fifth street to Ninth St. | | | | | | Wyoming Highway Dept. |
| 2. R.R. Overpass & Bear River Bridge (U.S. 30) | | | Aug. 30 '83 | | | Wyoming Highway Dept. |
| 3. Paving: | | | | | | |
| Aspen Groves I and II | | | | | | City of Evanston |
| Cheyenne Dr. from Yellow Creek Rd. to Overthrust Road** | | | | | | City of Evanston |
| Elm to Monroe St. | | | | | | City of Evanston |
| Frontage Rd. at E Hill** | | | | | | City of Evanston |
| Red Mountain Rd. from Wyo. 89 to pavement** | | | | | | City of Evanston |
| 4. Resurfacing or surface improvements: | | | | | | |
| Center St. from 11th to 17th Sts. | | | | | | City of Evanston |
| 1st Ave. from D Ave. to end of Sims Lane | | | | | | City of Evanston |
| Lombard from 6th to 11th Sts. | | | | | | City of Evanston |
| Sage St. from 9th to 19th Sts. | | | | | | City of Evanston |
| 2nd Ave. from Holland Dr. to D St. | | | | | | City of Evanston |
| 5. Construction of W. Main, west of 19th St. (finished to subgrade) | | | | | | City of Evanston |
| 6. Storm sewer projects: | | | | | | |
| Aspen Groves I and II | | | | | | City of Evanston |
| Elm to Monroe | | | | | | City of Evanston |
| 2 blocks of Sage St.** | | | | | | City of Evanston |
| 7. Sanitary Sewer: | | | | | | |
| Aspen Groves I and II | | | | | | City of Evanston |
| Riverside Ave.** | | | | | | City of Evanston |
| 8. Schools | | | | | | |
| Davis Middle School, at 9th and Lombard St. | | | | | | Uinta School District #1 |
| North Evanston Elementary, at Monroe and Washington Avenues | | | | Aug. 83 | | Uinta School District #1 |
| Uinta Meadows Elementary, on Cheyenne Dr. at Arapahoe Ct. | | | | | | Uinta School District #1 |
| 9. County Courthouse addition | | | | Jan. '84 | | Uinta County |
| 10. County Library | dates are undetermined | | | | | Uinta County |
| 11. Public Safety Building at Front and 12th Sts. | | | | June, '83 | | City of Evanston |
| 12. Public Works Garage on Bear River Dr. | | | Aug. '83 | | | City of Evanston |
| 13. Recreation Center at Uinta View Dr. and Saddle Ridge Rd. | | | | | | City of Evanston and Uinta County |
| 14. Sewage Treatment Plant | | | | | | City of Evanston |
| 15. Senior Citizen Housing | | | Aug. '83 | | | Evans. Housing Auth. |
| 16. Moderate Income Housing | | | | Sept. '84 | | Evans. Housing Auth. |
| 17. Hospital at Tomahawk Dr. and Yellow Creek Rd. | | | July '84 | | | Lutheran Hosp. & Homes Soc. |
| 18. Human Services Center | | | May '83 | | | Joint Powers Board |
| 19. Airport relocation: site preparation | | | | undetermined | | Evanston Airport Board |
| 20. Bus Maintenance Facility at Kirlin Bldg. at High School on Summit Ave. | | | Jan. '83 | | | Uinta School District #1 |
| 21. Renovation of old High School at Morse Lee and 10th | | | | Dec. | | Uinta School District #1 |

\* 1982 unless otherwise noted.   \*\* Subject to 1982-83 budget approval.

# CONSTRUCTION ACTIVITY IN EVANSTON

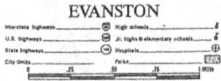

EVANSTON

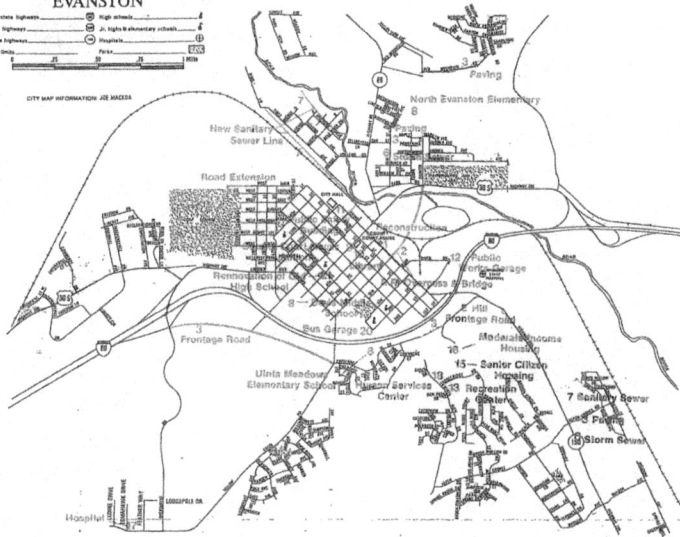

Evanston map with major construction sites indicated in brown. Project numbers are correlated with those on Construction Schedule, page 2.

## Uinta School District #1 has Five Projects

**PROJECT DETAILS:**

Uinta School District #1 has five projects underway this summer, funded from three sources: a $10,000,000 bond which was issued in 1980, part of $20,000,000 in bonds authorized by voters in 1981, and a $3,343,000 grant from the Wyoming Farm Loan Board. The five facilities will add classroom space for a maximum of 1,325 elementary students and 850 middle school students, along with a bus maintenance garage and new space for central services.

**North Evanston Elementary School.** When it is completed in August of next year, the school will have classroom

space for a maximum of 550 students from kindergarten through fifth grade. The building will have approximately 50,000 square feet of space and will cost about $2,500,000, in addition to the $358,000 spent acquiring the land. Located at Washington and Monroe Avenue, the school will have 22 classrooms and a full-sized gymnasium, plus space available for community use.

**Uinta Meadows Elementary School.** A maximum of 775 students from kindergarten through fifth grade could be enrolled this fall when the school opens. The school's approximate 60,000 square feet will have 31 classrooms, a full-sized gymnasium and meeting rooms available to the public. In 1980 the land at Cheyenne Drive and Arapahoe Circle was acquired at a cost of $240,728. The building itself will cost about $3,000,000.

**Davis Middle School.** Started in April 1981, the new middle school will be

open this fall and able to accommodate a maximum of 850 students in grades six through eight. The 111,000 square-foot building, with 34 classrooms and an auditorium, will cost $6,000,000. Facilities for swimming will add $2,300,000 to that cost. In addition, land costs at the Lombard Street site were $168,966.

**Bus Maintenance Facility.** A 20,000 square-foot building is under construction adjacent to the Kerlin Building at the present High School on Summit Avenue. The building will cost $1,235,000 and offer work room for bus maintenance and some garage space when it is complete in January 1983.

**Renovation of the Old High School.** The old high school at 10th and Morse Lee will be renovated this summer and in service by December of this year. One million dollars will be spent to gut the building and add an interior steel framework, while keeping the exterior intact. Before construction can begin,

the building must be emptied of everything which has been stored there over the years. A public auction will be held for this purpose, a sort of District #1 Garage Sale. When it is completed the building will house central services, a Board Meeting Room, additional administrative space, and some storage areas. A total of 18,000 square feet will be available on three floors.

These five projects, each of which would be called ambitious by itself, together will add nearly 260,000 square feet of useable space to the District's facilities, at a total cost of $16,802,694. By August 1983, 87 new classrooms will be added to the District. About 2,800 students are expected to enroll this fall, while an average of 2,450 attended last year.

Davis Middle School

Uinta Meadows Elementary School

North Evanston Elementary School

# CONSTRUCTION ACTIVITY IN EVANSTON

## Wyoming Highway Department Projects in Evanston: It's going to be easier to get around

The Wyoming Highway Department has two major projects in Evanston, one under construction this summer on U.S. 30S, and one next summer on Wyoming 89 which, together, are expected to cost over $8,000,000.

The first project will rebuild U.S. 30S at Front Street from 6th to 9th Streets. (An earlier stage of this project, Front Street from 9th to 11th Streets, is finished and in use.) Sidewalks, curbs, gutters and four concrete driving lanes and a turning lane will be complete by the end of July. One lane of traffic will be allowed in each direction during construction.

Also included in this project is a new 202-foot-long bridge for U.S. 30S over the Bear River, near Painter Lane, and 669-foot-long overpass to bring traffic above the railroad tracks at 6th and Front Streets. New traffic signals will be installed at three intersections: 6th and Front Streets, 9th and Front Streets, and at the intersection of U.S. 30S and Wyoming 89 near Painter Lane.

Roughly eleven acres of new right-of-way were necessary for this project. Total cost of the project is $5,500,000, paid out of Wyoming Severance Tax money.

The second project, the relocation of Wyoming 89, will begin in the spring of next year, and may be finished by the

Construction on bridge over Bear River at Painter Lane

Front Street after completion of construction

Concrete being laid on west side of Front Street

fall. The new roadway will be just a little over a mile long and has an estimated cost of $2,652,000 for construction. Acquiring right-of-way, which is now expected to total about 13.5 acres, will add to that cost. Like U.S. 30S, this project will offer four concrete driving lanes, a turning lane and sidewalks, curbs and gutters.

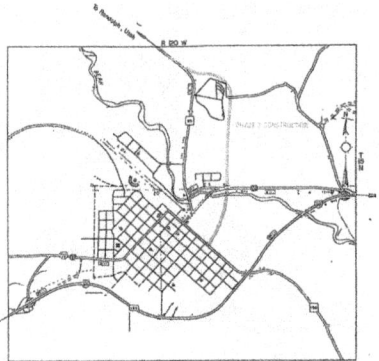

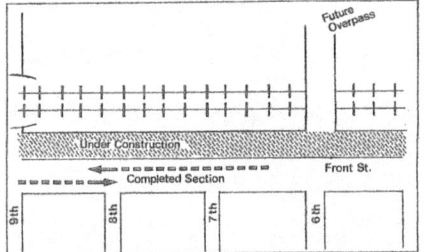
Diagram of traffic movement during construction this summer on Front Street between 6th and 9th Streets

## Relocation of the City-County Airport

Bid specifications are being drawn for a relocated City-County airport about three miles northwest of the intersection of I-80 and Overthrust Road. Construction will begin in August and will continue as funds are available for five or six years. The Wyoming Aeronautics Commission has designated the airport as its top priority, and granted $760,000 this year toward a project which could cost as much as $6,000,000. This year's construction will include site preparation, grading of the runway and, from city-county matching funds, work on an access road. About 500 acres of land from the Bureau of Land Managment and 170 acres of private land will be acquired at an expected cost of $130,000.

The new airport will have a terminal, parking, taxiways, hangers and a 7,000 foot runway. The runway will be able to accommodate medium-size jets such as a 737 or DC9. The site will allow the expansion of the runway to 8,000 feet at a later date, although an expansion is not now planned. The project has been overseen by the Evanston Airport Board, while a Uinta County-Evanston Joint Powers Board is being formed.

## The City of Evanston's Three Projects will Total $13,000,000

Three projects which total $13,000,000 will be begun by the City of Evanston this summer: a $10,700,000 sewage treatment plant, a $1,500,000 public works garage, and an $800,000 public safety building.

**Project Details:**

**Sewage Treatment Plant.** The sewage treatment plant will increase both the capacity and the effectiveness of sewage treatment in Evanston. Present capacity is 2.7 million gallons per day (mgd); the new plant will have the capacity of 2.9 mgd and will be built to allow an increase in capacity to 5.8 mgd at a later date. When complete in the fall of 1984, the plant will be able to treat the sewage of a city of 18,000 people and, with an increase to 5.8 mgd to serve over 36,000. The project is proposed to be funded by the City of Evanston, the Environmental Protection Agency, a maximum loan of $3,400,000 from the Wyoming Farm Loan Board, $250,000 in advance purchase of sewer

taps by Amoco Production Company and Chevron U.S.A. Inc. and a $250,000 grant from the O.I.A.

**Public Works Garage.** About 42,000 square feet of space will be available to house the water, sewer and street departments' repair shops and some garage space for city equipment, following the construction of a public works garage next summer. The building will cost $1,500,000 and will be jointly financed by the city ($500,000), the Overthrust Industrial Association ($250,000) and the Wyoming Farm Loan Board ($750,000).

**Public Safety Building.** A building for the Police Department will be built south of City Hall on Front Street at a cost of $800,000. The building will have offices on two floors and a basement, each with 3,600 square feet. The basement will house the squad room, dispatch facilities, and a shower room. The building is expected to be available by September 1983.

## A New Hospital

A new $10,300,000 hospital, to be built by Lutheran Hospitals and Homes Society of America, is expected to be in service by July 1984. The building will have 63,125 square feet with 42 beds, compared to 22 beds in the present hospital. The brick building is designed on one level, while allowing an additional two floors to be added later above the patient wing. Horizontal expansion at a later date is also a possibility.

The facility will have a large emergency suite with a landing pad for helicopters near its entrance. The location of the hospital is at Tomahawk Drive and Yellow Creek Road, on ten acres of land which were donated to the Society. Financing details and long range plans for both the old facility and the nursing home are under study.

Sketch of new hospital

The city ended up relocating Mrs. Condos to a new one-story house in the M Bar B Subdivision. Nobody likes to be relocated from their home, but I think once Mrs. Condos got moved and settled, I believe she was more than happy.

The purpose of buying her home was that it was right next to the city shops on Front Street across from where the police station is at present, and with the city growing so much with additional and larger equipment, as well as manpower, the city was seriously in need of the additional space. We had to do something. A motion was made and seconded to direct City Engineer Wayne Shepherd to draw up plans and specifications for a shop building and have it put out for bids as soon as possible.

A special meeting was called on July 20th to hold a public hearing to consider and finalize the 1982-1983 Budget, and other business that might come up during the meeting.

The budget hearing had very few folks present and there was very little discussion. Therefore, I sponsored Ordinance 82-96 passing the tentative budget and Councilman Albrecht introduced it.

The total appropriations for the fiscal year ending on June 30, 1983 were just over $19,000,000. That included all grant monies received, special assessments, cash reserve, federal-reserve sharing, and water and sewer funding. It was the largest budget that Evanston had ever had, but we had no deficit, and we had an attractive cash reserve of almost $4,000,000 that could be used as a cushion for almost anything the city council should decide was needed. Councilman Fruits made the motion to pass the ordinance on an emergency basis, seconded by Wall, with all voting in favor.

During the regular city meeting on July 22nd, Ordinance 82-59 permitting the city to vacate 8th Street between Main and Center Streets, and vacate the alley running through Block 17 of the Original Town of Evanston, came up for third and final reading. After a short discussion, Councilman Bills made a motion to pass the ordinance on the third and final reading, seconded by Wall, with 5 yes votes, 1 no vote (Davis) and 1 absent. The motion passed by a large majority.

There was a public hearing called for during this meeting concerning the Centennial Valley Annexation. The hearing was recorded and the tape was filed at the City Hall. After the public hearing, Ordinance 82-76 annexing the 82.622 acres of Centennial Valley requested by J. D. Kindler and Evan H. Reese, Partners, came up for its third and final reading.

Councilman Bills made the motion to pass Ordinance 82-76 on third and final reading, seconded by Morgan. More discussion followed, and Councilman Morgan made the motion to table the ordinance until the August 19th meeting, seconded by Davis, with all voting in favor.

Ordinance 82-92, allowing almost 40 acres of additional property to be annexed was brought on the floor for first reading. This ordinance was also tabled until the August 19th meeting.

During the previous month of July we acted on the removal of junk and disabled vehicles around town by applying a warning sign to the vehicle and giving the owner time to have the item removed. If the vehicle was not moved by that date then the city would have it moved and the cost would be charged back to the owner. The only problem was that the city could not always find the owner. Therefore, in a lot of cases, the city ended up having to pay the towing cost. During the past few years there had been many appeals to the Evanston City Council because the council was also acting as the Board of Adjustments to the Evanston Planning and Zoning Commission. Whenever the Commission denied someone the right to do something on their property or denied a zone change request or something similar that did not conform to the ordinance, the party that was denied had the right to appeal to the Board of Adjustments.

This meeting was no different from previous meetings. We had several appeals to consider and no decision seemed to be easy. Most of the time the appeals would pass or fail by split votes of the board. Sometimes the Board made the P & Z Commission pretty upset when the Board went against their decision, but this was the way the system was set up. I thought the P & Z was doing a terrific job, and told them that. They were doing a great service to the community and receiving no compensation. It was a very thankless job.

During the meeting I appointed Willis Rose and Jake Williams to the Evanston Police Department. Motion was made and seconded to confirm these appointments, with all voting in favor.

Motion was made and seconded to authorize General Superintendent of Public Works Allen Kennedy to look into a sprinkling system for the Evanston Cemetery and to call for bids for the project. The motion passed with all voting in favor.

There was talk about using sodium vapor rather than mercury vapor in the installation of new street lights. City Attorney Lancaster recommended that we use the sodium; therefore, a motion was made and seconded that we go with the attorney's recommendation, with all voting in favor.

When we finally got Overthrust Road through to Yellow Creek Road, we used an old right-of-way that had some S-curves in it that proved to be a little dangerous, especially in the winter when roads got slick. I mentioned to the council that the city ought to obtain new right-of-ways and straighten those curves out.

After some discussion a motion was made and seconded to authorize City Engineer Wayne Shepherd to proceed with the redesign of Overthrust Road, to get the road straightened out. The motion was passed unanimously.

The *Uinta County Herald* issue of July 9th came out with an article titled, PLANS DOWNTOWN IMPROVEMENTS. The article read: *Mayor Dennis Ottley and the City Council have appointed a Downtown Task Force to help prevent downtown Evanston from falling victim to the "ghost town" syndrome.*

*The task force, and Overthrust Industrial Association funded architect Ronald Straka met Wednesday to formulate a plan of action in Evanston. In attendance were the members appointed: John Deru, Beverly Coles, Sandy Ottley, Rick Sather, Julie Lehman, Cathy Hileman, Janice Bodine, Lynn Fox, Albert Bradbury and Dennis Farley.*

The article continued with Straka telling the task force, *"I think there is a great potential in Evanston to do something with the downtown area. You haven't screwed up yet."*

*Straka told the task force that downtown Evanston possesses a number of "good old buildings" and admonished the group to save them. "If those historical buildings are torn down you will have another Anyplace, USA. I don't think you want that,"* said Straka.

*The Task Force also supported the further development of the abandoned Union Pacific roundhouse land and the acreage adjacent to the Bear River Industrial Park (the land where the ice ponds are),* the article continued.

Ron Straka was an architect from Denver brought in by the Denver Research Group and hired and paid by the O.I.A. He was brought in to assist the city and their committees to come up with a plan to save the downtown area as "the heart of Evanston." Mr. Straka appeared to be well qualified and worked with everyone with a lot of respect.

A public hearing was held on July 22nd concerning the annexation of the Centennial Valley subdivisions. Landowner and developer J. D. Kindler filed a petition of annexation with the city which would mean that the city would take over Kindler's water and sewer system. Three years ago the residents of Centennial Valley didn't want to be annexed into the city when the city requested it. That was before the subdivisions got too big, but now it had more than tripled in size.

The City Engineer's office told the council that it would cost the city approximately $206,500 to upgrade the Centennial Valley sewer system, $17,550 to fence the lagoons, and $75,650 to upgrade the water system.

The City Engineer's report indicated that the Kindler water system was currently discharging wastewater illegally into the Yellow Creek drainage system.

City Councilman Bills spoke up and said, *Our first obligation is to the people of the city. We have city residents who use that system. The bottom line as far as I'm concerned is that those people are served. I'll admit that the cost estimates made me question this, but that's my position on it,* he said.

But in a sense, Councilman Bills was wrong. Those people in Centennial Valley were not citizens of Evanston; they paid no city taxes, and no one in Evanston used their system. I told the group that the city wanted the Centennial Valley subdivisions annexed, but I questioned the cost. I said, *We want them in, but we still have to address the question of who is going to foot the bill.* No other action was taken at this time, but it would come up again at a later date.

Amoco District Superintendent Tom G. Doss announced that Amoco Production Company was going to move their District office from Salt Lake City to Evanston and would be in operation by summer of 1983. Mr. Doss said he expected Evanston to remain a center of western energy development for many years to come. *We feel there are enough oil and gas reserves here to merit our bringing the district office here,* said Doss. *I do think Evanston may be more of a hub for energy activity as a result of this move,* he added.

After hearing this announcement, the Evanston City Council and I felt a lot better about the future of Evanston. More announcements were coming in about how the industry was planning big things, although the drilling and exploration of the industry seemed to be slowing down. Some folks were starting to leave Evanston, but we were looking for more to come in. In the month of July three more people announced their desire to run for mayor. They were Eugene "Gene" Martin, Miles J. Alexander, and Keith Grover. In addition to me running for re-election, we also had Councilman David Bills, former County Commissioner Gene Martin, businessman Alexander, and Keith Grover, who ran against me the first time. I was sure the election was going to be interesting.

The editorial "Perspectives" by David Fierro came out in the *Uinta County Herald* on July 23, 1982 talking about the Oath of Office prescribed by the Wyoming Constitution that each member of the city council, including the mayor, must take before going into office.

He said that *Mayor Dennis Ottley admitted that the conflict of interest issue will be a major one in the mayoral race against challengers David Bills, Gene Martin, Miles Alexander and Keith Grover. But, to his credit, Mayor Ottley has recognized the conflicts of interest and excused himself from those segments of the council meetings in which the items he had a business interest in were being discussed.*

*Opponents of Mayor Ottley admit that he has addressed the conflicts but maintain that the very existence of the conflicts make it difficult for him to govern effectively.*

*When Mayor Ottley took the Oath of Office he pledged to the people of Evanston that he would uphold it.*

*Until it is proven otherwise, he deserves to be treated with respect due someone who has lived up to that commitment.*

That was a nice article Mr. Fierro wrote. I believe it is the first time he had ever said anything halfway decent about me since he started "Perspectives." I thanked him for what he said in the article.

During the August meetings, other than taking care of pending ordinances on second and third readings, the Centennial Valley Sub-divisions came back on the floor for discussion, when the question of cost to each residence came up. Councilman Albrecht made a motion to direct City Engineer Wayne Shepherd to notify all residents living in the area to be annexed that the proposed cost to each established family would be an assessment in the amount of $150.00 per meter with a one-year time limit to pay, seconded by Morgan, with all voting in favor.

Councilman Albrecht also made a motion for City Engineer Shepherd to notify Mr. J. D. Kindler concerning the improvements needed at the sewage lagoon. The motion required Shepherd to inform Mr. Kindler that if he made the improvements to the lagoon, estimated at approximately $380,000, at his cost and then, if and when the time came that the city no longer needed the lagoon, then the land would revert back to Mr. Kindler. However, if the City of Evanston did the improvements at the city's cost, then the property would revert to the city. Motion was seconded by Fruits, with all voting unanimously in favor.

During the discussion of the proposed annexation of Centennial Valley I voiced my concern about the utilities. I said, *Over and above the estimates that Mr. Shepherd has come up with, we don't know if the water and sewer lines under the streets are deep enough to keep from causing freeze-ups and other problems, plus we don't even know what condition the streets are in.* City Engineer Shepherd agreed with me that those utility lines should be checked before going any further. Again, no other action would be taken at this time.

Ordinance 82-98 was sponsored and introduced by Councilman Fruits, turning over the Evanston Airport, located in Almy running parallel to Wyoming State Highway 89 North, to the newly formed Evanston/Uinta County Airport Joint Powers Board, providing for the dissolution and discontinuance when the new airport was constructed. The new airport would be controlled under the new Joint Powers Board. Motion was made by Councilman Morgan to pass Ordinance 82-98 on first reading, seconded by Wall, with all voting in favor. The ordinance went on to pass on second and third readings with all in favor.

⚜

Over the years the Town of Evanston had tried many locations for an airport. When I came to town in 1947 the Evanston airport was located just north of the Uinta County Fairgrounds. That apparently didn't work out so well, so they moved it out in Almy where it had been in use until the new present airport, located a few miles west of the city, was constructed and completed for use.

The property of the old Almy airport was owned entirely by the City of Evanston, however years ago, when the city purchased the south part of the airport and runway property from the previous owners, Bear River Coal Company, there was a condition in the deed, "that once the city ceased to use the property as an airport the property then would be deeded back to the Coal Company." That is why the city no longer owns that portion of the old Almy airport.

However, the north portion of the runway was deeded to the city by the U.P.R.R. years ago with no conditions attached to the deed. I have no idea whether the railroad donated the land or whether the city paid them for it, but the city needed the extra property to extend the runway. That portion of the airport is still owned by the city and is presently used for various programs by different local groups.

⚜

Resolution 82-98 was introduced by Councilman Fruits to establish policies and procedures for Environmental Protection Agency Projects. This resolution assured that the city would conduct all aspects of any project according to rules and regulations set by the E.P.A. if financial assistance was given to the City of Evanston from the U.S. Environmental Protection Agency. Motion was made by Morgan to adopt Resolution 82-98, seconded by Wall, and passed by the majority with 5 yes votes, 1 no vote, and 1 absent.

This resolution had to be adopted before Evanston could receive any grant funds from the E.P.A. Therefore, it was very important that we adopt the resolution in order to get financing for the new Evanston Sewer Treatment Plant, as well as funds for new sewer trunk lines.

At this time I introduced Evanston's new City Planner, Mr. Bruce Wright. He had great credentials and was well accepted by the city council. I was very impressed with Mr. Wright when interviewing him. Hopefully he would continue with Evanston's master plan and have good relations will everyone.

Ordinances 82-76 and Ordinance 82-92 were both tabled in July until the August 19th meeting. Ordinance 82-76 had been passed on the first and second readings, but Ordinance 82-92 was tabled on the first reading before being passed.

Councilman Bills made a motion during the meeting of August 19th to take Ordinance 82-76 off the table, seconded by Fruits, with all voting in favor. This was an ordinance annexing approximately 83.0 acres of the Centennial Valley Subdivisions, as requested by the developers, Mr. J. D. Kindler and Mr. Evan H. Reese, as well as the homeowners.

After a short discussion Councilman Albrecht made a motion to table Ordinance 82-76 once again, but indefinitely this time. The motion was seconded by Fruits with a unanimous vote. However, during a meeting in October, a motion to bring Ordinance 82-76 back on the floor was made and the ordinance was passed unanimously on third and final reading. The discussion of annexing the 83.0 acres of Centennial Valley was over and the ordinance had passed. Welcome Centennial Valley!

Councilman Albrecht also made the motion to take Ordinance 82-92 off the table, seconded by Fruits with all voting in favor.

This ordinance pertained to the annexation of 40 acres called Centennial Village, in the same area as the Centennial Valley Subdivisions, and would also have some pretty extensive costs—but would not be as costly as the Centennial Valley Subdivisions. However, we had the same concerns.

After a lengthy discussion, Councilwoman Wall made a motion to allow up to 36 months for payment of meters in Centennial Village, seconded by Bills with all voting in favor.

Vote on the main motion to pass Ordinance 82-92 on first reading was passed with all voting in favor. This ordinance went on to pass on second and third readings in October by a unanimous vote with no more problems.

I reported to the city council that bids had been opened for the first phase of the new airport work. The low bid was from Jim's Water Service in the amount of $1,055,160.

I also reported that the City of Evanston had received a check from the Overthrust Industrial Association in the amount of $131,905 for the motor grader that we had previously requested in a grant from O.I.A.

During this same meeting, I reported sending a letter to the Wyoming Highway Department recommending routing and planning at the Interstate 80 and Wyoming State Highway 150 South interchange at the location near the Wyoming State Hospital. Councilman Fruits made a motion for approval to my actions, seconded by Albrecht, with the motion passing by a majority.

I received a letter from Mr. Harold Young concerning his release from the city as City Planner. The letter spelled out some of his concerns and requested that the city not blackball him, which we had no intentions of doing. The letter was acknowledged and recommended to be placed in Mr. Young's personnel file. But Councilman Bills made a motion to place a copy of Mr. Young's letter in Bills's personnel file as well.

# Uinta County Herald

Evanston, Wyoming 82930     Friday, August 6, 1982     Volume 48, Number 60     Price 25c per copy

## Wyo. Highway Department took interchange case to the people

by David Fierro
of the Herald staff

Wyoming Highway Department officials took their case for a proposed interchange at the intersection of Highway 150 and I-80 to the people of Evanston Wednesday at a public hearing in the City Council chambers.

Highway Department engineering William B. King told the crowd of more than 50 people that the proposed design was "not the best nor the worst; it is a compromise."

The compromise aspect came into play in the Highway Department proposal because of a limited right of way situation with the land near the proposed interchange.

The department's proposed design does not call for the relocation of any residences on First Street, as was included in earlier proposals.

"We do not plan to relocate any of the residences in the area. We felt that had to be a major consideration in our planning," said King.

The proposed plan calls for a diamond interchange at the Highway 150-I-80 intersection with ramps at each of the four quadrants.

First Street would be divided in the center with the east side of the street converted into the westbound on ramp for the interstate.

The interchange, coupled with the planned Sixth Street overpass, is being designed to alleviate traffic congestion on Highway 30 through the city and offer better access to the downtown Evanston area, according to Highway Department officials.

Construction on the project is estimated from $2.7 to $3.3 million,

depending on final design selection. The project is targeted for a fiscal year 1984 completion.

A number of residents spoke against the interchange proposal, citing the hazardous winter driving conditions at the current Highway 150 underpass and the close proximity of an interstate on-ramp to residential housing units.

"As it is I can't get my car up Highway 150 in the water. How are you going to have an interchange there?" asked resident Arlene Hirst.

Apartment complex owner Jae Dee Kindler told the highway department representatives that he is "totally against it." "The traffic on those ramps will devalue all of the housing in that area," said Kindler.

Some residents of the vicinity suggested the interchange be

Continued on page 10

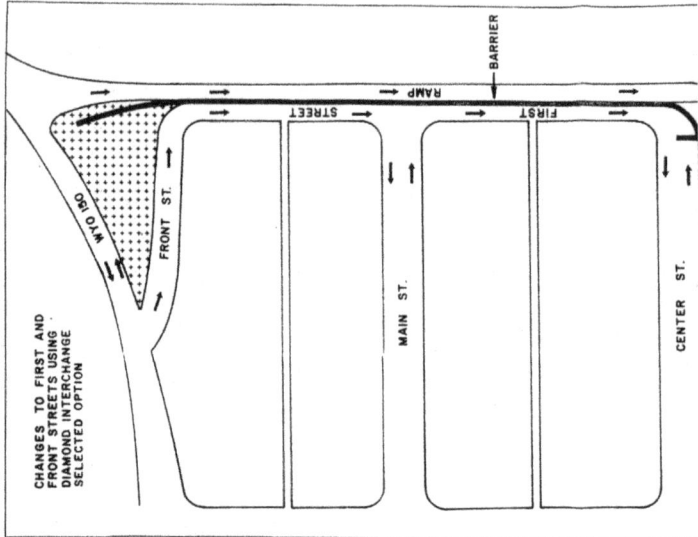

CHANGES TO FIRST AND FRONT STREETS USING DIAMOND INTERCHANGE SELECTED OPTION

Why? The only reason I could imagine why Bills would want a copy in his file was because he was the only one that voted against the resignation of Young and he wanted something that he could use against me in his campaign for mayor. But the motion was seconded by Albrecht with all voting in favor.

During a special city council meeting at the end of August, Dr. Roger Ranta, Superintendent of School District No. 1, was in attendance requesting that the City of Evanston participate with the school district in getting street improvements completed on No Name Street. After a short discussion, motion was made and seconded for the City of Evanston to provide an amount not to exceed $20,000 plus engineering, inspections and testing to assist the School District No. 1 in the improvements of No Name Street.

But a motion to amend the main motion was made and seconded to increase the amount to the school district to $30,000 and require sidewalks on both sides of the street where practical. The motion as amended passed by a unanimous vote.

At this time Dr. Ranta was preparing construction for the new Davis Middle School located on No Name Street, and the school district was also starting their plan for the North School on Washington Avenue and Wyoming State Highway 89 North.

During the city council meetings of September we acted on several pending ordinances on second and third readings and other regular business. Councilman Albrecht introduced Resolution 82-112 authorizing the City of Evanston to enter into an agreement with the Evanston Chamber of Commerce and the Uinta County Library Foundation to provide certain services to the city. The city would pay an annual amount of $8,600 to the Chamber of Commerce and $8,200 to the Library Foundation. Motion was made and seconded to adopt Resolution 82-112 with all voting in favor.

During the meetings the Centennial Valley annexation came up for discussion again with Councilman Davis making a motion for City Attorney Lancaster to negotiate a contract with Mr. J. D. Kindler and Mr. Evan Reese concerning the number of structures, taps to be paid, and so on, setting October 1, 1982 as the deadline for an agreement on costs and how costs are paid. The motion was seconded by Wall, with all voting in favor.

I sponsored Ordinance 82-104 and Councilwoman Wall introduced it. This ordinance pertained to a hearing on the vacating of 10th Street on the south side of Interstate 80. When the interstate highway was constructed it cut off 10th Street, which was part of a subdivision that Mr. Jack "Dub" W. Mills of the Best Western Motel (Dunmar Inn) had approved by the city but later vacated. The 10th Street extension on the other side of the interstate highway actually was owned by the city as a dedicated street, but as the original subdivision was vacated, I felt that this part of 10th Street should also have been vacated at the same time. With the interstate cutting it off, it had not been included, but I thought that the council would look at it the same way and agree to deed it back to Mr. Mills as the only fair thing to do. Mr. Mills would also own additional property attached to the street, which was part of the subdivision, and he also owned all the mineral rights. Finally, there was a producing oil well already on the property.

The ordinance just needed to be cleaned up by vacating the street. Therefore, Councilman Morgan made the motion to pass Ordinance 82-104 on first reading, seconded by Wall. However, Councilman Bills said he would like to go on record as opposing this ordinance. He was in favor of condemning the entire property owned by Mr. Mills, and retaining the street property. Motion was called for with 4 yes votes, 1 no vote (Bills), and 2 absent. Motion passed by a majority and went on to pass on second and third readings with all voting in favor accept Councilman Bills.

A resolution was introduced authorizing the city to enter into a five-year lease agreement with the U.P.R.R. for the site on China Mary Road and County Road on the north side of the underpass to use for a city shop building. A motion was made for adoption and seconded with all voting in favor. However, that did not happen that way, but the city did end up buying the property.

Originally, Utah Power and Light Company leased the property from the railroad and constructed the building for a power plant for their use, but when the power company had no more use for the building, the City of Evanston bought the building from the power company, and later purchased the property from the railroad. At the present that location is being used for the Recycling Center.

At this time plans were being made by the Wyoming Recreation Commission to create Bear River State Park on state land located east of Evanston and just off Interstate 80. Albert Pilch from Evanston, and a member of the state commission, made the announcement. He had been working on this project for years.

During our September meetings the city council made a motion to write a letter to the Wyoming Recreation Commission requesting that they consider annexation to the city. The city's request was honored, enabling the park to hook into the city's water and sewer system. After the park was developed it had become a great asset to the City of Evanston, and it became one of the state's most visited state parks.

Resolution 82-123, authorizing the City of Evanston to enter into a contract with Kean Recreation Company to provide light fixtures to the Overthrust Baseball Field #1, was introduced by Councilman Bills, also during the September meetings. This was the start of providing lighting to all the baseball fields. Motion was made by Wall for adoption and seconded by Bills, with all voting in favor.

Early in September it was announced that the new replacement hospital would be built in Evanston by the Lutheran Hospitals and Homes Society with assistance from the local community and other donors. New construction would start immediately and was scheduled for completion in early 1984.

A motion was made by Councilman Bills to authorize Superintendent of Public Works Allen Kennedy to work with the Hospital Board in providing city equipment to assist with some of the dirt work as long as city projects were not interfered with. The motion was seconded by Wall and passed with a unanimous vote.

Also during September, the Wyoming Highway Department took the case of the interchange to come off Interstate 80 and on to Wyoming State Highway 150 South, to the people at a public hearing. Those in attendance opposing the project were mostly those who had businesses located on Bear River Drive. But most of the folks in attendance were in favor of the new interchange. They thought it would really help with the traffic problems Evanston was now having, and several folks wondered why the interchange wasn't put there to start with when the interstate was constructed.

On September 9th, the *Uinta County Herald* came out with an article titled, FIVE-YEAR BUDGET PROJECTION FOR CITY OF EVANSTON NEARS COMPLETION. The article went on to say, *Mayor Dennis Ottley today announced that a five-year fiscal budget projection for Evanston being prepared by the Overthrust Industrial Association (O.I.A.) is "nearing completion" and will be presented to Evanston officials in the near future.*

The article continued: *Ottley said the five-year projection will "give us an idea of how we will stand down the road." The O.I.A. project is being conducted in response to an Evanston request for financial and technical assistance.*

*The five-year projection is being funded under a $100,000 O.I.A. grant for masterplanning in Evanston. "I'd hate to have a mayor in here in five years and have a bankrupt position. We don't want to wait until there is a problem to start planning solutions," said Ottley.*

*Ottley said that the city has short-term and long-term plans for land use and streets underway with the overall master plan expected to be completed this fall. "We had a stall in the planning process but things are back on track now," he said.*

*"Plans for the $10.7 million sewage treatment plant have been submitted to the E.P.A. for approval and the engineering department is currently negotiating for land acquisition and right-of-way," he continued.*

*"As for water, we are working with a $2 million Farm Loan Board grant to upgrade our water system. We are concerned with water and we know Gov. Herschler is concerned about water in Wyoming," said Ottley.*

*Ottley said these projects have been accomplished with an 18 percent budget increase, the smallest increase in five years. "We had a budget of $1.5 million my first year in office and this year we have* *a $10.5 million budget. That's the kind of growth we've had here,"* he said.

During this time of the year of 1982 an article recently came out in the *Uinta County Herald* with the headline: AMOCO BREAKS GROUND IN EVANSTON: The article said, *Tom Doss, Amoco District Superintendent, said the 100 employees currently staffing the district office in Salt Lake City will be offered positions in Evanston when the 45,000 sq. ft. building is completed, hopefully in early summer of 1983. He noted, however, that there will be some job vacancies to be filled by Evanston area residents after the move from Utah is complete.*

*Doss said,* the article continued, *plans are to have the structure located on Overthrust Drive south of Interstate 80, enclosed before the Wyoming winter breaks so interior work can continue during the colder months.*

NOTE: At present, the building that Amoco Production Company built for their headquarters was also used for Chevron USA personnel. However, today that same building is now occupied by the Uinta Boces #1 Education Center which is also a big asset for Evanston.

Japanese weekly magazine named
*"Asaki Graph,"* which means "Morning Sun."

Japanese weekly magazine named
*"Asaki Graph,"* which means "Morning Sun."

Holding the model of the pump, operated by solar battery. Someday
oil will be depleted, but the sun's heat is perpetual. Therefore, solar energy
is the energy of the future. Jack Mills is an 83-year-old rancher. He is 3rd
generation man with some Indian blood in him. He leases to an oil company
and derives substantial revenue from this.

Japanese weekly magazine named
*"Asaki Graph,"* which means *"Morning Sun."*

テ ー ー ー ・ ー ｜ ｜ ｜ ＿町長（四十九歳）と採油施設　米国では人口の少ない

Dennis Ottley is the mayor (49 years old). The picture is the pumping
machine. In America's small populated city, he does not receive a large
salary. His occupation is real estate.

About this time we also had a Japanese writer from Tokyo visit
Evanston. He had come to Evanston to write an article for his mag-
azine concerning our oil and gas boom. He also took a few pictures.
He took one of me standing by an oil pumper and one of Mr. John
Mills, "Dub" Mills's dad, standing by the oil pumper that was on his
land and which he was getting royalties from.

⟨⟩

Several weeks after the writer left to go back to Tokyo I received two
or three copies of the magazine. The magazine was in Japanese so I
couldn't read it, but the pictures looked good and it was a 3- or 4-page
article. I gave a copy to Mr. Mills and he couldn't read it either. I also
gave a copy to the Uinta County Museum with the translation.

Japanese books open from the back cover, and the front to us was their back cover, opposite from the American way, and they write their sentences differently as well. Through my business, Uinta Realty, I had gotten acquainted with a Japanese-American, who appraised property from Salt Lake City by the name of George Fuji. Sometimes he would come to Evanston to appraise commercial property. That is how I got acquainted with him. He was about the same age as I was, and his family spent their time during World War II in a Japanese camp when he was between 10 and 13 years old.

I talked to him a little about that, but he didn't seem to want to talk much about it, though he never seemed to be upset about it, or hateful or vengeful. He was really a nice guy, and over the years we became good friends. I showed the magazine to him and he said he would take it and get it translated for me and have it back to me in a week or so. So he took the magazine and did get it back to me just like he promised.

During our September meetings, Ordinance 82-110 was sponsored by me and introduced by Councilman Fruits. It authorized the issuance of Special Improvement Bonds of the City of Evanston, for Special Improvement District No. 3, to pay the cost and expenses of the construction and installation of all street paving, grading, curb, gutter, sidewalk, drainage, and sanitary sewer improvements, together with all other necessary appurtenances; and providing for the payment of said bonds and the interest; and declaring an emergency.

This was a $350,000 bond issue that was to be paid back through grants and loans from the Wyoming Highway Department. It was to pay for street improvements for new city streets in the 40-acre Haw Patch Subdivision owned by the city.

A motion to suspend the rules was made by Councilman Morgan so we could pass this ordinance on an emergency basis, which was seconded by Fruits with 6 yes votes and 1 no vote (Bills). The motion passed by a majority.

Motion to pass Ordinance 82-110 on an emergency basis was also made by Morgan and seconded by Davis, with the same vote. Ordinance 82-110 passed by a majority.

We were now able to start on construction of roads and construction of the Recreation Center and the Human Service Center had already broken ground. The Elderly Housing Project, the Pioneer Counseling Building, and the safe house were also in the process of getting starting. The Youth Alternative Home (Y.A.H.A.) came in later and was built on the same 40 acres of the city's Haw Patch Subdivision.

Commissioner John Fanos said to me the day of groundbreaking for the Human Service Center, *Hell Denny,* he said, *we are causing our own impact with all this construction going on.*

*Yeah,* I said, *ain't that great!*

Ordinance 82-76 to annex the 82.622 acres, which included the Centennial Valley Subdivisions, was brought off the table by regular motion. The main motion to pass Ordinance 82-76 was called for with all voting in favor.

I voted in favor of the ordinance, because I was concerned about the residents that lived there, but I <u>was</u> a little reluctant to vote in favor, because I was worried about the depth of the underground utilities, and how much it was going to cost the city in correcting some of the lapses in city standards that would show up in the near future.

By this time, Evanston had every street in the city either already improved or in the process of being improved. This even included Greek Street and Schwitzer Court, the last two streets to get the improvements. Thanks go to the Wyoming State Highway Department and the Wyoming Farm Loan Board for making it possible.

The primary elections were now over and I came out on top with 655 votes and Gene Martin came in second with 535 votes. David Bills came in third with 459 votes, with Miles Alexander and Keith Grover lagging far behind.

**CELEBRATION**
On hand for groundbreaking ceremonies for the new recreaton center were, from left, Dennis Poppinga, Dan Wheeler, Keith Sorenson, Kevin Smith, Jerry Wall, Bonnie Weber and Dennis Ottley.

On hand for groundbreaking ceremonies for the Human Service Center, located on City View Drive and Saddle Ridge Road, were Joint Powers Board Members, from left to right: John Fanos, Uinta County Commissioner; Jerry Wall, Evanston City Council Member; Denice Wheeler, Board Member; and Dennis Ottley, Evanston Mayor - September, 1982.

Therefore, Martin and I would be running for the mayor's seat, and Jerry Wall and Rick Sathers would be opposing each other for the city council seat in Ward 1; Lance Voss would oppose Marilyn Miller in Ward 2 (Roy Fruits did not seek re-election); and Ron Davis and Jerry Revelli would go against each other in Ward 3.

Campaigning started immediately and it looked like the City of Evanston candidates were entering the most underhanded election season in the history of Evanston, and the issue of "conflicts of interest" was to be one of the big campaign issues. But as I said before, almost everyone would have a conflict somewhere down the line. Mr. Martin was a businessman and he was also a real estate agent with Main Realty, and he owned property that would eventually become a mobile home park.

A few of the candidates running for city council seats also would have conflicts, but it's hard to find anyone to run for office that wouldn't have any conflicts at all. What mattered would be in the way you handled them while in office. I know I had a lot of conflicts, but I declared myself on every conflict and did the right thing by avoiding any kind of influence or special favors on any of them in and out of the meetings. I know I was accused of a lot of things such as being in the pockets of the oil companies, and rigging the bidding on the sale of the old town hall so I could end up owning it. What a lie!

Like I said before, every time an issue came up where I had a conflict of interest I dismissed myself. Almost every one of those issues where I had a conflict was passed by the council unanimously, and a few passed by a large majority.

So I asked myself, *Where the hell are the conflicts?*

I don't know why Gene Martin and some of the council candidates were spreading so many lies, half-truths, innuendos, and (putting it politely) "bullshit" about me indicating I was getting so rich being Mayor when I had just gone broke in our store, "Lockeroom Etc." My real estate agency, Uinta Realty, Inc., wasn't doing all that great, either. They were also accusing Councilwoman Jerry Wall of having a lot of conflicts, and spreading lies and innuendoes about her, just because her husband Cloey was a surveyor working on many of the new subdivisions and just because they owned some property.

Quoting Former President Harry S. Truman, *"You can't get rich in politics, unless you are a crook."* Well, I hadn't gotten anywhere close to being rich, so I must have been either a pretty honest, or a pretty stupid politician.

Gene Martin made the comment, *All is fair, because this is just politics!!* I said to him, Well, *I don't believe that, I don't believe spreading lies about people, where it hurts their reputation, is fair in politics, or at any other time.* But the dirt and lies kept flying from the competition. I guess they just figured that was the only way they could win, but I admit that I had stepped on a lot of toes over the years trying to do the right thing for the community. So at this time I wasn't sure just how the election was going to turn out, but it was one of the most underhanded and unethical elections I had ever been involved in. When I ran for office I always tried to run on my record. I never spoke ill about any of my opponents. I just figured they would do the same, but this year was really different and it wasn't turning out to be much fun; but I stuck to my guns and just tried to run on my record.

I also tried to defend myself as much as I felt necessary, but one of my supporters, Willis Barnes, chewed me out after getting beat in the election for not sticking up for myself more. He told me that you've got to be meaner and play their game. Willis was a great guy and he and his wife, Marie, both were real patriots for Evanston and did a lot of good for the community.

I had a lot of support and asked Kathy Cue, who was one of Uinta Realty's agents, to be my campaign manager, and she accepted. She was doing a great job and got a lot of my fans to help her. I had a large committee and they received a lot of donations from dedicated folks who were in favor of me being elected. But city business went on as usual. During our October city council meetings we worked on a lot of ordinances and introduced several resolutions. A lot of the ordinances concerned land acquisition for the new sewer plant, storm water runoff, rezoning, extensions and acceptance of some streets, sewer and water hookup increases, and water rights transfer. All passed by at least a majority vote.

Concerning the property for the new Evanston Sewer Treatment Plant, the City of Evanston had to acquire land from a few ranchers, such as Edith Stewart, Vivian S. Hayduk, Arthur and June Sims, Lowham Land Limited Partnership, Nixon Investment Company/ Red Mountain Partners, and Anne M. Black, Elmer Leon Black and R. T. Black. The city was very grateful to these folks for being so understanding in giving up their land at an agreeable and fair price.

Councilman Morgan introduced Resolution 82-125 declaring the City of Evanston's support for the State of Wyoming's proposal for the development of Bear River State Park. A motion was made by Albrecht to adopt Resolution 82-125, seconded by Fruits, with all voting in favor.

We were working hard trying to keep the post office in the downtown area while other developers were trying to get the U.S. Postal Department to move into other areas where they were building commercial shopping areas. In fact, a couple of the developers even offered the Postal Department free donated land if they would consider moving into their subdivisions.

Steve Snyder, Administrative Assistant, and I made a trip to San Francisco, California to meet with the Postal Department and talk to them about keeping the post office in the downtown area, because Evanston was trying to keep the downtown area as the "heart of Evanston." I told them that we had heard that they wanted to build a new post office in Evanston because of the growth from the boom, and we were very concerned about losing it from the downtown area. We told them that there were two full blocks that could be made available to them for a fair price and the city would participate as much as they could wherever the laws allowed.

By this time, Amoco said that they would be moving out of their shop located in the Evanston Industrial Center on Allegiance Circle soon, and the City of Evanston could take it over for a reasonable price, or maybe they would just give it to the city. It was a nice shop and it would be almost exactly what Public Works needed.

We mentioned that to the Postal Department and that the old city shop was on one of those blocks that would be available. They talked favorably about trying to stay in the downtown area, and Snyder and I felt good about our trip to San Francisco.

During the October meeting we talked about it, and Councilman Morgan immediately made a motion for the city to start negotiations with John Aanerud and Jerry Cazin who owned property on the one block where the post office is at the present. The motion was seconded by Bills, with all voting in favor.

But we had to take it slow and easy because the Postal Department could also look at the block where the old town hall was. They would have their choice of the two blocks, and they had not had the opportunity at that time to consider either block.

There were several mothers who had called me during October because Halloween was scheduled for October 31st and that would be falling on a Sunday. They requested that the mayor declare Saturday, October 30th as Halloween because they didn't think it was right for kids to be out halloweening on a Sunday. I brought this up to the city council during one of our October meetings.

I actually had some problems with this because I didn't think we should mess around with the calendar, but after a lengthy discussion with the council a motion was made and seconded with all voting in favor of proclaiming Halloween to be on Saturday, October 30th. Boy, what a mistake that was. I caught all kinds of hell from a lot of folks because they didn't think I had any business or right to change the date of Halloween. A lot of it was because of their religion. I kind of agreed with them, but the city council went along with the change. This also hurt me in the election.

I told myself, *That's something I'll never do again, election or no election,* and I didn't. *What a stupid thing to do,* I said to myself.

The city election was getting hot and heavy with lies, untruths and innuendos. It was becoming a very uncomfortable election. Although, my campaign chairman Kathy Cue was trying to run an honest campaign for me, it was difficult not to try to stand on my own two feet and back up my actions as mayor. I tried to run on my own record in getting things done, but with all the B.S. that was being put out, I was often being put in a position where I had to justify my actions.

I had a large committee working for the "Ottley for Mayor" campaign. I even had a pickup truck running around the city asking people to "Vote Ottley for Mayor" over a loudspeaker for a few days before election, and KEVA Radio took a poll on the mayor's race about three days before the election, showing me way ahead.

Gene Martin was accusing me of "pork barreling". Sandy asked me what that meant, and I told her, "Hell, I don't know, but I'm sure we'll find out real soon." We did, but we weren't much acquainted with the political jargon, so it had us in the dark for a while. Martin had been active in the Democratic Party for quite some time and he knew politics, or he thought he did. But we had never been very active in our own political party, the Republicans. So we were a little naive in political lingo.

But his accusations were way off base; the only money we were trying to raise was for certain projects that were needed to meet our mitigation plans which were funded almost 100% through grants from the state of Wyoming, the oil companies, and their affiliates. Other than that we pretty much stuck to our budget, and by the next budget hearing for fiscal year 1982-1983 there would be well over $4 million in cash reserve.

City Attorney Lancaster gave his report to the city council concerning the Wyoming State Supreme Court's decision on the Whirl Inn, Inc. lawsuit, and as I feared, the city lost. It cost the City of Evanston a huge amount of money, money that the city really couldn't afford. The decision was a big disappointment for the city council and for those folks who lived near the Whirl Inn.

Attorney Larry Lehman was on my committee and working hard for me to get re-elected. We scheduled a large public forum for my campaign and Larry asked if he could write my speech for me. I had never had anyone write a speech for me before, but I thought that he had worked so hard setting up the forum, I told him to go ahead. This was another big mistake, because when I got up and delivered the speech Larry had written for me, I made one hell of a mess out of it. The speech just wasn't me and it did not go over well at all. I learned a good lesson from that and never let anyone write one of my speeches again. From then on I wrote all my own speeches as I had in the past.

My campaign chairperson, Kathy Cue, wrote a letter to my opponent for mayor, Gene Martin, inviting him to a debate between him and me sometime in late October concerning the upcoming problems and projects the City of Evanston would be facing in the next several years, but he declined the invitation. I was very disappointed because I really wanted to debate him one-on-one before election.

My committee was also in the process of holding a big "victory party" election night at The Three Knights restaurant, because taking everything into consideration, it didn't look like there was any doubt that I would win, but quite disappointingly, I didn't.

When we heard the final results come in, the large attendance of my supporters at the party just couldn't believe it. It was a bad evening with all the disappointed people at the event, some crying, others wondering what happened. Sandy and I were both feeling pretty bad.

I thought of the old saying, *"How to win friends and influence people."* I guess I just forgot how to win friends, but I did a lot of good influencing people, and the right people, because Evanston had gotten a lot of funding and assistance from some top decision making people that I had proven to have had some clout with, because I did use my influence to get whatever we were going after. Of course, I did have a lot of help. I certainly didn't do it alone.

The November meetings were not much different: more ordinances to pass on second and third readings and additional new ordinances that were sponsored and introduced with all passing on first reading. Regular business was also taken care of with no problems.

During the meeting, Resolution 82-130, awarding the construction of the Evanston Public Safety Building to Newland and Turner Construction, Inc. of Evanston was passed, with motion made and seconded, and all voting in favor.

It was announced that there would be a groundbreaking ceremony at the new hospital site at 2:00 p.m. on Saturday, November 20, 1982. That was good news.

On Wednesday, November 3rd the *Uinta County Herald* issued the following headline: EUGENE MARTIN UNSEATS MAYOR DENNIS OTTLEY. The article went on to read, *Challenger Eugene Martin unseated incumbent Mayor Dennis Ottley in a close election Tuesday. He received 1182 votes to 1087 for Ottley.*

*Other results* (the article continued) *were City Council: Ward 1, Rick Sather 422, Jerry Wall 233; Ward 2, Lance Voss 441, Marilyn Miller 426; Ward 3, Ronald Davis 386, Jerry Revelli 343.*

In the County Commissioner's race, John Stevens beat out Dan South, incumbent Clark Anderson got re-elected, and Governor Ed Herschler got re-elected for a third term. Governor Herschler would be the only Wyoming governor ever to serve 3 terms. After this election the state legislature passed legislation that a governor could not serve more than two terms.

Ed Herschler was a good governor and served Wyoming well, especially Lincoln and Uinta Counties. He really helped Evanston through the tough boom times. He was instrumental in helping Evanston, Uinta County, and Uinta County School District No. 1 obtain the state and federal funding for the many projects now being constructed in the area.

I was quite disappointed that I didn't get re-elected for Mayor. I was hoping to serve another term so that I could see the completion of the many projects that my administration had worked on and the city had planned for, including the new Water Treatment Plant, the Elderly Housing Project, the Public Safety Building, the new Fire Hall, Evanston's new Recreation Center, the new overpass, "Ottley's Folly," off 6th Street, the Bear River Project including the ponds, the Wyoming Highway 150 Interchange, and the water project including additional water resources from the Upper Bear River.

Other projects that would be completed in the near future would be the North Elementary School and Evanston High School, the new Memorial Hospital, and the new Uinta County Courthouse and Library.

Commissioner John Fanos was absolutely correct when he said that *we were creating our own impact.* There would be a lot of construction, private and government, in the next few years, but we had hit the peak of the boom this year of 1982. Because of the drilling and exploration slowing down, some folks were starting to leave Evanston, but others would be coming in because of the production which would be going strong until things start leveling off.

When the two sour gas plants were up and running the man-camps will be removed and those workers living there will be leaving. So the economy will be taking a slump in the next few years, especially when all these projects are completed.

Although being a bit disappointed about the outcome of the election, I was confident that all these projects were far enough along in the construction and the planning that they would not be stopped, though there could be some changes. I was thankful for that.

The *Uinta County Herald* issue of November 24th came out with headlines reading, GROUNDBREAKING SATURDAY FOR NEW MEMORIAL HOSPITAL. The article went on to read: *Ken Bloomfield, Hospital Board Chairmen, welcomed guests and participants to the ceremonies. Brief statements were made by Evanston Mayor Dennis Ottley; Joe French, President of the Evanston Chamber of Commerce; Dr. Steven French of the Memorial Hospital Medical Staff; Robert A. Anderson, President of the Lutheran Hospitals and Homes Society of America; Keith Mesmer, LHHS Regional Vice; Norman Campeau, Memorial Hospital Administrator; and Gerda Robinson, representing the Hospital Ladies Auxiliary.*

*Mary Emerson, Chairman of the Fund Drive for the New Memorial Hospital of Uinta County, turned the first shovel of earth, followed by Bloomfield, Anderson, Dr. French, and Mayor Ottley.*

The article did state that: *The cold snowy weather during the ceremonies was no deterrent to the participants and spectators.* Also, in the same issue of the *Herald*, it was announced that *the groundbreaking event of the new Pioneer Bank Building* (presently the Wells Fargo Bank building) *had been recently held with Bank President Harry Palmer turning the first shovel full. This was a six story office complex and now would be the tallest building in the City of Evanston.*

A group of us from the city and county wanted to make a trip to Omaha, Nebraska to meet with the Union Pacific Corp. Board of

Directors, so I had Steve Snyder, Administrative Assistant of the City of Evanston set the meeting up sometime in early December. Snyder also chartered an airplane to fly us to Omaha. The plane would hold fifteen passengers, and the manager of the Evanston Airport would be the pilot. It would be a one-day trip; we leave early in the morning and get back that same day, quite late.

The group making the trip included me, Steve Snyder, Councilwoman Jerry Wall, Ron Straka, representing the Downtown Commission, County Commissioner Clark Anderson, and others I don't recall, but there were several of us from the city and county.

The purpose for the trip was to talk to the U.P. about obtaining the depot side of Front Street from 9th to 12th Streets, owned by the railroad, plus the purchase of the depot. It was a good meeting and U.P. did agree to work with us on purchasing the Front Street frontage. They also tentatively agreed to sell the old Uinta County Library and Museum property to Uinta County, but they excluded the Old Timers building. The Old Timers kept that for their organization. The railroad also tentatively agreed to sell the depot to the city, but only the building, because the depot was sitting on the railroad right-of-way, and by federal law they can't sell railroad right-of-way property.

The trip going and coming was a pretty smooth flight, though we were all dead tired and anxious get back. We all felt good about the meeting, but now it would be up to the next administration to deal with it. It would have to be Snyder and Straka, with the help of the Urban Renewal Agency to follow up on the project and work things out with the railroad, but over a period of time the entire deal did work out.

Miles Alexander and his son Bill Alexander started another newspaper in the city called *The Evanston Post*. Their December 22nd issue of the *Post* headlined: CITY BAILS OUT COWBOY DAYS. The article read, *The Evanston City Council voted unanimously during their December meeting to give the Evanston Cowboy Days Committee $20,000.*

The *Uinta County Herald* had a similar article titled, COWBOY DAYS IS IN TROUBLE. The article noted that *the 1982 Cowboy Days Committee chairman Dennis Heap requested financial help from the city, through the Evanston Chamber of Commerce, but committee member George L. Robinson, a past chairman, said the problem lies with the management.*

Evanston Chamber of Commerce President Joe French submitted a letter to the city requesting the financial assistance from the City of Evanston. He explained that the Labor Day weekend celebration was good for Evanston and that, if the council agrees to contribute funds through the Chamber, the Chamber would take over the program and rewrite the bylaws and reorganize the entire program. Mr. French recommended that the organization hire a part-time director to coordinate Cowboy Days activities.

The city council agreed to pay the Chamber of Commerce the $20,000 to get the Cowboy Days Committee back on their feet, but the recommendations that Mr. French presented never worked out and eventually the committee just went back to their usual method of running the program.

Other business that came up in the December meetings was the usual passing of a number of ordinances on second and third readings, and new ordinances and resolutions were introduced. Mr. Doug Matthews made application to be a police officer. Mr. Matthews had been recommended by the Personnel Board; however, he lived outside the city limits, but Councilwoman Wall made a motion to waive the requirement of living within the limits as set by ordinance if Matthews were hired. The motion was seconded by Fruits with 5 yes votes, 1 no vote, and 1 absent. Motion passed by the majority.

I then appointed Doug Matthews to the Evanston Police Department. Councilman Fruits made the motion to confirm my appointment, seconded by Wall, with 4 yes votes, 1 no vote, and 1 absent.

The only stipulation on police officers living outside the city limits was that they had to leave their patrol car somewhere visible to the public in the city. We wanted all city police cars to remain in the city for the purpose of being visible to help discourage any unlawful activity.

Therefore, now that the city acquired a marked patrol car for almost every Evanston police officer we had come up with a ruling that each officer living in town could take their car home and park it, but it must be where the vehicle was visible to the public. It could not be parked in the garage or anywhere out of sight. We felt that while marked police cars were visible to the public it kept crime, speeding and other criminal acts down. I believed that it was just human nature that when a person sees a police car they think twice before doing something they shouldn't be doing, and I firmly felt that it worked.

I also read a letter from Dennis Lancaster resigning as City Attorney effective January 5, 1983. His letter read:

*I would like to take this opportunity to express my appreciation to Mayor Ottley and the Council for the opportunity I have had to serve as City Attorney for the past 6½ years. I would like to pay special tribute to Mayor Ottley for the dedication and effort he has put into the position of Mayor and the efforts he has made to make this a better community. Very few people know better than I the time and effort Mayor Ottley has put into this job. I would also like to thank Jerry Wall and Roy Fruits for the association I have had with them during my tenure as City Attorney and the dedication that they have shown to the City. In addition, I would like to express to the other members of the Council my appreciation for the support they have given me.*

The letter continued: *When I first became City Attorney 6½ years ago, the City did not have any existing codification of ordinances, since the last codification had been done in 1916 and that all ordinances passed since 1916 were located in various offices of the City. The City Attorney's office, under my direction, first codified the ordinances in 1977 and which culminated in the 1982 codification, which was recently passed by this Council. The City, during my 6½ years as City Attorney, has experienced tremendous growth, which I feel this Council has effectively dealt with. Since I have been City Attorney, the City has passed approximately 540 ordinances, which is more ordinances than were passed from 1916 through 1966. I feel that several of these ordinances have been "model ordinances" which have been adopted and followed by other communities.*

*Specifically, the drug paraphernalia ordinance that was drafted by my office has been adopted almost verbatim by several other communities in the State of Wyoming, as well as by the Wyoming state legislature. A few other ordinances which I feel this Council can be extremely proud of would be the oil and gas ordinance, which established a standard for drilling of oil and gas wells within certain areas of the City, as well as needed regulations relating to the same.*

The obscenity ordinance and the subdivision ordinances of the City, specifically the provisions relating to transfer of water rights and bonding requirements, have been adopted as models in other communities.

Other major accomplishments of the City Attorney's office have been the adopting of a policy resolution relating to industrial revenue bonds, wherein the City has established a framework for the issuance of said bonds on a uniform basis and has established an application and financing fee which has greatly benefited the City of Evanston. The City has also established extraterritorial zoning ordinances dealing with subdivision, water and sewer hookup controls.

The City Attorney's office has attempted to uniformly enforce the ordinances of the City against any and all violators regardless of their standing in the community, which has not set well with certain "permanent" residents. I have appreciated the support of the Mayor in my office's attempt to uniformly enforce all ordinances without any political interference.

When I first became City Attorney, the City of Evanston did not have a planner nor a full-time engineer, and there were certain times when the city did not have an engineer at all. During this time, the City has approved approximately 60 subdivisions, which necessitated the review by our office from both a legal and planning aspect. Our office has developed a model subdivision contract, which has been adopted by Uinta County and several other municipalities as a model contract to guarantee the completion of subdivision improvements and the warranting of the same. In approving these subdivisions, the City has required the subdivisions to have the water rights transferred, and this is a major project which we have started and, hopefully, the new City Attorney will follow through on.

I would like to also express my appreciation to John A. Thomas, who for the past year has served as my assistant after this office was approved by the Council. In closing, I would like to point out that the citizens of the City of Evanston have been fairly represented by Mayor Ottley and Council, in that all decisions have always been made in an open and fair manner after due hearings. Hopefully, under the new administration, this policy will continue and that City decisions will not revert to "backroom power group politics," some of which decisions I have noticed since the election.

Sincerely yours,

Dennis W. Lancaster

Attorney Lancaster was one of the most honest and thorough attorneys that I have ever been associated with, and I told him as much. The City of Evanston would be much better off if there was some way the new mayor could talk him into staying, but I'm sure Lancaster was pretty tired, because he worked very hard during his tenure as the city attorney.

Motion was made by Councilman Albrecht to accept his resignation. All members of the city council and I expressed our thanks and appreciation for his service, and felt that the city had been very fortunate to have had the expertise and professionalism Attorney Lancaster had given to the city. The motion was seconded by Bills with all voting in favor.

This was my last official meeting as Mayor of Evanston. However, I would be opening up the first meeting in January, 1983 to get some old business taken care of and getting the newly elected officers sworn in. I would also be giving my year-end State of the City report. I was not looking forward to that.

I heard that Councilwoman Jerry Wall was blaming me for her losing the election; she told folks that the reason she lost was because the voters thought that she was running on my shirt tail. I was really dumbfounded and a little pissed off. I told Sandy, *If Jerry was running on my so-called shirt tail, I sure as hell didn't know it, and it would have been her own fault for doing it.*

I went on to say, *She must not have done her math, because I only lost to Martin by 95 votes in the entire city, and she lost to Sather in just Ward 1 by 189 votes. So who the hell should she really blame?*

Jerry had been a good member on the council and had helped me a lot, so I had a hard time believing that she could stoop to blaming me for her defeat, but the report came back to me through what I considered good and honest sources. Therefore, I had no reason not to believe them.

When a mayor has stepped on as many toes as I have, with all the growth and construction going on, and when he has initiated projects like the installation of water meters after citizens had been on a flat rate water usage for over 100 years, the removal of the parking meters, vacating some of the streets, implementing one-way streets for traffic control, being associated with Ottley's Foley, the I-80 interchange at highway 150, the Whirl Inn lawsuit, and the dismissal of Jerry Cazin as Fire Chief of the Evanston Voluntary Fire Department—one of the state of Wyoming's finest, the Recreation Center that some folks in Evanston thought was just a waste of money, and other projects that some folks were against, I guess a person shouldn't expect to be re-elected.

My son Dave said to me, *Dad, you'll never make a politician. You are just too damn honest.* And years ago someone told me, *A good mayor pleases no one.* How right they were. I was a good mayor, showing favoritism to no one. I didn't play politics. I upheld the Oath of Office the best I could by serving the people of Evanston with honesty and loyalty. I was a people's mayor, and very proud of it. I actually believe that Evanston's history would prove it, acknowledge it and attest to it. It will be very evident.

# ACKNOWLEDGEMENTS

This book would never have been written if it hadn't been for a number of people who had assisted me in remembering some of the events and occurrences mentioned in the book, and making minutes of meetings and other materials available to me. In showing my appreciation I wish to name those folks.

First of all, I would like to thank my wife Sandy for all her support and encouragement she gave me to help me through this book. There were many times when I was ready to quit, but with her encouragement and her editing, I was able to get it finished.

I also wish to thank Maryl Thompson, Receptionist and Administrative Assistant of my real estate agency, Uinta Realty, Inc., for all the assistance she gave me in using my computer. When I had a computer problem, she was always on hand to help me through it, as did Tonya Dennis, Associate Broker in the office, who also assisted me on the computer when necessary.

Also, I want to thank the Executive Assistant to the Mayor of Evanston and Deputy City Clerk Nancy Stevenson for her time and hard work in providing me with 16 years of copies of the minutes of all the official meetings of the Evanston City Council during my tenure as Mayor of Evanston, 1979-1983 and 1987-1995, plus the term of Mayor Gene Martin, 1983-1987.

Other folks I wish to thank and show appreciation to are Shelly and Deann Horne of Creative Ink Images for their assistance in preparing the book cover; and Former City Engineer Brian Honey for information he provided me concerning the Sulphur Creek Dam Project and many other projects that were constructed during my term as Mayor. Brian was City Engineer under me for my last eight years in office. Thanks are also due to City Attorney Dennis Boal for straightening me out on a few matters. Dennis was my City Attorney also during my final eight years of my term as mayor. Thanks also to retired Urban Renewal Agency Director Jim Davis for providing me with information for my book; and former City Councilmember Tom Hutchinson for the information and input that he provided me. Other city employees that I wish to thank are Paul Knopf, former city planner, Public Works Superintendent Allan "Oop" Hansen and Engineering Tech Bob Liechty for their input to my story.

I also want to thank the Uinta County Library in Evanston for the use of their equipment, the Uinta County Museum in Evanston and the Evanston Chamber of Commerce for materials provided me to be used in my book; and the Uinta County Herald for giving me the opportunity to look through many of their old newspapers.

I appreciate all those named above for the completion of this book Evanston, Wyoming...Boom-Bust-Politics.

However, I want to let you, the reader, know that almost all of the material used in this story was from my personal collection of photos, newspaper clippings, letters, etc., and from the actual minutes of the Evanston meetings during the period from 1967 to 1995. But some material is also from my own memory and from talking to some of those folks I mentioned above.

*Thank You...*
*April 25, 2018*

# ABOUT THE AUTHOR

Born January 28, 1932 in Salt Lake City, Utah, Dennis ended up in Evanston, Wyoming. He quit high school and joined the 141st Tank Battalion of the Wyoming National Guard.

When the Korean War started in 1950, his unit was called to active duty in September, but he and his wife, Sandy got married on July 26, 1950 before he left for active duty, and to serve time in Korea.

Dennis and Sandy settled in Evanston, where he served three 4-year terms as a member of the Evanston city council and three 4-year terms as mayor. Dennis retired at the age of 81 from his real estate agency, and after raising four sons and over 68 years of marriage, he and his wife Sandy still reside in Evanston.

> **Be sure to look for**
> **Volume 3 of Evanston Wyoming**

www.ingramcontent.com/pod-product-compliance
Lightning Source LLC
Chambersburg PA
CBHW030409100426
42812CB00028B/2890/J